T0334587

Negotiating in the Leadership Zone

Negotiating in the Leadership Zone

Ken Sylvester
Colorado Springs, CO, USA

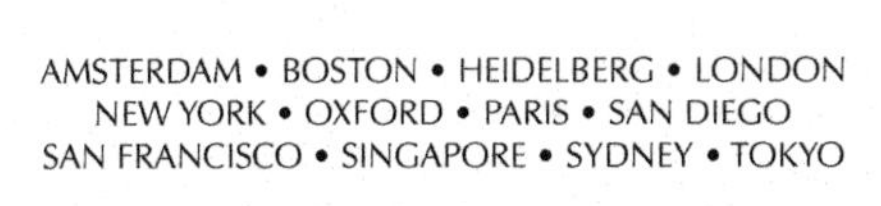
AMSTERDAM • BOSTON • HEIDELBERG • LONDON
NEW YORK • OXFORD • PARIS • SAN DIEGO
SAN FRANCISCO • SINGAPORE • SYDNEY • TOKYO

Academic Press is an imprint of Elsevier

Academic Press is an imprint of Elsevier
125 London Wall, London EC2Y 5AS, UK
525 B Street, Suite 1800, San Diego, CA 92101-4495, USA
225 Wyman Street, Waltham, MA 02451, USA
The Boulevard, Langford Lane, Kidlington, Oxford OX5 1GB, UK

ISBN: 978-0-12-800340-4

British Library Cataloguing-in-Publication Data
A catalogue record for this book is available from the British Library

Library of Congress Cataloging-in-Publication Data
A catalog record for this book is available from the Library of Congress

For information on all Academic Press publications
visit our website at http://store.elsevier.com/

Publisher: Nikki Levy
Acquisition Editor: Scott Bentley
Editorial Project Manager: Susan Ikeda
Production Project Manager: Jason Mitchell
Designer: Maria Inês Cruz

Typeset by TNQ Books and Journals
www.tnq.co.in

Printed and bound in the United States of America

Contents

3. Systems-3 Leadership

Section II
Identifying Assumptions using Effective Questioning (EQ)

4. Introduction to Effective Questioning (EQ)

5. Using Effective Questioning Strategically

10. Troubleshooting the Collaborative Process

Section IV
Managing Conflict

11. The Context of Conflict

12. Diagnosing and Managing Conflict

Section V
Hidden Traps

13. Closing Words: Hidden Traps

Section VI
Appendices

Preface

I made a choice before writing this book to maintain the confidentialities entrusted to me by those organizations that employed me. Whether written or implied, each organization expected confidentiality. I know this is an *old school* attitude. Nonetheless, it is with their trust that I write this book. Therefore, the stories in this book have been shared without naming the company, its leadership, or the company's industry. Some of you will read this book and recognize your existence in the stories. When we meet again, I prefer to meet you in the disposition of integrity and loyalty; not with a request for an apology.

I have worked with and learned from many great men and women who as leaders have made great contributions and, have some flaws. The lesson for me is that *all people* have both strengths and limitations. The core competencies of leader-negotiators involve solving complicated problems, making relevant decisions, taking effective action, building competent teams, and crafting strategy. These competencies require persistence and shrewd wisdom. My preference for how I wrote this book involves passing on the lessons about how the leaders with whom I worked developed success, recovered from failures, and learned to cope with imperfections.

Acknowledgments

I could not have written this book without the help of many people. First, I would like to thank those who have supported me. **First and foremost,** to my wife, Mary Ann—the words *thank you* do not express the appreciation I have for your gifted support throughout the years and specifically, in getting this book to print. In addition to the cookies and milk that were lifesavers, waking me while I fell asleep in front of the computer, there have been years together in conversation about the topics covered in this book that have helped shape my thinking and hours together recently organizing and editing content. After all the thousands of words used to write this book, there is *not one word or an entire book of words* that are adequate to acknowledge your tireless and persistent focus at making it possible for me to complete this book.

In addition, the following are people who have accompanied me in the long-term process of thinking about and writing this book. In particular, thank you to Dr Jacqueline Hooper, a friend and business professional, who helped me formulate and refine my doctoral dissertation. My doctoral dissertation is where this book was born. Thank you to Dr John Milliman, Professor of Management, who prodded me to write this book. Thank you to Zoë Emmanuel, a highly skilled technology professional, who patiently, year by year, encouraged me to communicate my ideas and reminded me of my contributions. Thank you to Ron Stratten, former V.P. of the National Collegiate Athletic Association (NCAA), who invigorated and reinvigorated me with reminders that I could write this book. Thank you to Julie Whitehead and Mun Choi, owners of Axio Design, who supported me through several false starts, yet remained committed through completion of this book.

Finally, thank you to those at the following educational institutions who provoked my thinking and enhanced the credence *that "I could be more."* To Pacific University, for my undergraduate degree that provided the foundation upon which all future steps depended; to Pacific Lutheran University for providing the underpinnings for managing my business throughout the world; and to Seattle University for providing me with the coursework needed, the supportive cohort of doctoral students, and the opportunity to write my dissertation, which is the essence of my Leader-Negotiator Theory. One by one, each institution *carved a "notch"* into the branches of my intellect. Independently, each institution influenced me differently, yet similarly honed a common pursuit—to be a lifelong learner, realizing that learning is a never-ending and worthy pursuit.

Dr Ken Sylvester

Introduction: The Alaskan Fishing Conflict—A Real-Life Negotiation

I developed a well-thought-out business plan. I built a competent team. The objectives were clear. I hired Joe Sullivan, the best fisheries attorney in Seattle, for excellent legal counsel. The question is: **How did it fail?**

THE CONTEXT

I was the lead negotiator for the Alaska fishing conflict from 1998 through 2002. The negotiation represented about 25,000 members of the Alaskan fisheries to obtain higher prices for their industry. On the surface, this appeared to be simple and straightforward.

THE SITUATION

From about 1990 to 2000, fishermen were struggling to make a livelihood in a once prosperous Alaskan fishing industry. As a result of the declining economic conditions, conflict among fisheries, processors, and Alaskan government officials escalated into intense confrontations. Communication and trust among the fisheries was nonexistent. The negotiation environment spiraled downward into unproductive behaviors. Both verbal and physical threats were frequent. Aggressive, hostile, and antagonistic behavior was chronic. Enmity existed among those in the fisheries, the processors, local government, state government, federal government, and international fisheries.

THE STRATEGY

To gain a better understanding of situation, I began by asking questions (E-Questions are discussed in Chapters 4 and 5) and then listened to the Kodiak Board of Directors (the United Salmon Association, USA). Further, I interviewed leaders among the fisheries, processors, and governments to help me understand the dynamics of the present fishing industry. I studied thousands of pages of economic, financial, and related data. Each conversation brought together the numerous components of a fragmented puzzle.

Subsequent to explaining my strategy to the Kodiak Board of Directors (who gave me their unanimous support), negotiations commenced among the Alaskan fisheries, the USA fisheries, Norway, South America, China, Japan, and Canada. In consulting with US Senator Mark Hatfield (Oregon, 1967–1997), I was encouraged to find that he agreed that my strategy for resolving the Alaska fisheries conflict was aligned with his more than 30 years of political work in the United States fisheries.

FRAMING THE NEGOTIATION

Progress was positive albeit not trouble free. The Alaskan parties began to realize that their adversary was not each other. Consequently, government officials, fishermen, and processors recognized that the challenge involved reframing their commercial marketing strategy. The reframe involved persuading grocery retailers, who preferred to purchase farm-raised fish more than naturally caught Alaskan fish, to buy the natural Alaskan fish products. The reason retailers preferred farm-raised fish is because they look better to consumers than fish caught in the turbulent open ocean environment. In other words, farm fish look pretty. Natural fish shows signs of being beaten up by the ocean. A second major part of the negotiation was lobbying government regulators who realized that expensive licensing fees created financial barriers to those trying to enter the fishing industry. This placed the entire Alaskan fisheries industry into a significant economic disadvantage with foreign competitors. Foreign fisheries did not require such restricted commercial fishing regulations and license fees.

THE RESULTS

After traveling to almost every nook and cranny of Alaska, an industry-wide meeting was held in Anchorage where 95% of all the fisherman and processors, and the Alaskan Attorney General attended. At this meeting, I presented a plan for internal collaboration among the Alaskan Fishing Industry with an aggressive competitive marketing strategy toward global competitors. The assumption was that the fishing industry would be willing to act in a collaborative and mutually beneficial way with each other.

- The first part of this assumption began to succeed when I disarmed the economic and geopolitical conflict by redirecting marketing efforts away from only the United States marketplace toward a global market. The objective was to reframe the conflict away from each other and toward a collectively motivated workforce that would result in increasing each fisherman's revenue (see Chapter 10: Troubleshooting the Collaborative Process).
- Second, the United Salmon Association (USA) replaced a local Alaskan marketing organization with the USA's nonpolitical but politically savvy marketing team.

- Third, I met with Alaska's government officials and business leaders to propose changes in regulatory policies that prevented Alaska's fisheries from competing with international competitors.
- Fourth, I launched a media campaign with retailers to reframe farm fish as an "unhealthy choice" and to promote wild Alaskan fish, rich in Omega-3 oils, as a "healthy choice."

The strategy was succeeding as expected by the end of 1998. However, within the first few months of 1999, the negotiation began to lose its momentum. *How could such a successful and well-executed plan fail?*

There were barriers that needed to be overcome to achieve this fourth initiative. One major barrier involved the predictable delivery of farm fish to retailers. Because the farm fish were in a protected environment, farm fish operators offered retailers a more predictable supply of "prettier" fish. The fact is that natural fish have scars on their skin and Wild Alaska salmon "run" but no one can predict when or how many fish will be available. Despite this challenge, the strategy was progressing.

SO WHAT UNDERMINED THIS STRATEGY?

In short, two overlooked assumption thwarted the plan. Both assumptions involved the "human behavior." The first assumption involved the Alaska fishermen's general psychological profile which was to maintain an autonomous and independent, self-determined way of life. Their collective mind-set opposed collaboration with anyone and everyone. This mind-set symbolizes the majority of the Alaskan fisheries. Of course, there were a small number of fishermen who realized that they needed to collaborate, but they were overruled by the majority. The fishermen's resistance to collaborate and become economically interdependent resulted in the collapse of the Alaskan commercial fishing industry. In essence, they preferred to fail rather than lose their value of self-determination. The industry has made strides to recover, but Alaska has not returned to its once dominant position as the world's most natural fish provider.

The second assumption also involved human behavior. As soon as the USA board observed the successful progress toward increasing revenue throughout the Alaska fisheries, they assumed that the negotiation would be sustainable. The fact is that momentum was growing, but far from completed. Refusal to work together and impatience caused this negotiation to fail.

SO, WHAT DOES THIS HAVE TO DO WITH THIS BOOK?

This book is not about how to fail. Rather, it is about minimizing failures by recognizing assumptions, that if not identified, may undermine even the best Leader-Negotiator's plans. One of the most unpredictable and uncontrollable factors in a negotiation is people. It has been said that if you could just remove people from the negotiation, negotiating would be simple. The focus of this book is:

SECTION I: The Mind of the Leader-Negotiator
SECTION II: Identifying Assumptions using Effective Questioning (EQ)
SECTION III: Negotiating in the Leadership Zone
SECTION IV: Managing Conflict
SECTION V: Hidden Traps

Thinking strategically is the competitive edge in business, politics, education, and everyday life.

Ken Sylvester

In selecting this book, you are about to embark on a journey that will transform the way that you lead and/or the way you build future leaders. The information presented to you will not resemble anything in the thousands of leadership books on bookstore shelves. That's because one-dimensional theories—however prettily they're packaged and repackaged—can only attempt to teach you what to think. They cannot teach you *how* to think.

To put it simply, in the unpredictable global business environment, it is not enough to follow last millennium's formulaic strategies. You have to learn to think multidimensionally. That means seeing the world through different lenses. It means reprogramming assumptions so that you are able to see doors where once there appeared to be walls. The leadership theories and negotiation strategies in this book have undergone years of rigorous field testing from boardrooms to courtrooms with the same results—success. Success for executives, for shareholders, for the bottom line, and—in identifying and cultivating leaders. The door is waiting…you're about to be handed the key.

Section I

The Mind of the Leader-Negotiator

Chapter 1

The Case for the Leader-as-Negotiator

INTRODUCTION: THE NEED FOR LEADER–NEGOTIATORS

There is a significant need for Leaders to be Negotiators in order for them to:

1. Negotiate within their organizations;
2. Extend opportunities beyond their organization's boundaries; and
3. Recognize the fundamental assumptions behind their industry, global economies, and the implications of worldwide competition.

Leaders from business, education, nonprofits, and government must use **negotiation** skills to succeed. When they look for assistance from literature and training in the area of negotiation, however, they are often limited to technique-based negotiation concepts and strategies. The technique-based, buy–sell theory of negotiation that dominates Western literature and culture is important to understand and useful in certain contexts. However, the complexity of organizations these days and the emerging global economic reality, characterized by its lack of a single, dominant political power, are at the heart of the need for the integration of leadership and negotiation. Answers, formulas, and techniques (AFTs) fail to consider the changing conditions that demand a more sophisticated approach to both leadership and negotiation.

The model for my Leader–Negotiator (L-N) Theory included the study and implementation of this framework to educate and train approximately 30,000 professional leader–negotiators. This material has been presented to large corporations, small companies, government agencies, and universities since 1990. It is important to note that this is the first public offering of this framework, its practical elements, and suggested applications to the education and business worlds. It is my thesis that the disciplines of leadership and negotiation should be inseparable when discussing effective leadership. As such, I argue that the behavioral attributes necessary for effective leaders are complementary to behavioral attributes for effective negotiators. After reviewing the literature, I am left with the inescapable conclusion that no significant research in terms of number as well as rigor exists that addresses the real-world skills that Leader–Negotiators must possess today. The following story in Box 1.1 serves as a case in point about why leaders need to be negotiators in a global economy.

Box 1.1 The China Story

Following a business trip to Shanghai and Beijing China, one of the 28 leaders I consulted with from the Chinese government contacted me and asked if I could arrange a conversation between him and the CEO of the US-based technology company I represented on my trip. This government leader told me that the regional representative for this US company had been positioned to negotiate with them, but the Chinese viewed him as a manager, *not a leader* who could complete a negotiated agreement. In fact, the Chinese officials were offended that this prominent technology company sent a manager *instead of* the company's CEO to negotiate with them. This choice by the US company is the equivalent in China to sending a boy to do a man's job. Subsequently, I had a conversation with the technology company's CEO who said, "No, they would have their regional director, viewed by them as an expert negotiator, manage this negotiation." (The potential for this deal involved 2½ billion potential customers.) The deal was lost because Chinese protocol is that leaders, not managers, negotiate important deals. This illustrates that the Chinese, in this case at least, perceive their leaders as Leader–Negotiators while many US companies separate the function of leadership from the function of negotiation.

Global economic pressure requires leaders to practice collaboration among diverse human and political networks if they are to realize a bold economic future. **Collaboration** implies a synergistic mind-set that engenders shared visions, alliance formation, and tolerates the ambiguity of managing complex, global relationships. Most leaders have not been schooled in negotiation skills, nor are these skills anticipated by academic institutions and most corporate systems. Shifting basic organizational assumptions is not just of interest but rather, necessary. This idea will be referred to in this book as **global interdependence**.

FOUR PROMINENT LEADERSHIP THEORIES

We owe a debt to the early theorists who pioneered leadership studies; they have guided us to where we are today. It is important, therefore, to briefly examine the four predominant leadership **theories** from which we have evolved.

Trait Theory: Personal Attributes Are What Determines a Leader's Effectiveness

Trait theory was developed in the late 1930s. Trait theory attributes leadership success to the extraordinary leader qualities, such as tireless energy, penetrating intuition, uncanny foresight, and irresistible persuasive powers. The assumption is that some people are natural or born leaders, endowed with traits not possessed by others.

Behavior Theory: What Leaders Do

Behavior theory caught fire in the 1950s. It was assumed that those who are most disciplined, who spend their time most efficiently, effectively network, mentor, and delegate, are most likely to succeed. Researchers thought that if they could discover what managers actually *did* on the job, the secrets of effective leadership might be revealed. Hence, they attempted to classify human behavior through the use of questionnaires. Researchers measured task-oriented behavior, relationship-oriented behavior, and participative leadership.

Situation Leadership Theory: The Situation Determines the Leader's Behavior

Situation leadership theory developed around 1975. It proposed that leaders are born of circumstance and are at their best in a particular context. Also called "contingency" or "path–goal" theory, this model attempts to help managers and leaders deal with hectic schedules, fragmented organizational structures, and political pressures. Researchers have difficulty in measuring situation leadership because the model does not account for more than one situational variable at a time.

Power and Influence Theory: Leaders Exert Power and Followers React

Power and influence theory was popularized in the 1980s. It examines the use of on-the-job rewards, punishments, and persuasion, assuming that effective leadership flows from the top-down; leaders act and followers react. Studies in this school of thought focus on types of power, the amount of power, how power is exercised, and power tactics. Similarly, attention is paid to how influence is exerted—through persuasion, inspiration, consultation, praise, loyalty, friendships, favors, and more. Followers of this theory frequently call on Machiavelli's The Prince and Sun Tzu's Art of War.

EXPLAINING THE WORLD FROM ONE POINT OF VIEW IS A PERFECT FORMULA FOR FAILURE

Although the leadership theories summarized above have become quite well-known, they still are not able to adequately describe or predict effective leadership. Further, they do not address leadership *and* negotiation. Most books, training, seminars, and people try to adopt one of these theories as though it is THE single operating theory for successful leadership. It is not the theory; it is the **critical thinking** attached to the theory that makes it work.

Successful leadership relies on the mind of the negotiator and effective questioning, to be discussed in detail in later chapters. The preponderance of leadership research focuses on leader–group relations, particularly leadership styles. However, "styles" ignore cultural assumptions that are inherent in global relationships. I want to emphasize that I am not disregarding the contributions of the numerous authors whose theories I have researched. Instead, each theory was reviewed and analyzed to identify gaps, resulting in the grounding of theoretical precepts included in my Leader–Negotiator Theory. The challenge remains to observe, describe, and understand the real world of leadership, and then develop a relevant and effective theory encompassing leadership *and* negotiation.

The Leader-as-Negotiator Theory

In a very broad sense, **negotiation** can be viewed as the changing of any relationship and can be viewed on a continuum spanning contractual and routine resource allocation to negotiating major organizational change. Formal literature about negotiation theory began more than 4000 years ago in Asia. Negotiation today has necessarily changed from what negotiation was, shifting to a primarily Western perspective. The major shift required today is a move from a nationalistic, technique-based approach to negotiations to one that must adapt to an interdependent world. This shift began at the conclusion of World War II, with subsequent landmark events, for instance, the establishment of the United Nations, the prominent role of the International Monetary Fund, the collapse of the Berlin Wall, the development of Greenpeace, the formation of the G-7, etc.

The Leader

Given the context of an **interdependent** world, the concept of leader takes on new meaning. For the purposes of my Leader–Negotiator Theory, a **leader** will be defined as "any person holding a managerial or executive position of influence." Leaders must be able to (1) solve problems, (2) make decisions, (3) take effective action, (4) build competent teams, and (5) craft strategy. The Leader–Negotiator Theory helps clarify what the significant issues are for an organization's success. It accomplishes this by focusing on questioning **assumptions**, which are necessary skills if leaders are to effectively manage his or her organization.

The Negotiator

Given the previously stated implications of an interdependent world, the term "negotiator" takes on new meanings and new functions. A **negotiator** is any appointed leader who interacts with and connects internal and external systems. Negotiation is not limited to situations such as attempting to obtain the best price for an automobile or to obtain a much-deserved raise. On the contrary, the ability to effectively negotiate is one of the necessary skills for leaders, corporations, and nations to successfully compete, prosper, and ultimately survive in an emerging global economy. This naturally implies an involvement with the structural concepts of politics, law, technology, demographics, economics, etc.

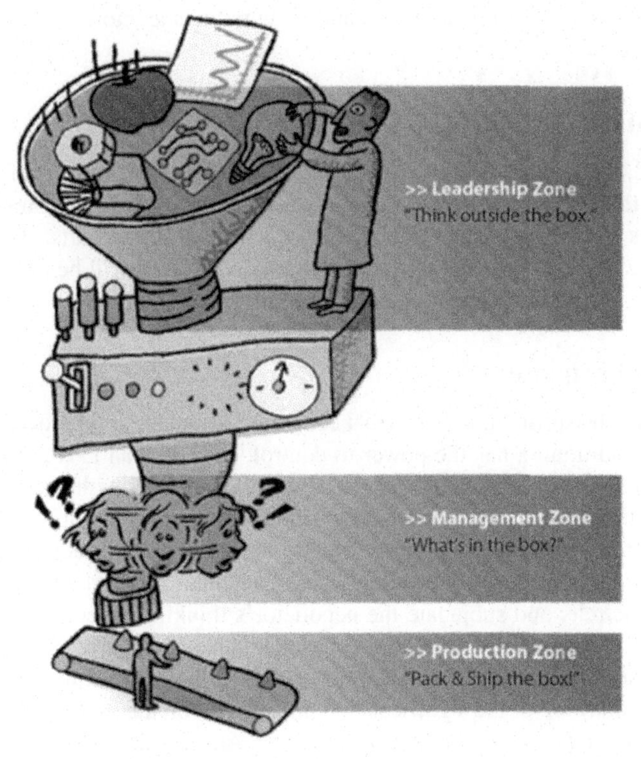

FIGURE 1.1 Systems-3 leadership model: Artist Unknown Following Extensive Search.

Questioning assumptions that may be outside of one's nationalistic box is the essence of the L-N Theory. The primary objective of the L-N Theory includes integrating the internal functions of the *three organizational zones* that are described in Chapter 3. The Leadership Zone (LZ), the Management Zone (MZ), and the Production Zone (PZ), pictured in Figure 1.1, form an organizational pattern that dominates organizations irrespective of nation and culture.

Leadership Zone (LZ): One of three organizational zones characterized by thinking out of the box, complexity, ambiguity, responsibility, and bottom-line orientation.

Management Zone (MZ): The middle of the three organizational zones, where management acts as a communicator between those in the Leadership Zone and those in the Production Zone.

Production Zone (PZ): The bottom of the three organizational zones; this is the level of the organization where goods and services are "packed and shipped."

Negotiating within the three zones requires leadership to support a fluid boundary spanning culture that ensures that products and services are effectively delegated from the LZ to the MZ and implemented by the PZ to customers. Leaders must insist that the three zones do not cross-purpose each other, hold information as political power, and view politics as more important than competence.

THE LEADER–NEGOTIATOR DIAGRAM

Figure 1.2, the Leader–Negotiator diagram, is comprised of three symbols that represent thinking skills involved in negotiations. The intended meaning of the diagram is best described by referring to each of its three parts, the middle square, the inside arrow, and the outside arrow. Note: L-N will be used to refer to "Leader–Negotiator" for the remainder of the text.

The Middle Square

It is not just the substantive issues that constitute the negotiation process. Accumulated conditioning has the power to control, or box-in an L-N as well. The middle square (the box) symbolizes the contextual complexity that exists during all negotiations. The idea of an **accumulated mind** refers to how a person's thinking process is conditioned over time by way of subtle influences. As such this square represents assumptions, biases, prejudices, and premises that may confine, encircle, and subjugate the negotiator's thinking process. The origins of these influences are infinite and involve all that has ever shaped an L-N's life. The Leader–Negotiator brings these influences to the negotiation table yet, is frequently unaware of the significance of their effect on the process. Awareness does not guarantee open-mindedness, however. As a result L-Ns get locked (or boxed) into:

- Their own thinking and logic patterns
- Their own assumptions that organize their course of thought and reasoning
- Their own ideological beliefs that frame their world view
- Their own emotional patterns that reinforce their reasoning
- Their own intuitive perceptions that are culturally unique
- Their own listening pattern(s) that subconsciously "filter" or control communications

FIGURE 1.2 The leader–negotiator diagram.

- Their prejudice for either a competitive (win–lose) or collaborative (win–win) negotiation
- Their acceptance or avoidance of conflict
- Their tendency to interpret the whole universe from their personal viewpoint
- Their predisposition to judge themselves by their intentions while judging others by their actions; a formula for increased conflict and possible loss of opportunities

The multiple influences on an L-N's skills are varied and complex. The middle square symbolizes this complexity and the limitations that can be imposed on a negotiation outcome if the L-N is unaware of the significance of these dynamics.

The Inner Arrow

One of the most demanding negotiations that L-N's conduct is with their own thinking. The inner arrow symbolizes the existence of personal assumptions that may sabotage one's thinking. This internal mind-set is referred to as a **psychological cul-de-sac**. One important power an L-N possesses is the ability to generate alternatives; but, when one's biases limit one's ability to generate creative alternatives, the L-N's thinking becomes a liability.

The Outside Arrow

The outside arrow symbolizes a willingness to be open to new ideas and perspectives beyond one's own. Thus, the outside arrow represents an effort to understand others' values as opportunities to improve negotiated outcomes. Effective Questioning (EQ) is an approach that is designed to sharpen one's awareness of others' thinking. This becomes essential if the objective is to maximize an optimal outcome for all parties.

This L-N diagram (Figure 1.2) is a symbol of the sophisticated complexities of human perception. It represents the cognitive skills of knowing oneself, knowing one's opponent, and knowing the negotiation context. One's perception of both past and present strongly influences the future. An L-N's perceptions and beliefs about the world will be inaccurate or distorted unless she or he takes active steps to verify their assumptions (Box 1.2).

The most inescapable principle of the future is continuous **change**; change that represents complex adjustments to complex systems that dominate our world. Business leaders must not only desire to adapt to change, they must know also how to think so that the assumptions that undergird increasingly complex change become understood and contextually relevant. Natural mind defaults, or assumptions, that limit success are:

- Assuming that the past has something to do with the future
- Assuming that reducing complex issues to oversimplified "bumper stickers" is advantageous

Box 1.2 The Leader-as-Negotiator Theory

The disciplines of leadership and negotiation are inseparable; the behavioral attributes necessary for effective leadership are complementary to behavioral attributes for negotiators. This theory contains three precepts, signified by the three parts of the L-N symbol: (1) Accumulated conditioning has the power to control or box-in an L-N (middle square); (2) Unexamined assumptions, biases, prejudices, and premises may confine, encircle, and subjugate an L-N's thinking process into a "psychological cul-de-sac" (inner arrow); and (3) Willingness to be open to new ideas and perspectives beyond one's own (through the use of Effective Questioning) can sharpen an L-N's awareness of others' and one's own thinking in order to optimize outcomes for all parties in a negotiation.

- Assuming that converting data to familiar patterns and habits will accelerate acceptance of change
- Assuming that accepting as true that all problems can be approached from a single problem-solving model that will result in simple answers and solutions
- Assuming belief in the "one great leader" theory
- Assuming that changing the way we do business involves only surface change (while not actually changing the way we think about business)
- Assuming that short-term problems will go away

Critical thinking is characterized by careful evaluation and judgment. It involves thinking about one's thinking and reshaping our minds to a different kind of habit—the habit of expecting change. Effective L-Ns have the skills to consistently produce in the context of the unexpected and problematic by turning systems upside down and inside out. This is a risky challenge for L-Ns; but, it is more risky to not make the adaptive leap. Why? Because not expecting change and/or not adapting only puts you further behind the change curve and will act as a time delay upon your business system. Delayed action does not favor survivors in a highly interdependent, fast-changing environment.

Chapter 2 will discuss the mind of the leader within the context of systems interdependencies.

"Old school" leadership assumed that proven *"AFTs"* would foster success.
"New school" leadership challenges assumptions to be able *to think* in terms of fast-changing strategy and disarming competitive threats.

Chapter 2

Attributes of Effective Leader-Negotiators

INTRODUCTION

How well Leader-Negotiators (L-Ns) think is the determining factor in how they perform five core leadership tasks:

1. Solving problems
2. Making decisions
3. Taking effective action
4. Building competent teams, and
5. Crafting effective strategy.

Yet, how L-Ns think, or **reason**, is one of the most overlooked components of assessing leadership competence. People learn how to reason so that they can draw conclusions or inferences from observations, experiences, or facts. This results in a personalized system of **logic**. This logic system functions as both a strength as well as a psychological prison, or "cul-de-sac." Psychological cul-de-sacs operate when we try to fit the world into our mental box in order to make sense of it. However, there are situations when our sense-making system must expand or change because it is not able to make sense of the situations of which we are confronted.

The demand for leaders to expand their "box" means that they must think critically. Thinking critically is the ability to examine contradictory lines of reasoning and using different lines of reasoning to cross-examine alternatives. This is the true sense of thinking strategically. That is, giving consideration of arguments for and against; point and counterpoint.

Critical thinking involves thinking about one's thinking. Critical thinking is a skill designed to help the L-N defend him or herself against self-entrapment. It involves being open to having one's viewpoint changed. People often have trouble changing their viewpoint because their dignity, status, or position depends on being right or, in having their beliefs and biases accepted without the threat of being challenged (Box 2.1).

The experience of being plagued by obstacles is common to leadership. In reality, judgments and decisions are made under conditions of **ambiguity** and **uncertainty**. Faced with incomplete information, pressured by time constraints and goal attainment, L-Ns often fall back on routine strategies, frames

Box 2.1 The Intoxicated Man

An intoxicated man left his favorite bar, strained his eyes into focus, and selected his homeward course. At the corner, he collided with a lamppost. Staggering back a few steps, he realigned his bearings and then, set forward on *the same* collision course. Inevitably, he struck the lamppost and this time he fell. Nevertheless, he gathered himself up with determined tenacity, retracing his steps once more. Colliding with the lamppost again, he clung to it and moaned in defeat, "I give up! It's no use, I'm surrounded."

of reference that become the unquestioned stratagems for how they lead their organizations.

> *If you always do what you have always done, you will always get what you have always got.*
>
> Ken Sylvester

Concealed traps can undermine the best of plans, the finest of intentions, and the greatest of organizations. Complex and important decisions are prone to **self-entrapment** because they tend to generate overconfident assumptions and lean toward overstated estimates. The greater the complexity of the decision, the greater the vulnerability of being snared into hidden traps—traps that are the product of the way we have been conditioned to think. There are numerous ways that human beings are conditioned to think. However, one's context determines whether or not the thinking pattern is advantageous or disadvantageous. **Strategic advantage** involves selecting a direction that is most favorable given the context. In other words, no single strategy is adequate in all situations. Alternate ways to think are necessary if one seeks freedom of choice. No choice, no freedom.

THREE POWERS OF EFFECTIVE L-NS

A L-N's greatest asset is his or her mind and will. One's thinking is seen in behavior and behavior is seen in the way a leader uses power. There are three "powers" that all successful L-Ns must possess: (1) **personal power**, (2) **professional power**, and (3) **situation power** (Figure 2.1).

- *Personal Power* includes knowledge of one's self, an awareness of one's strengths and vulnerabilities, and the willpower to persist under stress. *This type of power is described throughout this book as an essential and often overlooked characteristic of leadership success.*
- *Professional Power is* an L-N's knowledge base and expertise. Professional power is revealed in shaping a negotiation that includes: listening to and sorting information, asking questions, clarifying ambiguity, and framing arguments. *This type of power is described in the Effective Questioning and Framing chapters.*

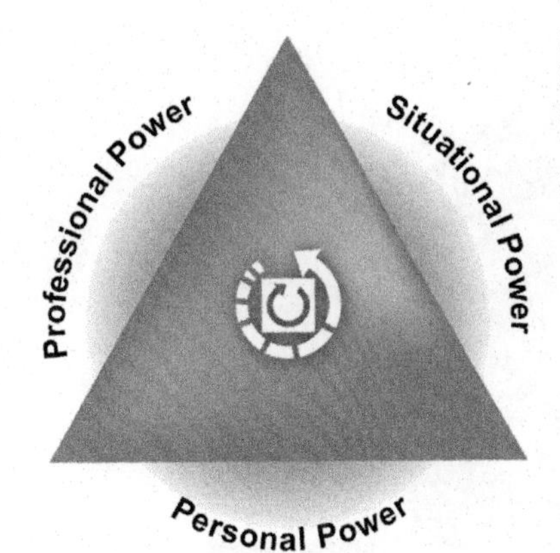

FIGURE 2.1 The Three Powers of Effective Leader-Negotiators (L-Ns) Personal Power: The mind and will of the L-N. Professional Power: The knowledge and expertise of the L-N. Situation Power: The wisdom of the L-N.

- *Situation Power* is the combined wisdom and judgment needed to select appropriate strategies and tactics. Wisdom cannot be replaced by AFTs (Answers, Formulas, or Techniques). As of this writing, computers do not provide wisdom; rather, wisdom continues to be an asset that is unique characteristic of the informed human mind. *This type of power will be described in the Strategies and Tactics chapters.*

THE FIVE ATTRIBUTES

A cluster of five inseparable **attributes** enhance or cancel out the L-N's powers (Figure 2.2). These five attributes are discussed in detail below. Sun Tzu, whose influence on twentieth century thinking is undisputed, reveals the importance of these five attributes. In his 2900-year-old manuscript, he puts forward these timeless L-N "secrets." Lessons implied from Sun Tzu:

> *If you know the enemy and know yourself, you need not fear the result of a hundred battles.*
> *If you know yourself but not the enemy, for every victory gained you will also suffer a defeat.*
> *If you know neither the enemy nor yourself, you will succumb in every battle.*
>
> Sun Tzu, The Art of War

Self-control: The Ability to Disarm Personal "Hot Buttons"

Self-control refers to a person's ability to maintain disciplined composure while under stress (Figure 2.3). The challenge to maintaining self-control involves being in command of our internal triggers or "hot buttons." Hot buttons are activated under stress and pressure. These hot buttons are unique to each individual.

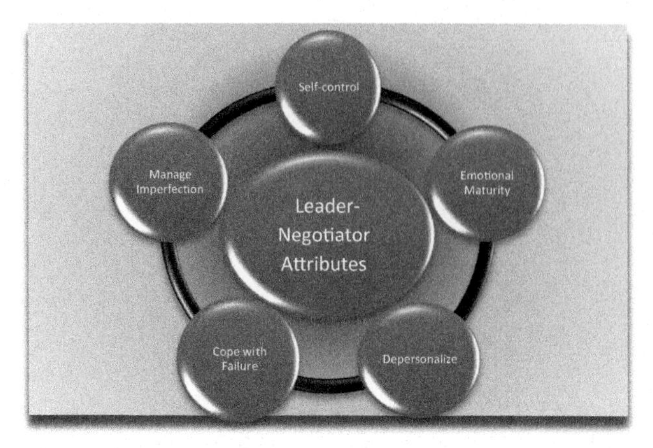

FIGURE 2.2 The five Leader-Negotiator Attributes **Research:** Organization Strategy Institute (OSI) research concludes that these five attributes not only endure the test of time, but are relevant to every culture. The only thing that differs is how they are articulated or prioritized in each culture.

FIGURE 2.3 Self-Control.

Two of the most contagious human emotions are anger and aggression. As a general rule, anger escalates unproductive behaviors. Anger can minimize our powers of reasoning and arouse counterproductive actions and words. *Why do people get angry when others get angry?* The answer is not about what the other party did or did not do. The answer involves asking why we allow others' behavior to provoke our emotions; it concerns why people answer others' anger with their anger.

An angry environment transfers energy away from common ground and emphasizes areas of disagreement and difference. A negotiation should focus on achieving one's objective. The challenge involves not getting trapped into an atmosphere of contagion where anger dominates reasoning. Rather than letting yourself *go into* anger, quiet your mind and emotions during moments of frustration and redirect your energy toward productive outcomes; these are the most effective ways of dealing with contagion (Box 2.2).

Expectations for a satisfactory negotiation may further lead to anger and frustration.

Why do we expect the negotiation process to be a satisfying experience? More often than not, the process of negotiating is not a satisfying experience. A negotiators' goal should be to reach a productive outcome, not to necessarily enjoy the process. This requires that we lead with our greatest asset—self-control of our mind. It is always a bonus if the negotiation process is enjoyable.

Box 2.2 To Regain Perspective, Use the 3×5 Card

During intense negotiations, I recommend that you retain a 3×5 card that concisely states or symbolizes your negotiation purpose. If you become emotionally aroused and are not sure that you can control your reactions, look at the 3×5 card to remind yourself: *Was it your purpose to get into an argument? Or, was it your goal to reach an agreement?* Use the 3×5 card idea to regain composure or even laugh. In addition, take three slow, deep abdominal breaths to relax and take your mind to a place that reframes your perspective. Your imagination will be helpful in visualizing how to restore your perspective. When you have time, find a way to write your "recovered perspective" on your 3×5 card.

Often, strong impulsive feelings create split-second reactions that result in saying words and doing things we wish we had not. Intense emotions increase the probability that we will incorrectly interpret situations. In a perfect world, we should be able to recover from these impulsive reactions by communicating regret or trying to absolve our behavior with the intent to move forward. However, there will be situations when our words and behavior will not be forgotten or absolved. If this occurs, make an attempt to restore the negotiation if the other party is receptive. If restoration is not workable, then—if possible—replace yourself with a different negotiator. There is an old proverb that says, "Cool heads prevail." This is excellent advice.

Consider an example provided by the national baseball icon, Jackie Robinson: Born January 31, 1919 in Cairo, GA; Died October 24, 1972 in Stamford, CT; Years with Dodgers: 1947–1956; Inducted into Hall of Fame: 1962 (Box 2.3).

Lesson learned: The attribute of self-control does not require L-Ns to be nonemotional. Rather, it requires not being sucked into and entrapped in nonproductive emotional scenarios.

Last, a negotiation is not a place to get one's personal needs met. If you have personal needs such as: the need to be listened to, to be respected, to have the right to speak your mind, or to be understood, appreciated, or esteemed, then it is recommended that you take care of those personal needs *before* you enter into a negotiation.

Table 2.1 below may help you maintain self-control. The three columns of Table 2.1 are:

> *Column 1* asks you to assess what you are able *to control.* This involves the ability or methods used to limit or restrict somebody or something from doing something. Typically, this column assumes that most of the time, one can only control oneself. Often, this list may be shorter than the two other columns. Be practical about what can be controlled and what cannot be controlled.
>
> *Column 2* asks you to assess what you may be able to *influence.* This assumes that you have the ability or potential to affect the course of events of someone else's thinking or actions. This involves a measurement of say, a 50–50 chance. Influence is infrequently a 100% probability.

Box 2.3 The Jackie Robinson Story

The social impact of Jackie Robinson's inclusion into Major League Baseball in 1947 resonates as one of the civil rights movement's most significant triumphs. For Robinson, the first African-American man to have the opportunity to participate in the major leagues for the Brooklyn Dodgers, it was all about *playing the game*. He was hand-selected by President Branch Rickey and the Dodger organization to cross the precipitous "color line." Robinson promised Rickey that he would not fight back, other than with his bat and glove, despite what teammates, competitors, fans, umpires, writers, broadcasters, and hotel managers might have said or how they tried to bait him into reacting.

Robinson agreed to take on this challenge. When he crossed the color lines at the ballpark, Robinson tried to relax and focus on the game, not on the constant catcalls. Off the field, the former UCLA four-sport star would also deal with bigotry, anonymous death threats, racial slurs, sitting in the back of the bus, "no colored" served or housed here signs, and opponents who were out to injure him.

Robinson, however, was bound and determined that he would perform to the highest level. And, that he did. In his debut season, he was named Rookie of the Year, an award which today bears his name. He became an immediate drawing card. While some just wanted to observe the only black player in baseball, others were truly enthralled by Robinson's daring and reckless abandon on the base paths and in the field. Robinson was the first African-American player to be inducted into the National Baseball Hall of Fame in 1962. All of Major League Baseball saluted him in 1997 (on the 50th Anniversary of his breaking the color barrier) and permanently retired his number from the game. On March 2, 2005, pioneer Robinson was recognized posthumously by receiving the Congressional Gold Medal during ceremonies in the rotunda of the United States Capitol Building in Washington, D.C. President George W. Bush made the presentation to Robinson's family members. The US Congress has commissioned gold medals as its highest expression of national appreciation for distinguished achievement.

Underlying Robinson's numerous awards was a world class demonstration of self-control and emotional maturity. If anyone ever had the right to lose emotional maturity, it was Jackie Robinson. Contrasting his challenges with mine, motivate me to exhibit self-control and emotional maturity.

Column 3 asks you to assess what you likely *cannot control*. This assumes that you have little to no chance of controlling or influencing someone else's thinking or actions.

Losing self-control may be associated with the perception of "powerlessness." If you are experiencing powerlessness, what are your alternatives? Loss of self-control often escalates negative or aggressive emotions. This is not a positive mind-set for L-Ns. Intense emotions tend to reduce one's *IQ* to something near their shoe size. In contrast, self-control gets the best out of one's thinking.

TABLE 2.1 Things You Can Control, Influences and/or Not Control

%	1. What are you able to control?	%	2. What are you able to influence?	%	3. What are you "not" able to control?

FIGURE 2.4 Emotional maturity.

Emotional Maturity—The Ability to Resist "Dancing to Others" (Psychological) Music

Emotional maturity requires that we control how we react to such things as others' personality traits, behavior, use of words, or ways of thinking that distract and sidetrack us from our goal (Figure 2.4). Negotiating with others involves recognizing that people often follow *predictable patterns* of behavior and rules. These "rules," expressed via behaviors such as: aggression, arrogance, deception, manipulation, disrespect, lack of consideration for others, procrastination, inflexibility, being uncommunicative, and/or argumentative, are often invisible to oneself. It is believed that to a great extent, human behavior is the result of conditioning. Often, the usual result of any or all of the behaviors described above is a failed negotiation (Box 2.4).

Lack of emotional maturity is often expressed in ideas that a negotiation must:

- be perfect, faultless, and precise
- be guarded, distrustful, cautious, or wary
- be suspicious of all authority and skeptical of everyone and everything
- be unwilling to admit mistakes and/or acknowledge being wrong
- be motivated to get even
- be defensive and be on guard against all inquiries that might reveal your position.

Box 2.4 How Behavior Can Cancel Out One's Intelligence

A major Fortune 500 corporation was involved in a lawsuit with an agency of the US government. During the early stages of negotiation, one of the company's attorneys, considered one of the brightest attorneys in his particular field of law, became embroiled in an argument with the government's spokesperson. In a split second, this bright attorney's "hot button" was activated. Without thought, he used emotionally charged, arrogant words that were unprofessional that stimulated an emotional reaction of anger and arrogance from the US government spokesperson. Essentially, both legal teams allowed their loss of self-control and emotional maturity to displace their very high intellect and the negotiation exploded into a highly charged, personalized climate even though the negotiation objective was to reach agreement, not to *feel* frustration. It was estimated that this altercation extended the legal case by 7 years at an additional cost of hundreds of millions of dollars.

FIGURE 2.5 Depersonalize.

The challenge involves not getting caught up in others' rules; in other words, the negotiator should not dance to others' "psychological music." When reason is countered with passion, it more often than not diminishes listening, escalates discord, and detracts from achieving the negotiated objective.

Depersonalization—"It's Not About Me"

Depersonalization refers to not interpreting others' words and/or behaviors as having to do with you personally (Figure 2.5). Depersonalization requires not getting caught up in the drama of conflict. In the intensity and passion of conflict, people tend to cling ferociously to stories that oversimplify problems and people, expand scenarios of good versus evil, and/or support themselves as righteous in their fight against those who are unjust, corrupt, etc.

The outcome of personalizing situations that are not personal is that people perceive themselves as victims who suffer at the hands of intolerable persons, and are powerless to protect themselves against unfair circumstances. This is not to imply that there are not situations where people are victims. Personalizing, however, only escalates conflict drama. Once you are "dancing to" someone else's music, you have decreased your ability

Box 2.5 This Has Nothing to Do With Me

A coworker passed me in the hallway in the early morning. I greeted him with "good morning!" He did not respond, passing by without making eye contact or saying a word. Within that split second, several personalized interpretations of his nonresponsiveness could have filtered through my mind; "Had I done something to offend him?" in other words, "Could I be the cause of his lack of response to my greeting?" However, I chose a different thought process. I thought, "I haven't seen John for several days. Something may have happened and he has a reason for not returning my greeting." Later that day I phoned John and asked how he was doing. He said he was glad I called, sharing that he spent the entire late night and all morning at the hospital with his 4-year-old daughter. A sudden and severe illness threatened her life. He was exhausted from the worry and lack of sleep. So I learned, when John passed me in the hallway, he did not have time or energy *to take care of me*. He was in a survival mode. John's behavior had nothing to do with me in fact. Depersonalizing this situation was not only healthy for me but positive for our friendship.

to manage a conflict and achieve your objective—a successful negotiated outcome (Box 2.5).

Aristotle said:

> *But to be angry with the right person, to the right degree, at the right time, for the right purpose, and in the right way - this is not easy.*
>
> Nichomachean Ethics

Managing Failure—The Ability to Be Rational About, and Accept Setbacks

Failure is a normal part of any attempt to achieve success (Figure 2.6). Consequently, one should not blame oneself or others for a normal experience of failure when it occurs. The human tendency to deny failure exists in all professions and in all areas of human life. Human beings tend to believe that others make mistakes. "Others may fail…but not us." The fact is, from time to time, all L-Ns fail. Not succeeding is a condition of life. We must acknowledge that the human mind is imperfect. An effective L-N must adjust to—but not surrender to—the potential of failure. We must accept that imperfections will invade everyone's life and plans. Expect imperfection! Better to be prepared than to be surprised (Box 2.6).

A common reaction to failure is to *catastrophize* the worst possible outcome. Ask yourself how many times the worst possible outcome has happened? Usually, it is seldom. The counter to this reaction is to look beyond the moment and, *look forward* to the *next opportunity*. Failure will occur.

FIGURE 2.6 Manage failure.

Box 2.6 Ten Steps to Memory Loss: A Lesson from the World's Most Successful Athletes

When world-class athletes fail to achieve their desired results, they practice *10 steps to memory loss*. This means that within 10 walking steps, they are to forget the mistake they made. How? Forgetting cannot be done by trying to undo the past. Rather, they reframe by *looking forward* to the next great result. They *replace* the failure by rehearsing success. The principle is to *control* what you can control and to put out of your mind what you cannot control. Ruminating about or clinging to failure usually increases the likelihood of failing again.

Failure cannot be avoided. However, the ability to recover from failure is the critical test of an effective L-N. No one enjoys failure, yet no person has ever demonstrated perfection.

Cope with Imperfection—The Discipline to Guard Your Expectations

There are two central perspectives involved in coping with **imperfection** (Figure 2.7). The first is to know the difference between high standards and perfectionism. The second involves knowing how to recover when we fail.

It has been said that the test of one's leadership is determined by what stops them from achieving their goal. This is termed stopping power. Stopping power comes from:

1. external situations, difficulties, and seemingly impossible challenges, and
2. personal flaws, defects, weaknesses, and mistakes that often dishearten, undermine, humiliate, and hinder one's pursuits.

L-Ns must be experts at managing disappointing performances as well as shortcomings. **Perfectionism** can be described as demanding the impossible. Perfectionism is not the same as high standards. High standards involve doing one's best and pursuing continual improvement.

FIGURE 2.7 Cope with imperfection.

Box 2.7 A Test of the Five Leader-Negotiator Attributes

1. A person organizes a picnic at the lake. It rains. They say, "I should have known that it was going to rain today. It rains a lot at this time of the year. I should have waited until later in the summer."

What is the Attribute? ____________________

2. "People will think that I am either a success or a failure. I've let everyone down. I will never live down this situation!"

What is the Attribute? ____________________

3. "What did I do to deserve that kind of behavior?"

What is the Attribute? ____________________

4. "Nobody talks with me like that! If it's the last thing I do I will get them back."

What is the Attribute? ____________________

5. "You can't say that to me! Who do you think you are? No, I am not listening to you, and let me tell you a thing or two."

What is the Attribute? ____________________

Answers: 1. Cope with Imperfection 2. Manage Failure 3. Depersonalization 4. Self-Control 5. Emotional Maturity

It is a stimulating exercise to imagine how the world might be better. This is a worthy use of one's time. However, an equally challenging exercise involves asking ourselves, "How unmanageable, problematic, complex, and fractious might people and situations be before it stops me?" Perfection usually accompanies expressions such as, "should" or "ought" and "must." Instead, state your expectations as preferences that symbolize high standards. Expect the best, but be prepared for less (Box 2.7).

Box 2.8 Five Attributes that Influence Leader-Negotiator Power

1. Self-Control—The ability to disarm personal "hot buttons" or triggers
2. Emotional Maturity—The ability to resist dancing to others "hot buttons"
3. Depersonalization—The ability to not take others, or things that happen, personally
4. Managing Failure—The ability to be rational and accept disappointments and setbacks
5. Coping with Imperfection—The discipline to guard your expectations.

IN CONCLUSION

The five attributes of effective L-Ns, summarized in Box 2.8 represent a cluster of important attributes that L-Ns must continually pursue. Knowledge of one's self, an awareness of one's strengths and vulnerabilities, and the willpower to succeed under stress are foundational for effective L-Ns.

- Remember, it is not a failure if you cannot control circumstances that are out of your control. All L-Ns will fail among the complexities of the world within which we live. Never fail, however, in maintaining your perspective and never fail to believe in yourself. It is not failure to have given your best and failed. All L-Ns have limitations; there are no exceptions. An effective L-N knows his or her limitations and deals candidly with them.
- L-Ns cannot effectively lead if they are caught up in the drama and stories of others.
- L-Ns are not perfect; the test of leadership is how you recover from mistakes, not did you make a mistake. Reframe your mind-set to recovery as soon as possible.
- The five leadership attributes are about being tough minded. *Leadership is not a flower to be picked; it is a mountain to be climbed.* Guard your expectations and remember, *There are no easy victories.*

Chapter 3 introduces The Systems-3 Leadership Model.

Chapter 3

Systems-3 Leadership

DISPELLING TWO LEADERSHIP MYTHS

Chapter 2 covered how to access and manage one's mind by developing five attributes that enhance (or cancel-out) an L-N's power. Knowledge of oneself, an awareness of one's strengths and vulnerabilities, and the willpower to succeed under stress are foundational for effective L-Ns. Having **contextual intelligence** is also paramount. Contextual intelligence is the ability to identify circumstances or background of a situation needed to gain insight into strategic planning and/or conflict management.

The Myth of the Magic Bullet

A frequent question I receive is, "What is the *one* secret to effective **leadership**?" The trouble with this question is not the question per se, but with the assumption behind the question. This question assumes that there is only one secret to being an effective Leader-Negotiator (L-N) and that knowing the secret will yield success. If there were just one secret and the secret were known, this "one magic bullet" strategy would have been revealed and the world would be at peace.

The Myth of the Lone Leader

On June 5, 1989, hundreds of Chinese civilians were massacred by the Chinese army during a military operation to quell a passionate uprising. Near Tiananmen Square, a small, unexceptional man in slacks and a white shirt, carrying what looked to be his day's groceries, positioned himself in front of an approaching tank. The tank swerved to avoid the man, but the man moved too, blocking its way. The lone man kept that tank—and the column of 17 other tanks behind it—at bay for more than half an hour (Figure 3.1).

That image, transmitted around the world, showed us all what we thought we needed to know about leadership—an unflinching hero standing in the face of brute force. The image endures in no small part because we are enamored with the mythology of self-sufficiency.

We've been conditioned to see our heroes as men or women in glorious isolation who, at crucial moments pull a hidden reserve from their psyches to reach transcendence. We see this in everything from Thoreau's escape to Walden Pond in order to live off the land, to the image of the lone chief executive or

FIGURE 3.1 Boy stopping tank.

head of state, to the star athlete making the winning play. The truth is, Thoreau frequently left his cabin, chief executives and heads of state rely upon skilled staffs, and the star athlete can only achieve immortality with a superb team.

The negative impact of these two myths is that they undermine what is expected of leaders and a leader's ability to implement most plans that require collaboration and cooperation. What we were not shown from Tiananmen is that moments before the tanks would have run over him, the man's friends drug him out of the way from being crushed by the tanks. These examples underscore a leadership secret that's beginning to catch on throughout the world. It's the concept of **team competence**. Team competence disposes the notion that a lone man or woman can be all things to all people.

To turn the conventional definition of leadership on its head even further, I'd like to suggest that a successful leader must do more than inspire others to follow. Motivation that is not competent is a formula for failure. The best leaders know when to use power and how and when to delegate it. The best leaders are not rigid, they are adaptable. They are aware of the assumptions through which they must see the world and, they can choose to abandon default modes of thinking when the situation demands. Most importantly, they know the value of diversity and not just in the classical sense. A great leader will actively set out to discover what qualities are missing in his or her team and then recruit to fill those holes. Great leaders must hire strategically. They must resist the temptation to hire or promote clones.

THE CHALLENGE OF WHERE WE ARE: DO YOU KNOW WHAT YOU ARE LEADING? DO YOU KNOW WHAT THE CONTEXT OF YOUR ORGANIZATION IS?

Leadership is an expression of the way L-Ns think. It is not enough to follow formulaic strategies, you have to think for yourself and think multidimensionally.

That means seeing the world through multiple lenses. It means reprogramming assumptions so you are able to open doors where once there appear to be walls. Once you see doors, you must find the key that fits. That's where the System-3 (S-3) Leadership Model comes in. You will have your assumptions challenged, your brain stretched, and you will learn new effective leadership methods. S-3 introduces the concept of an L-N's competence. Competence is as much about cultivating individual potential as it is about building competent teams. Where the S-3 Leadership Model breaks from the previous theorists—and other new ones—is that S-3 identifies *three zones* through which L-Ns understand their organization and the context within which their organization does business.

THE THREE ORGANIZATIONAL ZONES: THE S-3 LEADERSHIP MODEL

Effective L-Ns are responsible for organizing everything from money to manpower to time to conflict management to directing energy toward expected outcome and goals. **Organizational Intelligence** is a term used to describe an L-N's ability to understand how all the parts of an organization can be transformed into a whole. Effective L-Ns know that it is folly to insulate themselves from an understanding of all three organizational zones (Figure 3.2). The three organizational zones are:

1. The Leadership Zone (LZ)
2. The Management Zone (MZ)
3. The Production Zone (PZ)

It is important to note that what happens in these three zones is not related to the people who occupy those positions. Whoever works there must perform certain tasks. It is assumed that the organization depends on their performance in these roles for survival and growth. The zones are best understood when viewed as a holistic system.

S-3 Leadership is about understanding and leading, ensuring that all three zones work as one. The thinking skills required are divergent and convergent. **Divergent thinking** involves brainstorming and expanding opportunities for organizational growth. **Convergent thinking** is a method of problem-solving that searches for known and correct rules to find a proper solution.

The Leadership Zone

LZ is characterized by complexity, ambiguity, and responsibility. Those who work in the LZ are responsible for designing logical organizational structures that can adapt to external competition. L-Ns must design organizations with the ultimate goal of maximizing the bottom line. Enlarging opportunity and solving complicated problems dominates most of the L-N's thoughts, energy, and time (Figure 3.3).

The LZ is characterized by **specialization**. Specialization tends to promote self-interest rather than the organization's collaborative oneness. LZ's specialized expertise refers to how they are intraconnected yet struggle to collaborate with others LZ's who are concerned about their areas of specialization. Specialized zone interests, or turf wars, often lead to protected boundaries and conflicting viewpoints regarding how to lead the organization.

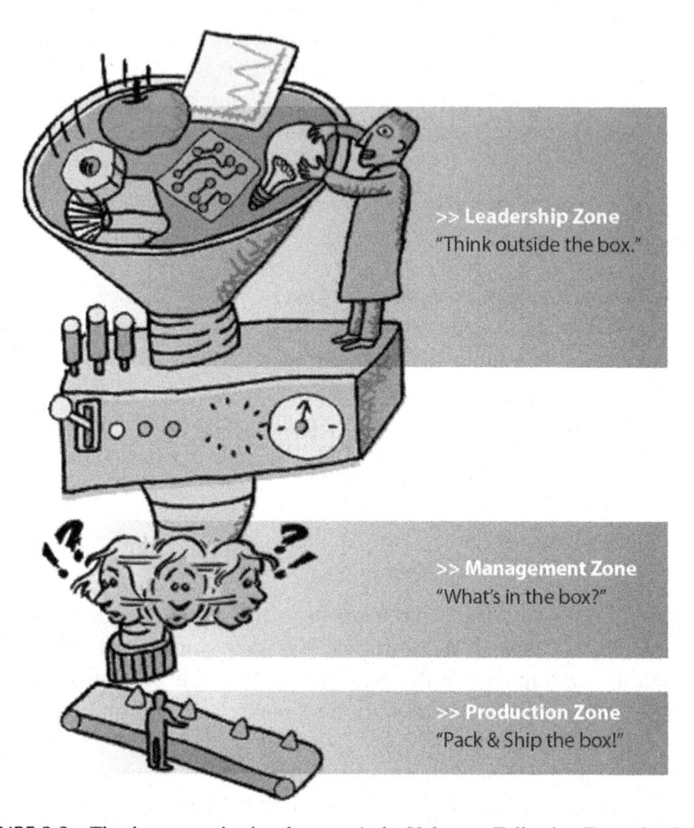

FIGURE 3.2 The three organizational zones: Artist Unknown Following Extensive Search.

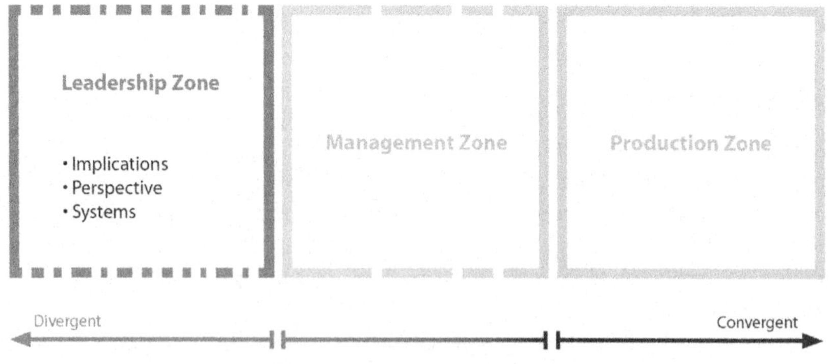

FIGURE 3.3 The Leadership Zone (LZ).

The Management Zone

The MZ is a pressurized place to be, but it is absolutely essential for an organization's success. This zone is distinguished by the need for managers to survive as they are caught between the LZ and the PZ. Management's task is to assume responsibility for strategic direction and then to find ways to implement that strategy in the PZ. MZs frequently feel torn between the LZ that communicates the big picture and the PZ where workers require specific direction in order to do their jobs (Figure 3.4).

Typically, managers in the MZ are given a limited and specialized glimpse of the LZ's big picture. This commonly results in managers being at cross-purposes with other managers. To make things complicated, MZs have responsibility for most everything but often have not been given the authority to resolve conflicts. This may cause them to isolate away from other MZs and closer to the groups or individuals they manage.

MZs are expected to view the organization from everyone's perspective and maintain 359° of organizational objectivity. However, organizations tend to "silo" into fragmented divisions, situating MZ's in the middle, wedged between what the LZ perceives as opportunity and what the PZ perceives as threat. Thus, the MZ is considered the "Tearing Zone."

Three Alternative Courses of Action in the Tearing Zone

1. MZs can slide UP to the LZ
2. MZs can remain in the Middle between LZs and PZs
3. MZs can slide Down to the PZ

Organizational Fragmentation Can Cause MZ Isolation and Distance Among Other MZs

Sliding tactics are used to cope with system **fragmentation**, but they only work for a short period of time as sliding does not resolve the fragmentation problem (Figure 3.5).

- If MZs move horizontally toward other MZs, they may risk being vulnerable to other MZ ladder climbers. Or, they may be perceived as incompetent if they reveal that they *need* other MZs.

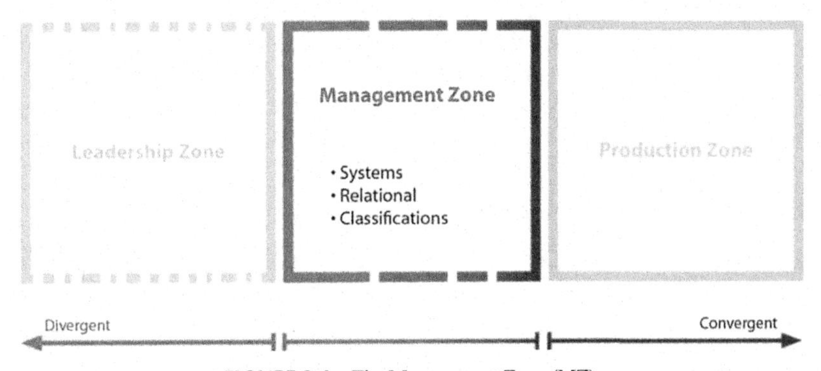

FIGURE 3.4 The Management Zone (MZ).

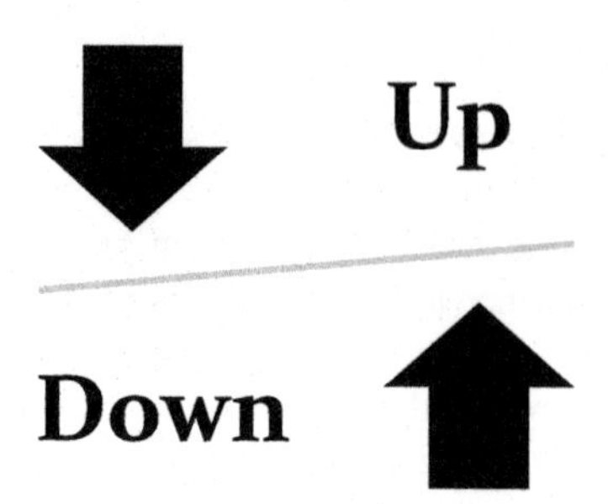

FIGURE 3.5 Management Zone (MZ) sliding Tactics.

- If MZs go down to the PZ, they may risk being perceived as breaching LZ confidentiality and perceived as not having what it takes to be an LZ.
- If MZs go up to LZ, they may risk losing trust among both MZs and PZs. They may be perceived as breaching confidentiality and losing trust.

MZ Dilemma: How do you cope when you perceive more problems and opportunities than can be resolved? MZs are often aware of more problems than they can resolve. MZs tend to cross divisional boundaries which allow them to see the whole organizational system more than either the LZs or the PZs who perceive the organization from the organization's perimeters. A 360° organizational view often overwhelms MZs. IF they perceive problems that impede the organization's progress yet they are prevented from crossing boundaries to resolve conflicts and improve organizational efficiencies, they can burn out.

The Production Zone

The PZ must implement the LZ's strategy as communicated via the MZ. However, production usually does not interpret strategic changes as opportunity. Rather, PZs usually perceive change as a threat to their job security. PZs have little or nothing to say about what comes down from the LZ and, consequently, feel vulnerable (Figure 3.6).

PZs tend to have an Us versus Them mind-set and feel exploited by them—the MZs and LZs. PZs are frequently not listened to and are not included in planning and decision-making. They tend to feel excluded from having a voice in the organization, which tends to reduce their sense of long-term loyalty. PZs are vulnerable to losing their job if LZs choose to reorganize.

ORGANIZATIONAL PUZZLES

Rarely are an organization's puzzle pieces organized from a master plan. Organizations grow as successes and failures force them to grow—randomly and

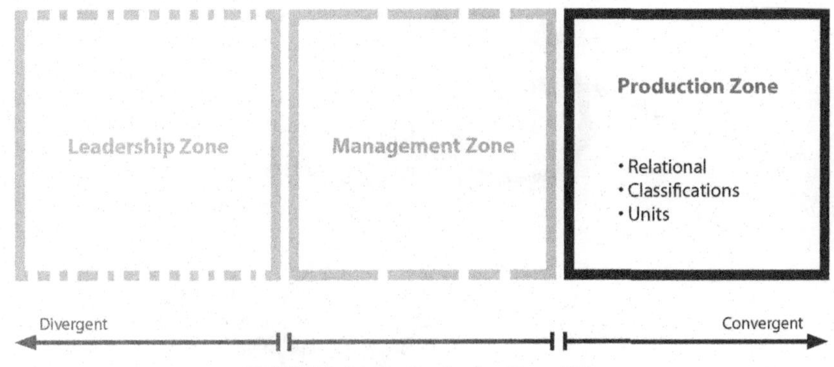

FIGURE 3.6 The Production Zone (PZ).

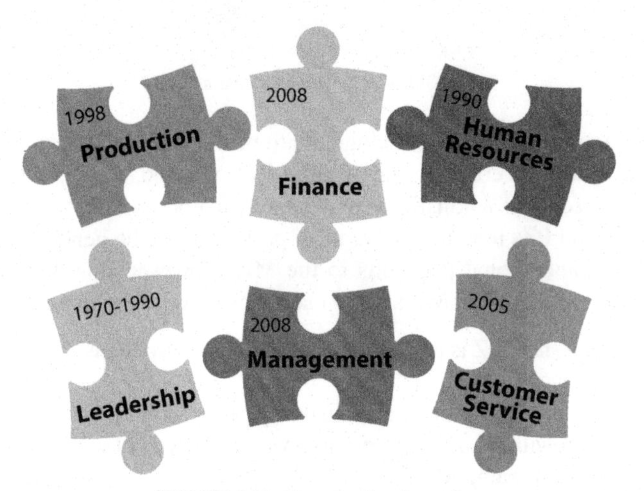

FIGURE 3.7 Organizational puzzles.

haphazardly. Most organizations are built over time, within different contexts, and by L-Ns who have different approaches to how organizations should be led. The spaces between each puzzle piece are where most conflict and misunderstanding occurs. Attempts to reorganize an organization tend to reorganize only certain puzzle pieces. As a result, divisions get reorganized, but system-wide pieces often remain disconnected (Figure 3.7).

ZONE BLINDNESS

Zone Blindness is the condition whereby each zone is so focused on their own needs, interests, problems, etc., that they cannot see the other zones. Each zone tends to perceive only their exclusive roles and responsibilities. This contributes to organizational fragmentation which frequently results in conflict (Figure 3.8).

FIGURE 3.8 Zone blindness.

Fragmentation results in not being able to perceive that one's zone contributes to organizational conflict (the "Blame Game"); and, the inability to perceive the three zones as a holistic system is likely to compromise the best efforts of L-Ns. LZs and PZs tend to resolve most problems via the general remedy of sending all organizational problems to the MZ. However, this domino effect results in bottle necks—the MZ simply cannot get everything done!

- LZ Myth #1—The MZ is the solution for solving all problems. In practice, this just does not work.
- LZ Myth #2—Delegating responsibility for MZs to resolve system fragmentation without the authority to do so, just does not work.
- LZ Myth #3—Blaming MZs for failed LZ plans does not solve the problem. Problems only get resolved when ALL three zones work collaboratively as one.

TEAM COMPETENCE

Why do so many of America's major corporations still continue to assemble executive teams full of clones? They simply don't know any better; that is, until the bottom line turns from black to red. Take the case of a major US car manufacturer. They were reeling from a $740 million loss when they hired us to help them stem the bleeding. The first thing they asked was, "How do we get out of this?" My response, "Let's take a look at how you got into it." Not surprisingly, our analysis revealed that their team of top executives were not proficient in any of the five L-N skills—problem-solving, decision-making, taking effective action, building competent teams, and crafting strategy; they were not aware that the S-3 organizational zones exist or how they function; and, they did not invest in team building within or among the three zones to create an effective organization.

Certainly, integration of the three zones represents a challenge to L-Ns. In the 1920s and 1930s, specialization was a major organizational approach (take the Ford Motor Company, for example). People seldom traveled more than 50 miles from their home, the culture of the United States was family oriented, people knew each other, etc. Similar values and familiarity with one another were the glue that allowed bureaucracies to work. Today, specialization has become a dominant characteristic such that teamwork is a much talked about ideal but an elusive practice. Specialization thwarts team competence, which refers to the integration of an organization to work as one.

In this era of global interdependence, new relationships are developing among nations. It's no longer enough for corporations to lead with like-minded thinkers who view problem-solving from the same assumptions.

The world can no longer be controlled and ordered from a single point of power. In fact, one of the surest ways to fail is to insist on explaining the world from only one viewpoint. However, the use of Effective Questioning (Section II) can help better understand organizational puzzles, soften the walls of specialization, and promote three-zone integration that is porous enough such that all three zones can boundary span. When information isn't guarded as power, employees, companies, and countries will be better able to develop resilient organizations and alliances. EQ describes how L-Ns can assess their thinking skills and avoid nine assumptions that result in thinking errors.

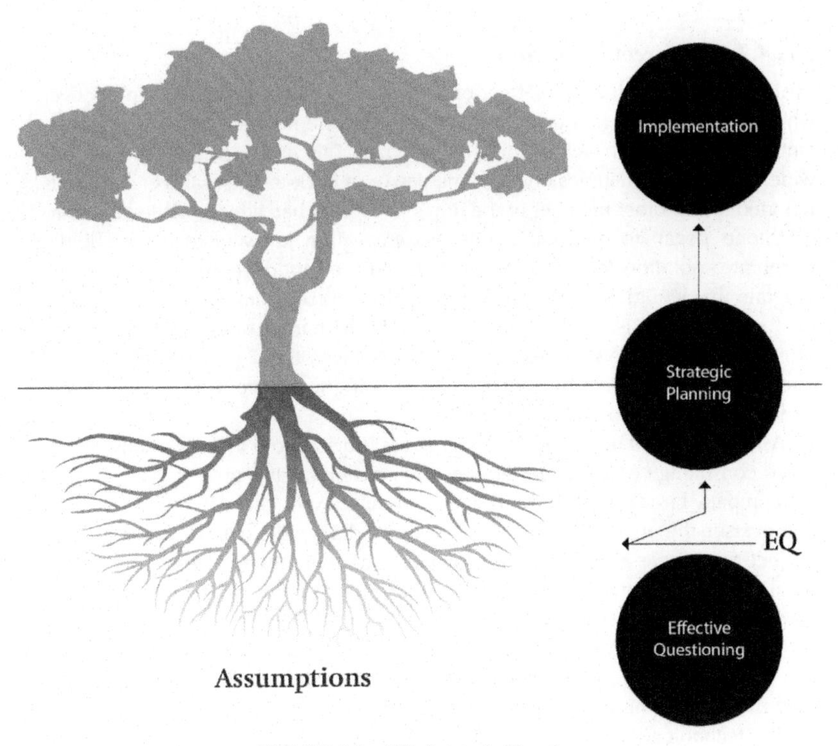

FIGURE 4.5 EQ: Strategic Planning.

FIGURE 4.6 The leader-negotiator diagram.

To summarize the Wall Street Conundrum (Box 4.2), let's review what the cause or causes of this $22 million failure were (Figure 4.7).

- The Wall Street firm unquestionably trusted the large consulting company with knowing the assumptions underlying the compatibility of the technology program to their situation.

Box 4.2 Wall Street Conundrum

I was consulting with a Wall Street brokerage firm, tasked by its CEO to uncover why so much money had been spent, timelines were not met, and a very important project had been delayed too many times. This firm's sales force is worldwide. However, sometimes on the same day or in back-to-back sales calls, clients reported that another member of the firm's sales team had already visited that day.

Clients began to question if this brokerage firm knew what it was doing. Corporate's solution to this problem included the introduction of a technology program that would prevent double-sales calls. This program was promised to be the "answer" to a customized, worldwide up-to-the-minute sales reporting system, promising to keep the sales team in touch with each other 24-7. The official word throughout the company was that this was going to transform their Wall Street operation, resulting in billions in profits.

As I investigated the technology's progress, I discovered that a globally recognized consulting company was employed to customize this project. This consulting company hired articulate, well-educated but inexperienced people to develop and oversee the project. The promised delivery dates were delayed several times, project costs were exceeding the projected $22 million, and costs continued to escalate. To better understand the cause for these problems, I convened 20 technologists who were working 10 h a day trying to deliver the technology on time. All 20 communicated to me that they were getting paid well, but there was no way that the technology selected for this project would work. More or less, their opinion was that this project was doomed to fail before it got started.

The technologists reported that they had shared this concern with the 22 VPs; however, the VPs chose not to communicate this concern to the CEO; the VPs had already invested more than $22 million in the project. The consequence of a *culture of fear* resulted in VPs passing on distortions that the project would be successful and, the CEO in turn passed these distortions onto his Board of Directors. Expectations of success based upon a faulty assumption continued to flourish.

In a meeting with the CEO, I suggested that we use EQ to resolve this problem. Within 1 week of learning more about the likely catastrophe of the technology project, the CEO requested an emergency meeting with the Board where I shared my findings. Needless to say, there was lack of enthusiasm to concede that the project was a $22 million failure. The Board asked, "Would further investment increase the success of this technology program?" My answer was no. I advised the Board and CEO not to "make this dead horse run again." Rather, I recommended cutting their losses and terminating the project. The Board accepted my advice. Unfortunately, as a result, several executives at the VP-level lost their jobs.

The lesson learned is, without asking any questions, 22 VPs accepted a "best practice" from an organization that sells best practices to the Fortune 5000 corporations. The project was doomed to fail before it began because underlying assumptions remained unexamined. In the final analysis, the best practice that was sold to this Wall Street firm originated from a manufacturing plant. The "context" of this best practice applied best to a manufacturing company, not to a Wall Street-type organization.

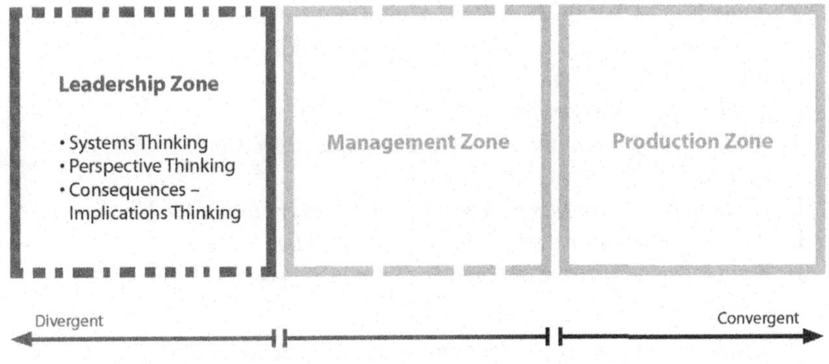

FIGURE 4.7 Leadership Zone Characteristics

- The VPs who had a long successful pattern of managing money were not qualified to make an informed decision about technology. They wrongly transferred their financial "acumen" to technology knowledge.
- The 22 VPs worked in an organizational culture that promoted "knowing" rather than "not knowing." If a person "knows" (like the fish), they have no reason to ask questions. However, the first step toward learning new information is to say, "I do not know."

Unquestionable trust, transfer of expertise from one field is not the basis of expertise in another field, and an organizational culture that promoted making "I know" statements—did not promote a culture of "asking questions." EQ could have saved this company more than $22 million. As to the consulting firm? They soon afterward went out of business.

WHAT IS THE IMPORTANCE OF QUESTIONS VERSUS STATEMENTS?

EQ was designed to stimulate corporate growth. Questions have the power to clarify tasks and identify problems. Statements, on the other hand, often signal a complete halt in thought. Talking cultures are the beginning of decline, especially when everyone talks and no one listens. What is the value of a great idea if no one is listening?

1. What is the EQ Advantage to the Questioner?
   a. EQ controls the focus and direction of conversation.
   b. EQ minimizes the use of basic analytical questions (such as when, where, who, what, why, when). Note: These six questions are not meant to surface assumptions. These questions are useful once assumptions are known.
   c. EQ gets to the "heart" of an issue fast and efficiently.
2. What Does the E-Questioner want to know?
   a. *Is there a dynamic interaction among several causes over a long period of time? Is this more complex than a single-cause and simple-effect?*
   b. *Is there a credibility problem with someone or some process?*
   c. *What is the source of these data, facts, or information? How can you verify the source?*

d. *What do we know and what do we not know? When do we need to know? How could we verify or test that new knowledge?*
e. *What is the time frame?*
f. *Is there a cost barrier? What is it?*
g. *What level of certainty is required to make a decision? 100% to 75%—50% to 25%?*
h. *What factors make this problem too challenging to pursue?*
i. *What are the major complexities of this problem?*
j. *What is the criterion that makes a decision (1) good, (2) unacceptable, or (3) outstanding?*

Remember: You can *only* learn more when you declare, *I don't know*. When an organization's culture supports "know-it-alls," an organization's advantage comes to a full stop because the culture supports the "status quo."

SIX CORE PRINCIPLES OF EQ

1. Be CONCISE—Aim for six to eight words.
2. Be PRECISE—Don't generalize. Generalizations result in oversimplified understandings.
3. Ask ONE QUESTION at a time—Multiple *machine-gun* questions confuse everyone.
4. NARROW THE TARGET—Ask for specificity.
5. Be PATIENT forming your questions—Excellent questions are the most difficult to compose.
6. Asking once may not be enough—You may need to persist ASKING SEVERAL TIMES.

WHAT IS THE "POLITENESS BARRIER?"

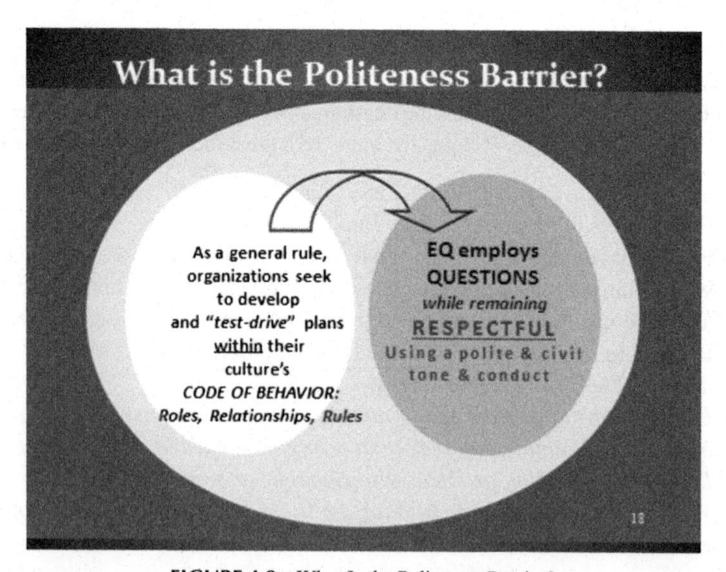

FIGURE 4.8 What Is the Politeness Barrier?

EQ organizes the focus and direction of communication. EQ can get to a "core" concern or problem quickly. As a general rule, organizations tend to develop and "test-drive" plans within their culture's (often unspoken) code of behavior comprised of roles, relationships, and rules (see Figure 4.8—What is the Politeness Barrier?).

There are situations where being polite and staying in one's organizational role could be problematic (Recall the Wall Street Conundrum—Box. 4.2).

Others not familiar with EQ may interpret EQ as impolite, rude, and/or disrespectful (see Box 4.3—CAUTION: EQ Could Be Perceived as Rude). EQ works best when others know that EQ is being used. Remember, E-Questions tend to stimulate thought. Statements tend to diminish or narrow reasoning and bring thinking to a full stop. In Box 4.4—A Typical Management Meeting

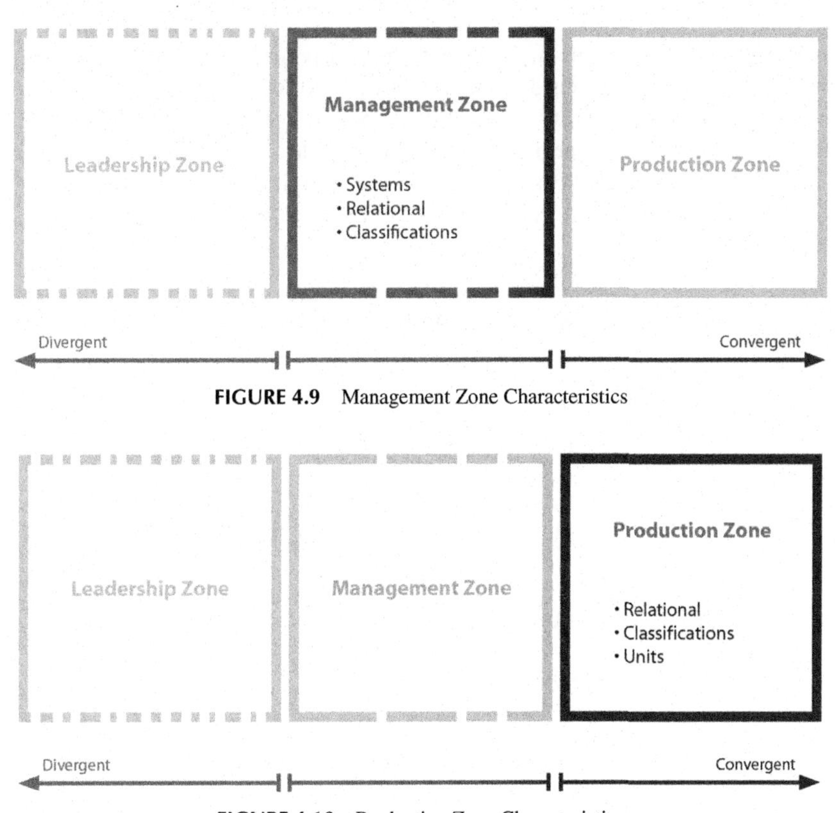

FIGURE 4.9 Management Zone Characteristics

FIGURE 4.10 Production Zone Characteristics

Box 4.3 CAUTION: EQ could be Perceived as Rude

When EQ violates the politeness barrier it may:

expose others' incompetence (a political risk)
reveal a limitation of one's expertise and skill
cause others to "lose face."

Box 4.4 A Typical Management Meeting Converted to EQ

Statement: We've collected statistics.

EQ: *How do you know the sample was large enough?*

Statement: That's what the committee decided.

EQ: *Do you believe the committee made the correct decision on the sample size?*

Statement: It's in the personnel report.

EQ: *What level of credibility do you give to this personnel report?*

Statement: Bill told me himself that it was a good report.

EQ: *What does "good" mean to Bill? Did Bill select information that was valid, reliable?*

converted to EQ—a series of statements from a typical management meeting and suggested E-Questions demonstrate how to convert a management meeting replete with statements to one of questions, in order to better understand the assumptions that undergird the statements made.

Lesson learned: Collecting data and classifying information without E-Questioning (examining its validity or reliability) is where most thinking errors occurs.

EQ is pushing thought in a V direction.

E
R
T
I
C
A
L ↓

So, is EQ rude?

- Is it RUDE *to seek clarity?*
- Is it RUDE *to desire concise answers?*
- Is it RUDE *to request relevance and significance?*
- Is it RUDE *to prevent someone from thinking aloud at the expense of a group's time and energy?*
- Is it RUDE *to ask that one person not dominate meetings?*
- Is it RUDE *to request clarification of ambiguity?*

The answer to all of the above is no. By being polite, assumptions go unexamined below the surface—the organization's "root system." Context shapes everything—how we ask questions is as important as what we ask. Interpreting a question as "RUDE" often involves nonverbal messages. Tone, pace of speech, volume, body posture, facial expressions, etc., all influence how a message is received. EQ could intensify:

- a Win–Lose competitive environment
- a preference for task that damages relationship
- strong emotions that obstruct impartiality
- a psychological *need* to win.

Note: If winning is the most important characteristic of a situation, there is no logic, no standard of fairness, no appeal to values or moral codes, no set of facts or persuasive arguments that will disarm a person's psychological need to win.

Never let EQ be an excuse for immaturity, anger, or personal attacks. The intent of EQ is to promote team competence, not to increase resistance or promote conflict. There are two interconnected but distinct components that comprise EQ. These two components underlie most decisions, actions, and plans. *The first* EQ component is "The Six Structures of EQ Thinking." *The second* is "The Nine Unexamined Assumptions that Result in Thinking Errors."

These components are discussed in Chapter 5—Using Effective Questioning Strategically.

Chapter 5

Using Effective Questioning Strategically

EQ provides a framework that enhances the creativity and potential of human problem solving and strategic planning.

Ken Sylvester

Effective Questioning (EQ) provides Leader-Negotiators (L-Ns) with a method of asking questions that helps minimize mistakes, and—the repetition of the same mistakes. The most common mistakes tend to come from unexamined assumptions. The challenging work of an effective L-N begins with an awareness of thinking patterns. Thinking patterns are strengths, weaknesses, and nonstrengths.

- *Strengths* become success stories when a particular context complements one's thinking pattern.
- *Weaknesses* become failure stories when the context does not complement one's particular thinking pattern.
- *Nonstrengths* are thinking patterns that cannot be developed; to be effective, they must be delegated.

THINKING AND PERCEPTION

It is interesting that out of the brain where logic and reasoning originates is also a place where dreams, nightmares, and fantasies originate. In the back of your head, at the base of your brain, there is a little area called the *reticular formation*. This mechanism is about half the size of a pencil eraser. It is where the selective **perception** system of your brain exists. Thinking skills first begin with the ability to perceive and extract accurate and relevant information; and secondly, with the ability to classify information accurately and to meaningfully explain classifications. The fact of the matter is that the reticular formation, this small brain area, is an emotional center of the brain that tends to reinforce strongly held emotion-laden assumptions that are capable of producing very sincere thinking errors. Therefore, E-Questioning (EQing) for collecting data and information as well as EQing of various interpretive scenarios that arise from a variety of perspectives on a topic or discussion point are necessary before conclusions are reached.

Perception

The perfect formula for failure includes trying to explain the world from only one point of view. For example, have a look at Figure 5.1—The two women.

Have you seen this picture before? It has been around for many years. If you have seen it, you know the questions I'm going to ask next. *What do you see?* Usually the answer is one old woman and one young woman. However, upon first glance, most people tend to see just one of the women's images, not both. *Did you see only one or both? Was the first woman you saw old and unattractive?* Take another look at Figure 5.1.

- Specifically, what characteristics made her old and unattractive?
- Many people say that her long, hooked nose renders her "old." (The question is, do *all* peoples' noses grow longer as they grow older?)

Was the woman you first saw "young" and "beautiful"?

- What makes her young and beautiful?
- Many people say that her slim jawline, petite features, and stylish hat render her "young." (The question is, do *all* young people have slim jawlines, petite features, and wear stylish hats?)

Obviously, if you've seen this picture before, you know that there are two women depicted. One suggests that she is "old"; one suggests that she is "young." The old woman has a large, hooked nose and is facing toward you. The young woman is wearing a large hat and appears like a profile.

If you saw only the older woman, or the younger woman, then you perceived only part of the information contained in the picture. If this is the case, you might prepare for a negotiation making your argument that there is only one

FIGURE 5.1 The two women.

woman in the picture, for example, the older one. If the other party perceived only the younger woman, it is probable that each negotiation party would begin with a *perceptual disagreement.*

Perceptual Disagreement

Either-or, right or wrong. If each party saw a different woman—one, the old woman and other, the young woman, then neither party has realized the full amount of information available at the negotiation. Thus, each party would likely begin negotiating from an either-or or a right or wrong mind-set.

Incomplete information. Which view of the two women in this picture is correct? The answer is that *both* viewpoints are correct. And, both parties would be negotiating from incomplete perspectives if they saw only one view or the other.

AVOIDING OVERSIMPLIFICATION

There is a reason that most of us use age as a descriptor of the women in Figure 5.1. It is that our brain is used to convergent thinking and thus reducing or oversimplifying information. If an L-N's preference for oversimplification is for the purpose of avoiding complexity, then this avoidance pattern represents an error in one's thinking. Moreover, if an L-N's thinking habits prefer oversimplification when there are complex problems to be solved, he or she will encounter problems leading within a multifaceted reality.

The way we interpret information and situations is a by-product of our assumptions. Either-or thinking results in disregarding potential middle-ground solutions because either-or thinking is *one dimensional.* It oversimplifies interpretations down to only one viewpoint, rendering null and void the need to ask questions. Not asking questions or not knowing what questions need to be asked limits the possible alternatives that might expand a negotiation "pie." The L-N's mind is their greatest asset and one of the greatest attributes of an effective L-N is the ability to generate alternatives within any context. Improved perception represents the quest of EQ. The E-Question that needs to be asked is, "Am I (the L-N) thinking from a complete view of the negotiation picture or a just *partial* view of the picture?"

GENERATING ALTERNATIVES

First impression interpretations usually generate resistance to additional perspectives. Typically, when two parties get locked into their limited perspectives, **conflict** results. Conflict contributes to an argumentative environment that often leads to impasse. Conflict is further described in Chapter 11: The Context of Conflict, and in Chapter 12: Conflict Strategies.

Question: who would have the greatest advantage in a negotiation? An L-N with two alternative interpretations; or, an L-N with 31 alternative interpretations? Most would agree that the greatest advantage belongs to the L-N who can generate

Box 5.1 Saving a College

A new college president faced a daunting financial dilemma. The college was $3.5 million in debt. I was asked to sit in on a meeting with his executive team. The president was at one time one of the special aides to a five-star Air Force General. He had learned how to generate alternatives, even within the worst life-and-death situations. His executive team (educators with no financial experience) saw nothing but financial disaster ahead. During the meeting, the president reframed the dilemma with his team by asking his team to generate as many alternative solutions as possible, no matter how stupid. Following 20 min of stating that the "sky is falling," the team finally generated 21 alternatives. 5 of the 21 alternatives turned out to be the solutions that saved the college from foreclosure. How did this occur? Because we used EQ to surface alternatives, instead of succumbing to fear.

the most alternatives within a given context. Now, let's consider alternatives. *Could either of the women in* Figure 5.1 *be a cross-dresser?* I gave this picture to a Fortune 500 corporation's executive team, asking them to generate as many interpretations as possible in their next executive meeting. One week later, they generated over 31 different interpretations. The story in Box 5.1—Saving a College—provides an example of how generating alternatives led to viable solutions.

TWO INTERCONNECTED, YET DISTINCT COMPONENTS OF EQ

There are two interconnected but distinct components of EQ that underlie almost every decision, action, and plan. *The first* EQ components are the The Six Structures of EQ Thinking. *The second* EQ components are The Nine Unexamined Assumptions that Result in Thinking Errors.

What Are the Six Structures of EQ Thinking?

1. Data Collection: Information of any kind.
2. Classification Thinking: How information is interpreted and organized. Note: This is where most errors and problems occur.
3. Relational Thinking: Linear-sequential reasoning versus complex circular reasoning that is based on "contextual intelligence."
4. Systems Thinking: How systems work; and how systems work among other systems.
5. Perspectives Thinking: Generating multiple and dissimilar viewpoints.
6. Consequences Thinking: Predictive expertise amid numerous alternative perspectives.

The Six Structures of EQ Thinking (6-ST) are not six detached, separate steps. Rather, they are six *interrelated* thinking classifications that assist

L-Ns to lead and resolve complex problems. Note: If any one of these six structures is *overused and/or overemphasized*, the value of 6-ST will be undermined.

The only trouble with a sure thing is its uncertainty.

Unknown author

DATA COLLECTION AND CLASSIFICATION

The purpose of the Six Structures of Thinking is to minimize thinking errors and repetition of those errors. The most important structures are data collection and classifications, because this is where most thinking errors begin.

Structure 1: Data Collection

It is not the purpose of this book to provide a comprehensive discussion about collecting data. Rather, this section will provide a concise overview of the *importance* of data in problem-solving and decision-making. Data include the collection of information of any kind. For the purpose of understanding EQ, two primary data categories will be described: (1) quantitative–numerical measures; and, (2) qualitative–characteristic measures. The focus here is not on the field of statistics; nor are the principles listed below intended to be comprehensive.

There are many processes used in data collection. The items listed below are more about the potential limitations of data collection than examples of data collection processes.

1. Statistics are valuable, depending upon how the numbers are interpreted. It is the unexamined interpretation of data collection that causes most errors.
2. Statistics are full of traps; yet, there is no absolute trap-proof statistical method.
3. The biggest trap in data collection is human involvement.
4. Numbers have no meaning other than what humans impose upon them.
5. Numbers will not absolutely prove something. However, numbers *could suggest* probabilities, likelihoods, chances, and odds. Using numbers still comes down to human judgment and contextual intelligence.

For further information about data collection and interpretation, refer to the resource section.

Structure 2: Classifications Thinking

The process of classifying information is also where most misunderstandings and miscommunications occur. **Classifications** are where our mind goes when deciding if there is a problem and/or how to classify the problem. Once classifications are assigned, all subsequent information comes from them. But where and when did we learn these classifications? The answer is, we learned them from family, friends, peers, teachers, bosses, institutions, and systems—over a long period of time. Most people are unaware of the classifications they use. These classifications are often culturally bound and buried deep within a person's unconscious. Unknown classifications are difficult to change because it is difficult to change what we do not know. If we cannot change with the future, then we can only do business in the status-quo past.

An L-N's effectiveness is diminished when he or she becomes a slave to their own mind-sets, philosophies, values, and tactics. Learning how to apply EQ will provide a mental checklist that reduces misunderstandings and miscommunications.

Structures 3–6

How we think is what we do. Thinking is the ability to adapt to situational demands. The following four structures of thinking will not be addressed fully in this chapter. References to these structures will be made in subsequent chapters. Most important to note here is that these structures are dependent upon the data we collect and the classifications we create.

Structure 3: Relational Thinking: Linear-sequential reasoning versus complex circular reasoning that is based on "contextual intelligence"
Structure 4: Systems Thinking: How systems work; and how systems work among other systems
Structure 5: Perspectives Thinking: Generating multiple and dissimilar viewpoints
Structure 6: Consequences Thinking: Predictive expertise amid numerous alternative perspectives

THE NINE ASSUMPTIONS THAT RESULT IN THINKING ERRORS

Decisions are determined within a **context**; and context influences an L-N's thinking. Recall the fish analogy from Chapter 4, that is—the last thing a fish knows is that it is *in* water. Effective L-Ns need to understand that assumptions *are* the "water" that surrounds their organization. Like a fish, L-Ns must uncover contextual assumptions before they are "caught" unaware.

The following nine assumptions represent the water an L-N swims in (Box 5.2). The checklist below was developed in recognition that human beings tend to forget under stress. All L-Ns need a mental checklist, similar to an airline pilot's flight preparation checklist, to make sure they don't get trapped in pursuing arguments based on incomplete, oversimplified, or distorted information.

Box 5.2 Nine Assumptions that Result in Thinking Errors

The Nine Assumptions:

1. Problem Identification: Unique Cause and Effect Characteristics
2. Previous Knowledge: Limitations of Knowledge
3. Assessment: Measurement Approaches
4. Time: Time Impacts Goal Achievement
5. Values: How Prioritizing What We Do
6. Context: Is the Context Relevant to an Existing Situation?
7. Audience: Six Unique Reasoning Patterns
8. Possible–Probable: What Might Happen versus What Is Likely to Happen
9. Final Interpretive Review: Have things changed—are they as you thought they were? Reevaluate and reconsider assumptions 1–8

The incorrect moment for a pilot to remember that he or she has forgotten to check something is when they are 36,000 feet above the earth. The same goes for L-Ns. Errors occur in the following nine categories when the following assumptions go unexamined. (Remember: Most errors happen at the Data and Classifications levels.)

Assumption #1: Problem Identification

EQ: *What are the unique characteristics of a problem or situation? Ask, is the problem*:

1. simple or complex?
2. easily identifiable? concealed or ambiguous?
3. a single symptom or multiple symptoms?
4. a new problem or similar to other problems?

Note: At times, there may be one single cause yet multiple symptoms. Problems like this are complex, less straightforward, and take more time to clearly identify. At times, there may be numerous causes yet only one symptom. These kinds of problems are also complex and will likely take time to resolve. The most common error in problem-solving occurs when the symptom of a problem is not the cause.

Assumption #2: Previous Knowledge

EQ: *Is what we know now relevant to resolve problems and challenges in the future?*

All knowledge is dynamic; that is, it changes over time. So the question is, is what we know still accurate? What knowledge will be needed to manage future

Box 5.3 Who was the First President of the United States of America?

When asked, "Who was the first President of the United States of America, thousands of well-educated people said: "George Washington." When asked why they said this, they indicated that they, "learned this in school, in history class." However, eight people were actually President of the United States *before* George Washington.

1. John Hanson, 1781
2. Elias Boudinot, 1783
3. Thomas Mifflin, 1784
4. Richard Henry Lee, 1785
5. John Hancock, 1786
6. Nathan Gorman, 1786
7. Arthur St. Clair, 1787
8. Cyrus Griffin, 1788

George Washington was sworn in 1789, technically making him the ninth President of the USA (http://www.historiography101.com).

forecasts and expectations? Case in point: See Box 5.3—Who Was the First President of the United States of America?

Bottom line? "Facts" *need to be questioned.*

Assumption #3: Assessment Measures

EQ: *How do we assess progress?*

- Is the situation or problem able to be measured? How much can it be measured? When will we know that the measurement provides accurate feedback as to progress?
- Should we use a quantitative or qualitative measure and how do we know that it will be adequate to assess progress?
- What knowledge is needed in order to manage future expectations?
  - Can we get it? How will we get it? When will it be available?
  - If it is not available, will that change plans? How long will the change in plans take? What is/are the consequences of a delay? Can this be measured? If so, how?

Assumption #4: Time

EQ: *How can we asses the influence of time on problem-solving and plan implementation?*

All plans are built with time in mind. When one says "time" it is important that everyone knows what kind of time is meant. In every step of the process then, time has to be assessed in the following ways. Time refers to:

- Time deadlines. Time enough (for completion)? Time span (reference to a historical period of time such an era, a period, a season, or a generation).

- A schedule or an agenda. Time zones. Time lines (e.g., Is time a five-day period of time including weekend days or five work days?).

Note: Some people are quick-start and begin with a bang but have trouble completing a task at the deadline. Other people are thorough; they start a task more slowly but complete the task they start. These two profiles each use time differently. These differences can cause conflict.

Assumption #5: Values

EQ: *What is the value, worth, or importance of something?*

- One's reputation and/or respect? The utility of something? The profitability of something?
- The advantage or benefit of something? How much risk is considered acceptable?

Assumption #6: Context

EQ: *What words or circumstances help explain or justify the meaning of something?*

Context refers to the circumstances or background of a situation that helps provide insight as to what happened. When considering context, consider the following frames: Economic, political, human resources, environmental, legal, sociological, psychological, among others.

Using the market frame as an example and purchasing a home as the context:

- Is it a buyers or sellers market?
- Is the market up or down?
- Has there been a policy change that will change an agreement?

Assumption #7: Audience

EQ: *How do L-Ns communicate with different audiences who have different frames of reference?*

An audience can be a person, a group, a nation, etc. L-Ns approach a negotiation with a set of values firmly in mind. There are approximately six ways that most people argue and explain their point of view (Figure 5.2). These preferences are best explained by using the acronym V.A.L.U.E.S. V.A.L.U.E.S stands for:

- Verified by Science
- Authority
- Logic
- Uses Intuition

FIGURE 5.2 Six world views.

- Emotive belief
- Sensory experience

The "V" in VALUES Represents Verified by Science

The scientific process is characterized by four steps:

1. Gather all the available facts through the use of your senses.
2. Immerse yourself in the facts until a solution/theory comes to mind: Intuition.
3. Think through all the implications: Logic-based consistency tests.
4. Evaluate test results: Sense perception.

The scientist's ideal is to be open-minded, but skeptical of claims that rest solely on faith or authority. He/she relies on empirical evidence and states hypotheses and predications precisely. Some of the tools of the scientist are case histories, naturalistic observation, laboratory observation, surveys, tests, correlation studies, experiments, and descriptive statistics. Each of these tools has strengths and weaknesses. Care must be taken to allow for findings that have hidden errors of observation, thought, and interpretation (Figure 5.3).

The "A" in VALUES Represents Authority

Authority is a very common way to assert that a belief is accepted as true. Children rely on parents and teachers to guide them in their thinking. Children tend to have faith in higher authority, somewhat unconditionally. Adults rely more on experts. However, trial and error experiences eventually teach adults to maintain a conditional, skeptical reserve about experts. They may no longer have unconditional respect for higher authority.

FIGURE 5.3 Verified by science.

FIGURE 5.4 Authority

Most adults agree that certain authority-based values should be treated conditionally. However, most are divided about which authority is to be respected, and which to be questioned. Many think that a skeptical, conditional stance is fine for everyday issues, but not the way to approach certain aspects of life, such as religion or politics. For some people, religious mandates should be followed literally (Figure 5.4).

Some see family and family surrogates (such as neighbors and schools) as especially trustworthy. Still others rely on economic systems and national governments for expert direction. For many people, the media has taken on a role expert authority.

Box 5.4 Logic

A woman requested her husband, a computer programmer, to do the following: "Dear, would you please go to the store and buy some bread. If they have eggs, buy a dozen." He agreed. A few minutes later he was back with 12 loaves of bread. The wife was flabbergasted! "Why on earth did you buy a dozen loaves of bread?" He logically replied, "They had eggs."

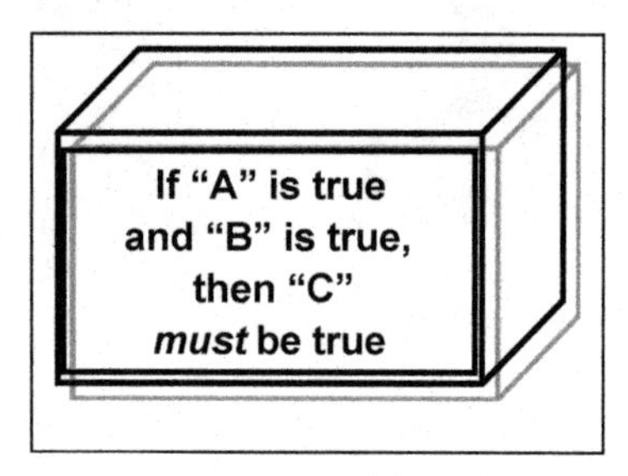

FIGURE 5.5 Logic.

The "L" in VALUES Represents Logic

In a syllogism, the conclusion must be true if the two premises are true. As evidenced in the story told in Box 5.4, not all thinking is logical. While some thinking does not have an obvious purpose (e.g., daydreaming), much of our thinking is goal-directed, requiring that we draw inferences from observations, facts, or assumptions. This kind of thinking is what is meant by deductive or inductive reasoning. When we reason, we use the concepts, experiences, and images we have stored in memory to review the past to make judgments and decisions and solve problems. There are two kinds of logic: Inductive and Deductive (Figure 5.5).

- **Inductive** logic, the thinker draws general conclusions from specific observations. Inductive logic has a weakness. No matter how much supporting evidence you gather, it is always possible that you have overlooked some evidence that could contradict your conclusion.

Premise #1:	All human beings are mortal.
Premise #2:	I am a human being.
Conclusion:	Therefore I am mortal.

- **Deductive** logic begins with general assumptions and draws "logical" conclusions. Deductive logic often takes the form of syllogism, a simple argument consisting of two premises and a conclusion.

We may often think that if people would only be logical, they could get along. But logic is not enough when L-Ns negotiate with different assumptions and values. *How can people who are operating from different premises reach*

Box 5.5 Kpelle Logic

In a study of the Kpelle tribe in Africa, researchers gave a farmer this problem:

Researcher: "All Kpelle men are rice farmers. Mr Smith is not a rice farmer. Is he a Kpelle man?" The Kpelle farmer insisted the information provided did not allow a conclusion.

Kpelle man: "I don't know the man in person. I have not laid eyes on the man himself."

Researcher: "Just think about the statement."

Kpelle man: "If I know him in person, I can answer that question, but since I do not know him in person I cannot answer that question."

agreement? Knowing if and when to apply deductive logic. This does not come easy. It is influenced by experience, education, and cultural teachings. Read (Box 5.5) Kpelle Logic.

The **Kpelle man** is reasoning deductively:

Premise #1: If I do not know a person, I cannot draw any conclusions about that person.
Premise #2: I do not know Mr Smith.
Conclusion: Therefore, I cannot draw any conclusions about Mr Smith.

Even when people are perfectly logical, they may disagree if they have different assumptions. Controversial issues tend to be those in which premises cannot be proven true or false to everyone's satisfaction. Thus, people of good will can reach opposite conclusions—"logically."

Logic is inadequate for solving some complicated real-life problems because there is often no single right answer. Many approaches and viewpoints compete, and you must decide which viewpoint is most reasonable *within a particular context.* To think logically about most issues, people need more than inductive and deductive logic. They also need the ability to think critically about opposing points of view.

The "U" in VALUES. Represents Uses Intuition

Intuition is the direct personal perception of some truth independent of any logical reasoning process. Intuitive knowledge is often nonverbal. It is the activity of the subconscious mind to categorize, associate, and relate experience into some systematic scheme, so as to arrive at a theory or view of how the world works (Figure 5.6).

Everyone uses intuition and hunches to generate theories about human behavior and how the world works. Scientists are required to confirm their theories through careful research and rigorous statistical analysis. In daily life, though, people usually test their ideas through casual observation and the use of "intuitive statistics"—notions about probabilities that may or may not be correct. Consider the situation in Box 5.6, Sherlock Homes and the Curious Incident of the Dog in the Nighttime. Not only are occurrences data; nonoccurrences can be as well.

FIGURE 5.6 Uses intuition.

Box 5.6 Sherlock Homes and the Curious Incident of the Dog in the Nighttime

Sherlock Holmes, the legendary detective, was aware of the value of nonoccurrences. In one episode he invited a police inspector to consider *the curious incident of the dog in the nighttime*. The inspector protested that the dog did nothing in the nighttime. Holmes replied that that was the curious incident. The dog's silence proved that the intruder in the mystery was someone well known to the dog. Like Sherlock Holmes, we all need to be aware of what nonoccurrences, as well as occurrences, can tell us.

FIGURE 5.7 Emotive beliefs.

The "E" in VALUES Stands for Emotive Beliefs

Emotive beliefs consist of physiological responses, interpretations of events, and cultural influences that shape experience. Western scientists often regard emotion as the opposite of reasoning; and, an inferior opposite at that. Thinking is often held superior to feelings. Reason, logic, intellectual ideas, judgment, and perception were deemed more credible than relying on intuition, hunches, and emotions, especially when it came to important issues. Human emotion is knowing via awareness, perception, and/or opinion (Figure 5.7).

The word emotion takes on a slightly derogatory connotation when people confuse it with emotional. In this book, the word emotion is accepted as an additional

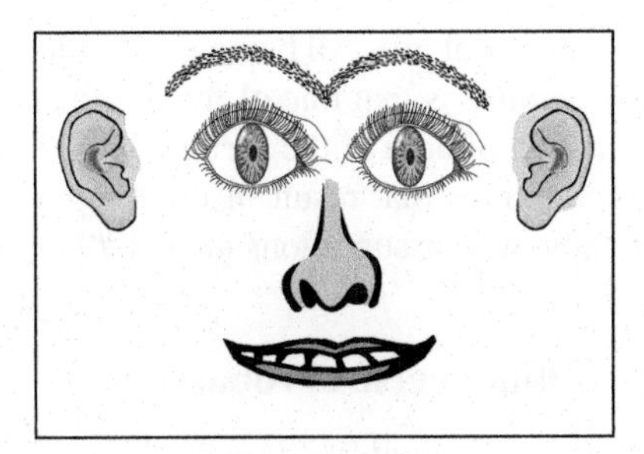

FIGURE 5.8 Uses intuition.

way of gathering information. Most people arrive at beliefs and judgments about the world through some aspect of feelings or emotion. However, few would admit or agree that their personal values are based on emotion. Value systems related to feeling include family, work group, neighborhood, national pride, class, race, certain groups, associations or causes (such as call to defend one's country), etc.

The "S" in VALUES Represents Sense Experience

Sense experience depends upon perception as its primary tool for interpreting the world. Perception is the process by which the brain organizes and interprets sensory information. Sensory experience refers to the knowledge we obtain directly by seeing, hearing, touching, tasting, and/or smelling. Since sensation is a subjective experience, our ideas about reality are affected by our sense experience. That is, things appear to us as they appear, not only because of *their* nature, but because of *ours* (Figure 5.8).

Most of us have been taught that human beings possess five senses. Although scientists often disagree as to the exact number of senses we have, they do agree we operate with more than the five mentioned above. However, our senses are only tuned into a narrow band of physical energies. For example, we are sensitive visually to only a fraction of all electromagnetic energy. Other species can pick up various signals; we cannot. Dogs can detect high-frequency sound waves beyond our range. Bees can see ultraviolet rays, and snakes can see minute changes in temperature. Sensory differences among species raise some intriguing questions about the nature of reality.

Obviously, all of us obtain general information as well as knowledge about values through sense experience. However, some people place greater reliance on their senses than the other modes of learning, knowing, and believing. They want to see and hear it themselves, either personally or vicariously through books and film, for example.

To summarize, Each of the six V.A.L.U.E.S. classifications stand separate and apart for the purpose of understanding each one. In real life, however, the six VALUES blend and interact together. Each individual combines his/her way of thinking into a uniquely personal mix. All human beings have more than a single VALUES system. The premise is that one of the dominant factors in reaching agreement is the satisfaction of both of the parties' VALUES.

Note: The nine assumptions that result in thinking errors are now continued...We will pick up now with assumptions #8 and #9.

Assumption #8: Possibility versus Probability

EQ: *Is everything possible (imaginable)? Is everything probable (likely)?*

As soon as you define the difference between possibility and probability, you have defined what the assumption is... What is the possibility that "x" will happen? If it's possible, how likely or probable is it? For example,

- It is *possible* that an airplane will go down.
- It is more *probable* that you will have an automobile accident than it will be to be in an airline crash.

It is critical that you prioritize agendas, conversations, and the resources you have around probabilities. It is a time-waster to talk about possibilities that have low to no probability of occurring. In other words, if the possibility of a problem or outcome is remote, question if we should move on to how likely (probable) it would be to occur. This may be a better use of organizational resources than imagining things that may never occur.

Box 5.7 provides an example of possibility versus probability at a large manufacturing facility.

Brainstorming explores possibilities. Problem-solving focuses on probabilities. Investing time on low probability scenarios should have a rationale, logical context for doing so.

Assumption #9: Interpretive Review

EQ: *Having assessed your thinking, has your thinking changed?*

In other words, has your assessment of the eight assumptions listed above changed your previous interpretation, understanding, or explanation of the

Box 5.7 Possibility versus Probability at a Large Manufacturing Facility

An engineering team spent 3 h discussing the possibility of something occurring. But, the question really was, "Was it probable?" The answer: "NO, the likelihood of this happening was calculated to be 1 in 43,000." In fact, in this industry there had been only two occurrences of this problem in a 90-year time span. This engineering team spent 3 h on something that had a very low likelihood of occurring; and, in so doing, neglected numerous other scenarios that had a greater probability of occurring—a waste of resource time and money.

problem? It is not uncommon for the review process to change one's point of view. You may need to repeat the review several times.

APPLYING EQ:

Effective L-Ns ask questions which is at the core of EQ. The question is—what are the questions? Most university business students have been taught the case study method. Frequently, what students have learned in school follows them into their professions. More often than not, via the case method, a rhythmic, default mind-set is developed that unquestionably accepts data as reliable. Trusting the assumption that data and its sources are unquestionably reliable may be helpful in case studies, but is not a good practice in the real world where asking questions about the source and the reliability of data is imperative.

EQ provides a framework for asking nine assumption-centered questions. Using the E-Questions in Box 5.8 will result in identifying, diagnosing, and accurately solving problems.

THE NIAGARA-MEDINA EXERCISE

The Niagara–Medina Exercise (below) was developed to advance effective reasoning by demonstrating how numerous assumptions go unquestioned

Box 5.8 E-Questions

Assumption #1: Problem Identification
EQ: *What are the characteristics of a problem or situation?*
Assumption #2: Previous Knowledge
EQ: *Is what we know now relevant to resolve problems and challenges in the future?*
Assumption #3: Assessment
EQ: *How do we assess progress?*
Assumption #4: Time
EQ: *How can we asses the influence of time on problem-solving and plan implementation?*
Assumption #5: Values
EQ: *What is the value, worth, or importance of something?*
Assumption #6: Context
EQ: *What words or circumstances help explain or justify the meaning of something?*
Assumption #7: Audience effect
EQ: *How do L-Ns communicate with different audiences who have different frames of reference?*
Assumption #8: Possibility versus Probability
EQ: *Is everything possible (imaginable)? Is everything probable (likely)?*
Assumption #9: Interpretive Review
EQ: *Having assessed your thinking, has your thinking changed?*

and undetected in everyday conversation and problem-solving. Recall, most assumption-related problems begin when L-Ns either unquestionably accept data or interpret data without questioning how it is classified. After completing the exercise below, go to Appendix B to check the assumptions you identified with the list of assumptions provided there.

DIRECTIONS: Niagara–Medina Case Study

Read the following scenario, then fill-in the table below. Assess the needs of three people: (1) the Niagara buyer, (2) the Medina seller, and (3) the Foremost rep.

Scenario:

Niagara Manufacturing is a large corporation that uses thousands of hinges of various sizes. For over a decade, the current Niagara buyer has purchased all of Niagara's hinges from Medina Hinge Company and the current Medina sales representative. The Niagara hinge account now represents 40% of the Medina seller's total dollar sales. Although the Niagara buyer is responsible for purchasing other items, the Medina hinge account is 30% of the buyer's total dollar purchases. Over a period of time, the price of Medina hinges has more than kept pace with inflation, and complaints from the factory supervisors about degrading hinge quality are increasing.

Niagara's hinge buyer places the orders with the Medina chief hinge sales representative, who happens to be fellow college alumni of the buyer. The buyer and the rep share a condo in Hawaii during winter months on a time-share lease plan arranged by the Medina rep's sister-in-law who figures prominently in the real estate business in the town where both the buyer and the rep live. Things are going OK at Niagara in spite of the rising costs and slipping quality, mainly because manufacturing is at plant capacity, orders keep pouring in and no one questions any of it, particularly no one in the accounting or quality departments.

In the same city as Niagara and Medina is the Foremost Hinge Company, whose hinges is unsurpassed in both quality and price competitiveness. Foremost started producing and selling hinges 4 years ago, and thanks to the efforts of a well-trained sales staff, has consistently gained market share of hinges. But not being able to crack Niagara is a sore point. The standing pun at Foremost is "Nobody from here sells to Niagara...Nobody!"

Foremost has its top producer working on the problem, though, and that rep found out about the Alumni/Hawaii connection! The Foremost rep accepted the Niagara case and is determined to crack it. This rep is consistently the winner of hinge sales contests and is a member of the Million Dollar Hinge Round Table, and organization of top hinge salespersons who are envied by every hinge sales rep in the country. This "hot dog" sales rep wants YOU to help!!!

Use the matrix below and *check the appropriate needs* of the Niagara buyer, the Medina seller, and the Foremost seller. These needs are Maslow's Hierarchy of needs. You should have convincing evidence to support your opinions.

Maslow needs theory	Niagara buyer	Medina seller	Foremost seller
Aesthetics			
Know and Understand			
Self-actualization			
Esteem			
Love and Belonging			
Safety and Security			
Survival			

The realism of the work world is that when employees enter their work area, they do not have case studies waiting for them on their desk. Instead, their competency involves first recognizing if a problem exists. If it exists, then they must diagnose the cause or causes of that problem. Diagnosing a problem may also involve crossing over and into others' divisional, silo protected, territories. Crossing boundaries to solve problems requires a manager to escalate a solution with other managers; and then, those managers would have to reach consensus on solving the cross-boundary problem. They may, depending on the complexities of interdependence, need to get *their* managers to approve the need to solve the problem. This will take time. In addition, if the person who initiated the problem-solving proposal has limited or flawed problem-solving skills, there may be more on the line here than a person's "academic grade." It may cost them a promotion or even their job. To me, case studies should invest their learning in real-world scenarios that include potential complications as posed above.

Chapter 6

Win–Win and Win–Lose in the Leadership Zone

AN INTRODUCTION TO THE WIN–WIN AND WIN–LOSE PHILOSOPHIES

It is important to note that the philosophies of "Win–Win" and "Win–Lose" are neither right nor wrong. Before you react to this comment, please read further. It may be uncomfortable to accept that both philosophies operate within our world. Furthermore, there are passionate, if not fanatical debates about preferences for and consequences and implications of each philosophical approach. What is inescapable is the need to acknowledge that both philosophies exist. This does not imply that you agree with their merits. However, just about everyone has a passionate preference for one philosophy or the other. In fact, many people become embroiled in arguments about which philosophy is best. It should not escape our notice that world wars have been fought over such differences in principles, standards, morals, and ethics. The point is to acknowledge that both approaches:

- exist
- have existed throughout recorded human history, and
- most likely will continue to exist at least until tomorrow morning.

"Our mind is like a chartroom of maps. The challenge is to select the best map for the situation."

Ken Sylvester

The intent of this chapter is to convey, among other things, that effective negotiators must possess knowledge of the other party's primary and preferred philosophy. If the other party has adopted a philosophical approach that differs from yours, then you should become skilled at working with those differences. Further, it is proposed that as a general rule, others are not willing to change their philosophy simply because we wish for them to do so. The Leader-Negotiator's (L-N's) challenge is to discover a framework that will convince those with whom we differ to agree to terms of common ground.

To help facilitate the understanding of the Win–Win and Win–Lose philosophies, two symbolic terms will be used: "Kansas" and "Chicago." These two

Negotiating in the Leadership Zone.

terms are symbolic terms and are not associated with the geographical locations of the states of Kansas and Chicago, Illinois.

The term Kansas references a stereotypical environment of peace and understanding; the Win–Win approach. The term Chicago symbolizes the numerous media images that convey Chicago's tough and rugged environment; the Win–Lose philosophy.

America's Heartland

It was one of those bright, sunny June mornings that seemed to invite drivers onto the open road and I was among them. I had finished some business in Denver and was anticipating a leisurely but full day's drive toward my next destination, Chicago, Illinois. My schedule allowed two days for travel, so I planned to stop in Kansas City, Kansas, for the night.

I've always enjoyed driving because it gives me time to think—to reflect on my life, my goals, my career, and my relationships. Many a problem has been solved, many a disaster averted thanks to that alone time behind the wheel. There's also a sense of freedom that can't be equaled in the middle seat of coach on an overcrowded airplane. This day, though, my thoughts would be rudely interrupted. The culprit was the nasty unwelcome circumstance known as car trouble. I knew the strange noises I was hearing were not good news, and I knew that the warning lights that began to glow meant 'find the next service station.'

I was several miles past Hays, Kansas, that charming town situated smack-dab in the middle of the United States. I decided it would be best to proceed to the next town on my route, a little spec on my Google map. So small was this town that the mapmakers didn't even note it, or its population, in their index. But I was certain it would have a gas station.

It did. It also had a grocery store, a drugstore, a small café, a hardware store, a farm implement dealer, a couple of churches, and a bar. I drove my clattering, rumbling car into the service station and pulled up in front of the service bay, at which point my engine promptly died.

I wiped the sweat from my forehead and went to the front door of the station where I was greeted by a sign. "Back in 10 min. Come on in." Sure enough, the door was open. I went in, bought a bottle of water from the machine and settled into an old vinyl-covered chair.

5 min later, a gentleman with a sewn-on patch on his uniform that bore his name "Arnie" came in. That's how I knew he was Arnie—he never actually volunteered that information. Arnie was a man of few words.

"That your car?"

"Yes."

"Broke?"

"Yes, how did you know?"

"If you wanted gas, you'd a-pulled up by the pumps."

Arnie the sleuth. I explained that my car had been making strange noises, but that it had died the moment I pulled into the station.

"I'll take a look-see," Arnie volunteered.

"Good. I was hoping you would."

As Arnie popped the hood and began to tinker, I decided to kill time by having a look-see around Small-Dot-on-the-Map, Kansas. Main Street was about a block and a half long. There were no stoplights. I didn't see a police station or even a patrol car for that matter.

As I was walking down the street, I happened to spot a car parked in front of the café with its windows open and the doors unlocked. I glanced inside and noticed that the keys were in the ignition. This, of course, concerned me.

I walked into the café and approached the waitress.

"Excuse me," I said, "but somebody has left the keys in the ignition of their car." I made my announcement loudly enough that a number of people in the café heard me and began to laugh. An older gentleman laughed quite loudly and said, "Son, everybody leaves their keys in the cars here." He went on to explain that in the 22 years he'd lived in Small-Dot, no car had ever been stolen. The reason was because it is 'gumpteen miles' to the next town. There would be no sense in stealing a car—there was no place to go.

Having heard the facts of life in Small-Dot spelled out to me in the café, I decided to pay a visit to the local drugstore where I spotted a pleasant woman stationed behind the counter.

"How's life in Small-Dot-on-the-Map, Kansas, today?" I asked.

"Great," she answered.

Must be Arnie's wife, I thought. *So few words.*

It turned out to be Betsy—I think that was her name, who moved to Small-Dot from the big city. She wanted a simpler life. She wanted to know her neighbors. She wanted to become part of a community.

Betsy was quick to volunteer what she meant by all that. It seems that Small-Dot is a farming community made up of hardworking, "God-fearing," "honest," and "upright people" whose word is "as good as gold." They say what they mean, and they mean what they say. That 'heartland' approach to life appealed to her.

Betsy soon discovered that her neighbors who lived on outlying farms usually worked until sundown, but then often needed something from her drugstore. Aspirin perhaps; or bandages or cough syrup. Possibly something to sooth a scrape or burn. But Betsy couldn't afford to remain open around the clock, so she came up with another strategy. She gave everyone keys to her drugstore. She told them to simply let themselves in, take what they needed, make a note on a tablet she left by the cash register, and she'd bill them later.

"It's a Win–Win," she explained to me. "I don't have to be here to sell things and they can get what they need when they need it. Of course, I keep prescription drugs under lock and key. They can't help themselves to controlled substances."

Good thing, I thought.

I thanked Betsy for her insights on the "Win–Win" and walked down the street to check on Arnie's progress. He had isolated the problem, had determined that it was minor and had concluded that he could fix it.

"How soon?" I queried.

"By sundown, if I don't knock off for dinner."

I found a park bench, settled in to watch the approaching sunset and hoped Arnie wouldn't knock off for dinner. Just as the sun was slipping down out of view, Arnie let out a loud whistle.

"Car's done."

"Will it get me to Chicago?"

"If you put more gas in it."

Arnie, the comedian. I paid the man without even attempting to negotiate his charges. I was just happy to get back on the road again.

All the way to Kansas City, I thought about what I had learned in Small-Dot, Kansas, just east of Hays, the city at the very heart of America. Here's a town in which everyone has the same outlook and shares the same values. Everyone plays by the same rules, and collaboration is stressed. "Win–Win" is the clear goal for everyone concerned. In Small-Dot, Kansas, the druggist can actually give keys to farmers and townspeople alike, and expect to come to work in the morning and find a note listing what was taken from the shelves in the middle of the previous night.

I thought about the negotiators I know who share the Small-Dot, Kansas philosophy toward life. They fully expect every negotiation to share the same philosophy and to work collectively toward a Win–Win outcome.

Small-Dot, Kansas, is a wonderful place filled with wonderful people, My guess is the local police office—if they ever have one in Small-Dot—doesn't have to wear a bulletproof vest.

If you grew up in a place like Small-Dot, you might begin to believe that the world is a very safe place—that you can actually trust other people. But the truth is, Small-Dot is not the only reality.

Characteristics of a Collaborative Negotiation

Collaboration is a negotiation approach through which L-Ns discover different aspects of a problem and explore solutions that go beyond their own independent approach. The objective of collaboration is to arrive at a more complete understanding from multiple perspectives.

"Collaborative" can be defined as the need or desire to work together. It accepts different perceptions, values, expectations, assumptions, behaviors, structures, processes, and outcomes. Collaboration does not imply that everyone enjoys or likes one another. Even though an amicable relationship may or may not exist between parties, there must be a need or commitment to succeed. All parties must be working toward a common goal albeit, there may be different outcomes. The term "collaboration" has been referred to in organizations

Box 6.1 When Should a Collaborative Approach Be Used?

1. When the negotiators' interests are mutually dependent
2. When negotiated issues can be resolved from various points of satisfaction, and resources can be expanded or equitably shared
3. When a long-term relationship is desired or required
4. When parties desire or need a Win–Win outcome

as "integration." Organizations must be integrated so that they work together. Anything less than integration represents a vulnerability to an organization's performance. Box 6.1 highlights when a collaborative approach should be used.

We're Not in Kansas Anymore

A few hundred miles to the northeast of Small-Dot, Kansas lies the sprawling metropolis of Chicago, Illinois. This vibrant, energetic city filled with stunning skyscrapers and great jazz and blues clubs also had what you might call a 'reputation.' Back in the 1920s and 1930s, in the era of prohibition, gangsters basically ran the city. The most notorious mobster, of course, was Al Capone, who operated widespread and very profitable gambling, bootlegging, and prostitution rackets. His style of negotiating with his rivals was Win–Lose. Capone once said, "You can get far more with a smile and a gun than you can with just a smile." Capone's competitors lost. His henchmen simply gunned them down.

Capone and his buddies have long since vanished from the Chicago scene. But like any large city, Chicago has its share of violent crime, drugs, and vandalism.

I left Kansas City early in the morning, eager to reach Chicago in plenty of time to check into my hotel, try out the health club and enjoy a relaxing dinner. As I neared my destination, I drove down a narrow Chicago side street. There, sandwiched between a jewelry store and a pawn shop, stood a drugstore. I noticed that there were bars and screens protecting all of the windows, and a large gate was being rolled into lockdown position in front of the entrance by a pharmacist in a white uniform.

What a contrast! Yesterday I was in Small-Dot, Kansas, where the druggist freely handed out keys to her store. Here in Chicago, my guess is that not one customer had a key to any drugstore. Steel bars and screens and grates encased the storefront to keep night visitors out. An elaborate alarm system was set to summon the police at the first hint of intrusion.

What do you suppose would happen if someone left the car windows open and the keys in the ignition in Chicago? Gone! What happens if a house were left unlocked? The TV, stereo, and computer would undoubtedly sprout legs. Chicago is a different environment than Kansas. If you were raised in Chicago, you might not trust anyone.

I thought about this throughout my quiet dinner. If the Small-Dot, Kansas drugstore could be used to symbolize the Win–Win, the Chicago drugstore could represent the Win–Lose. That little town in Kansas offers a collaborative Win–Win environment; Chicago is a competitive, Win–Lose environment. In Kansas, the druggist makes it easy for customers to meet their needs. In Chicago, the druggist has to rigorously protect the contents of the store from an unsavory element that would most certainly take advantage of any weakness in the store's defenses.

Characteristics of a Competitive Win–Lose Negotiation

The competitive, Win–Lose strategy is one in which each side emphasizes only their position. The primary interest is to win. The Win–Lose approach is referred to as the "Chicago" approach. Win–Lose occurs when there are limited resources in which a win for one party means a loss for the other party—referred to as a fixed sum, or fixed pie. The emphasis is that the parties cannot or will not divide the pie.

The goal of a Chicago negotiation is to win as much as possible and not lose. Typically, in a competitive negotiation, concessions are viewed as indications of vulnerability, and the other party is viewed as an opponent to be conquered.

Each party considers themselves correct and considers the other party "wrong." Both sides operate from an aggressive position. Questions are not asked and alternatives are not probed. Exploratory problem-solving and decision-making is not tolerated or is viewed as a weakness. The goal is winning, control, power, and domination. Box 6.2 describes when a competitive negotiation strategy is used.

You might say that the difference between Kansas and Chicago is one of philosophy. The people in these two distinct environments perceive things differently. All negotiators bring their own personal philosophies to every negotiation. Their actions and decisions are based on their experiences and perceptions, whether they are inherently aware of these factors or not.

- A Kansas-style negotiator is going to enter the negotiation process thinking that the world is a collaborative place where the Win–Win is the operative goal.
- A Chicago-style negotiator is going to approach the negotiation with a Win–Lose mentality, because in the big city, one is either a winner or is a loser.

This is important to remember as you work your way through this book. I will refer to Kansas style and Chicago style in a variety of illustrations so

Box 6.2 When Is a Competitive Negotiation Strategy Used?

1. When there are limited resources, therefore the negotiation is definitely a fixed-sum situation
2. When the parties are not interdependent or mutually supporting

that you can see how these two philosophical approaches affect a negotiation process as well as the outcome.

Most negotiators ascribe to one overriding philosophy, even though they may effectively feign the opposite. A Kansas negotiator may try to play hardball like a Chicago negotiator; but will usually back down in a competitive setting. A Chicago negotiator may dress in sheep's clothing during the negotiation, only to devour the Kansas negotiator in the end.

That's not to say that there isn't a valid place for both styles. There are times when all interests are best served by handing out keys to the drugstore. There are other times when bars, screens, and grates should be the order of the day. The astute L-N knows whether he or she is in Kansas or Chicago.

In Small-Dot, you could probably stand on a downtown corner at 1 o'clock in the morning flash a roll of $100 bills, and leave that spot 20 min later with the roll of bills still firmly in your grasp. Try that in downtown Chicago and you'll likely end up in the nearest emergency room, sans your cash.

The lesson here is very straightforward. When you enter a negotiation, figure out where you are as soon as possible. Are you in Kansas or are you in Chicago?

SO WHERE ARE YOU?

When you are in downtown Chicago, you do not expect to be surrounded by cornfields. Similarly, when you're in Small-Dot, Kansas, you don't expect to look up and see skyscrapers. Just as there are characteristics of the middle of Kansas or of the city of Chicago that signal to you where you are, so there are characteristics of the Kansas and Chicago-style negotiators that tell you where you are. At this point, I will discuss the clues—some obvious and some more concealed—that will tip the L-N as to what kind of opponent he or she is facing.

- Box 6.3 lists five characteristics of collaborative L-Ns.
- Box 6.4 lists six characteristics of competitive L-Ns.

If you are going to be a truly effective L-N, you need to consider operating under a dual philosophy. Your natural instinct may be that you are a "Kansas negotiator." Or, your conditioning may be to be a "Chicago negotiator." I'm suggesting that you need to have one foot in Kansas and one foot in Chicago.

On the other hand, there are times because of the context—the philosophical environment—that those of you from the Chicago school of negotiation may find yourself in Kansas. What you need to do is be as trusting as you can be and open up the situation. Right now you're probably thinking, "You have got to be kidding! It is naïve to trust people. You can't trust anybody."

Recall the quote by Al Capone, *You can get far more with a smile and a gun than just a smile*. I'm not going to suggest that Chicago-style negotiators put their guns down. There are times to use a win-lose approach and there are times not to. The effective L-N knows when to be armed and when to conceal the gun with no intention to take it out.

Box 6.3 Five Characteristics of Collaborative Leader-Negotiators

Most often Collaborative L-Ns:

1. focus on satisfying as many interests or needs as possible for each party
2. view negotiation as a problem-solving process as opposed to a contest to be won
3. promote Win–Win agreements rather than Win–Lose outcomes
4. model cooperative nonverbal behaviors that complement words
5. consider the "long view" by foreseeing future opportunities, anticipating unintended consequences and implications, and recognizing the value of a relationship that might be strategic at a future point in time.

Box 6.4 Six Characteristics of Competitive Leader-Negotiators

Toto, we aren't in Kansas anymore

Dorothy

Most often Competitive L-Ns:

1. make very high or, unreasonable, opening positions. These positions are employed to identify the high stakes required to reach agreement.
2. employ secretive maneuvers and offer little or no disclosure of information. They typically wait to reveal their agendas late into the negotiation and take a nontrusting stance toward the other party. They are compelled to question, scrutinize, and document everything. Documentation is a useful method in all negotiation. However, the "general feeling" or atmosphere of a competitive negotiation is distrust, suspicion, misgiving, and personal attack—not just documentation and proof.
3. have no intention to share resources or develop a doctrine of fair-mindedness. Their goal is to increase only their part of the "pie"; and, at the same time to decrease the other party's portion, if not in fact giving "no pie" at all to the other party.
4. utilize tactics of bluffing and threatening, which are used to emphasize risk if an agreement is not reached according to *their* terms. They may well use misinformation and/or half-truths. This is not a win-win environment; rather, it is a winner take all, situation,—as much as possible. Win–Lose negotiators have a short-term frame of mind. This approach limits the potential for any long-term opportunities.
5. make small concessions while requesting that the other party makes large, major concessions.
6. use threatening behaviors to intimidate the other party and/or to stimulate emotional reactions. This tends to escalate hostility, conflict, and aggression.

Kansas-style negotiators understand that the collaborative process involves problem-solving, long-term relationships, synergy, and opportunity. When two Kansas negotiators negotiate with each other, their "style" is to cooperate.

Chicago-style negotiators understand the competitive environment. Two Chicago negotiators realize that one of them will walk out winning and one losing. That is just the way the Chicago way of life is.

A COMPARISON OF COMPETITIVE AND COLLABORATIVE ORGANIZATIONS

At this point, let's transition from a focus on individual L-N characteristics to organizational characteristics. The formula for success in today's business climate is to be completely collaborative internally and aggressively competitive outside of one's organization.

The intent of Table 6.1, Characteristics of Competitive (Win–Lose) and Collaborative (Win–Win) organizations, contrasts the thinking that dominates competitive Chicago-style (Win–Lose) and collaborative Kansas-style (Win–Win) organizational environments. Each philosophy is described in either-or terms for the sake of clarity. However, in practice, characteristics of each philosophy are usually blended.

Competitive Organizations

The basic competitive motto is:

"Winning isn't everything. It is the only thing."

Vince Lombardi

Competitive organizations are generally characterized by the following.

Territorialism (Tr)

Organizations characterized by a territorial (Tr) culture typically establish ways to protect their departmental boundaries. In a Tr culture, a large amount of time and resources are expended on such things as clarifying who has what kind of power, where control begins and stops, and how rules and policies safeguard departmental boundaries. Territorialism becomes a central focus in management

TABLE 6.1 Characteristics of Competitive (Win–Lose) and Collaborative (Win–Win) Organizations

Competitive (Win–Lose)	Collaborative (Win–Win)
Territorialism	Strategic Thinking
Group Think	Learning and Diversity
Tribalism	Open System
Silo Conflict	Cross Functional
Fragmented	Integrated

meetings. Managers, on average, spend about 80% of their time safeguarding their Territorial interests against loss of power, working to increase their span of control, and/or working out plans to retain authority. This regularly interferes with management's ability to concentrate on increasing productivity, creating meaningful value, and strategizing about external competitive threats.

Group Think

Negotiators must maintain an open mind regarding possible solutions and points of common ground. A danger to an open mind is termed "Group Think" (GT). GT is when team members agree with one another at the expense of discernment. The pervasiveness of GT organizations can hinder achieving a productive outcome. The purpose here is not to repeat others' coverage of GT. This information can be accessed in the resource section of this book.

Tribalism

Tribal organizations are characterized by intimidation, bullying, and threat. A Tribalism (Tb) culture contributes to putting distance between organizational divisions. It is common behavior for employees to identify with their department, or "tribe"; not with the whole organization. It becomes difficult to know how to work and network with others outside 'their' department without bumping into departmental lines of Tb. Tb plays a role in not considering whether a particular action profits the whole organization and results in "fragmentation" (Fg). Fg concerns itself with only the immediate division of responsibility.

Silo Conflict

Because an organization is a system, no two groups within an organization can exist truly independently. Within a cross-functional structure, a particular group can succeed only when other cross-functional groups perform collaboratively. As interdependence increases, the potential for conflict increases.

Silos refer to parts of the organization that have specific job functions and do not prefer to be interdependent for their success. In order to fulfill departmental goals, a particular department may create a sense of pride and a spirit-décor about "belonging" to and identifying with a particular department. This can build morale; this can also result in a siloed organization. Siloed departments have low loyalty to the employing organization, but high commitment to specialized skills.

Conflict arises when mutually exclusive goals or values, a desire to win at others' cost, misunderstandings about how each silo needs to operate differently, and/or how each group seeks favor from authority. Additional factors that contribute to silo conflict are illuminated in Box 6.5.

Fragmentation

A characteristic of Figure 6.1 involves promoting one's department at the expense of all other interests. If the focus of everyday operations concerns only one group's interests and is indifferent to others' well-being, Fg occurs. Departments and

Box 6.5 Silo Conflict

1. Actions are made with no regard for other departments or employees.
2. Team members are encouraged to have negative attitudes toward outsiders.
3. Dislike and distrust toward others outside their team is promoted and reinforced.

FIGURE 6.1 Fragmentation.

employees find ways to promote their own success and achievement even if this is detrimental to others' departments. Managing internal politics and disarming internal competition becomes the primary description of job success (Figure 6.1).

In a competitive, Win–Lose scenario, all parts of the organization exist; however, few parts actually work together and may in fact work against each other. Note: Further characteristics of competitive organizations will be discussed in Chapter 11, The Context of Conflict, and Chapter 12, Diagnosing and Managing Conflict.

Collaborative Organizations

Collaborative organizations demonstrate the following characteristics. They:

1. **Engage in Strategic Thinking**—Strategic thinking implies openness to success anywhere within the organization. Differences in structure are permitted and encouraged if it results in strategic advantage. Territorialism is not tolerated or supported.
2. **Value Learning and Diversity**—Individuals are empowered to determine their course of action within the stated corporate parameters. A potential downside is that they equally accept the risk and consequences of not producing.
3. **Operate as an Open System**—An open system allows for continuous job mastery that improves expertise and quality. The need to control others is not a priority. Control comes from the desire to master one's job, as opposed to an exclusive goal to move up the corporate ladder.

4. **Promote Cross-Functional Communication**—Evaluation is based on measuring up to organization-wide standards. Problem-solving is a team effort, resulting in continuous quality improvement, stimulated creativity, and increased innovation. This is a key factor in both future growth and survival in an interdependent world.
5. **Are Integrated**—When interdependence is a central aspect of the reward system, then risk-taking is valued and rewarded as an expected, consistent organizational process. The result is increased productivity, better quality control, and a reduction of operating costs.

The Law of Opposites

The law of opposites (Figure 6.2) states that if two opposing forces exert pressure against each other, that somewhere in-between those two extremes exists a point of balance. An old negotiation adage states that once both parties establish a position about what they want, everyone knows what they cannot have. A realistic process of negotiation begins by moving somewhere toward the balance point in-between the extremes, referred to as "balanced tension." The L-N's skill involves managing unbalanced tension, or conflict, until achieving balance. Achieving balance demands a great deal of the L-N. It is important to note that permanent "balance" is seldom achieved. In fact, I have yet to observe a "balanced" organization. Continuous *balancing* is needed.

In terms of balance, there is a philosophical mismatch when you have a Kansas-style negotiator on one side of the table and a Chicago-style negotiator on the other side. Philosophically they are in each other's faces, and they can't believe the other person is acting the way he or she is. Generally, in this philosophical mismatch, the "Chicago" L-N will dominate the "Kansas" L-N. Not all the time, of course, but generally. The real problem is this— the Kansas negotiator who tends to see synergistic opportunity walks into a negotiation and says something like, "Look at what we can do. Look at the possibilities." And just

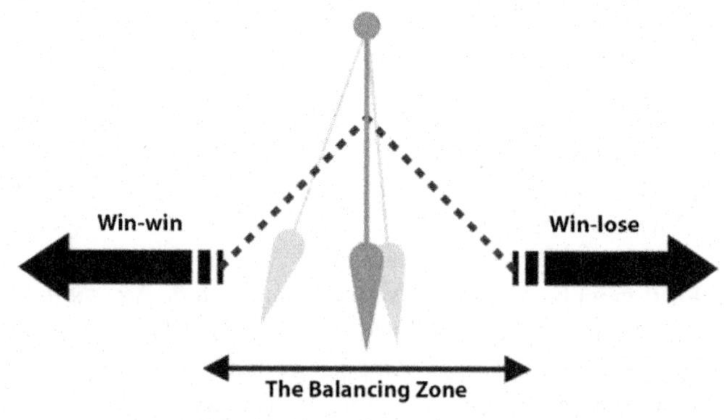

FIGURE 6.2 The law of opposites.

the time they say this, a large burning hole develops in their chest. When they look down, they are shocked. "My goodness, that's a bullet hole!" Their next response usually is, "That's not fair." Of course, that observation is completely irrelevant— the hole is already there.

Chicago negotiators, on the other hand, walk into the room and fire away. The outcome is that they usually do win. But they still have limited success because they never take the time to explore opportunity and possibility. As a result, when they win, they win a limited piece of the pie. Kansas negotiators see the whole pie but often are unable to explore potential alternatives because of the strong Chicago style.

How then can Kansas negotiators enjoy the collaborative environment they desire? The demand for balancing brings us back to Chapter 2 and the attributes of effective L-Ns: (1) self-control, (2) emotional maturity, (3) depersonalization, (4) the ability to manage failure, and (5) cope with imperfection. If collaborative L-Ns want to get to Kansas, one of their primary strategies is to disarm the Chicago win-lose environment.

HOW TO IMPLEMENT A COLLABORATIVE NEGOTIATION

1. Begin by identifying and understanding each party's needs:
   - **a.** Tangible requests (time, money, goods, and resources)
   - **b.** Operational requirements (the way something has to be done)
   - **c.** Relational needs (conditions that support an ongoing relationship)
2. Create solutions that equitably represent each party:
   - **a.** Avoid discussions that exclusively favor one party over the other
   - **b.** Look for agreement in principle if a specific one cannot be found
   - **c.** Identify objective criteria that both parties can agree to
   - **d.** Allow for various proposals to be introduced before one decision is selected
3. Generate proposals that consider various viewpoints:
   - **a.** Avoid being locked into rigid assumptions or "either-or" thinking
   - **b.** Discover ways to integrate solutions for mutual advantage
   - **c.** Don't lock into "fixed-pie" assumptions; if possible, explore ways to expand the pie
   - **d.** Each party gets what they want, but maybe at different times:
     - Consider two or more agenda items at the same time
     - Divide agenda items into higher and/or lower priorities
     - Each L-N gets his or her way on one issue
   - **e.** Keep proposal generation separate from the evaluation process
4. Find ways to agree with each proposal in principle:
   - **a.** Avoid arguing about specific issues. Consider higher level principles upon which each party can agree
   - **b.** Break the proposals into small, manageable pieces. This helps identify areas of disagreement as differentiated from the entire proposal

c. Avoid threatening each other. This takes self-control and emotional maturity
d. Respect all viewpoints and needs; this does not imply agreement, only understanding
e. Do not take advantage of weakness or vulnerability of others
f. Demonstrate trust; begin with a problem-solving approach rather than a competitive approach

Ironically, the Win–Win oriented L-N often ends up losing more than would have been lost had a competitive mind-set ruled their actions. The Win–Lose oriented person, however, unwittingly leaves unexplored opportunities on the table, obtaining much less than may have been gained had the negotiation been approached from a collaborative mind-set. The key, then, is to know *when* to be competitive and *when* to be collaborative; and, to understand that the stance of each party can shift many times within a negotiation as line items are individually considered and resolved. It is a balancing act to effectively negotiate by being consistently collaborative or consistently competitive. It requires a constant back-and-forth balance between Kansas and Chicago. I view collaboration and competition as highly fluid concepts, and every successful L-N I know perceives negotiations this same way.

One of the objectives of this book is to hone your critical thinking skills so that you can't be set up and duped. These skills represent a cognitive framework that explains how an L-N needs to think in order to be effective. Chapter 7 will unpack the influence of Frames. *Have you ever been framed?* Read on.

Section III

Negotiating in the Leadership Zone

Chapter 7

The Power and Influence of Frames

Whoever controls meaning controls others' viewpoints.

WHAT IS A FRAME? FRAMES ARE MENTAL MODELS

It has been said that those who know how to influence others benefit the most from negotiation. (Figure 7.1).

Frames are mental maps. A **frame** is a particular way of thinking within a particular context. There are many ways to describe a frame, such as: "a cognitive map," "a mental window," "a point of reference," "a persons' way of thinking," "a scheme," or, "a lens." A frame is what energizes a Leader-Negotiators (L-N's) communication and persuades people to want to do what the L-N needs or wants them to do. It follows, then, that the L-N must be able to select frames that are most advantageous to their organization. Frames influence, if not control, what a person sees, hears, and experiences as well as what he or she does not see, hear, and experience. (Figure 7.2).

FRAME RECOGNITION

The world cannot be made sense of and facts cannot be understood without frames. Every communication has a frame, conscious or not. **Framing** is how communication tools such as words, metaphors, examples, diagrams, and numbers are used to design an agreement. For example, in a negotiation someone uses the phrase "market forces," which is an economic frame that offers a solution to an economic problem. Effective Questioning (EQ) suggests asking questions to reduce perceptual disagreement, avoid oversimplification, and generate alternatives; broadening the context of the problem beyond only "market forces." Table 7.1—Common Frames in Business Environments—lists common frames that need to be recognized in everyday problem-solving and decision-making.

Frames construct value from a preferred point of view. Framing can organize a person's perspective so that it influences their acceptance of an offer or, if not framed well, the rejection of an offer. Using the "executive" and "production" frames from Table 7.1, let's see how they relate to risk and opportunity. During a negotiation, executives often frame information as an

FIGURE 7.1

FIGURE 7.2

"opportunity" for future growth; however, the production zone (PZ) may look at the same information and concludes that "opportunity" (aka change) represents an unacceptable risk. The frame is *NOT* the information. The frame is how one *interprets* the information.

People often see identical situations differently. For example, one person might look upon a situation in terms of its similarities, while another person looks upon the same situation in terms of its differences. Although "similarities" and "differences" are equivalent descriptions of the same situation, these two viewpoints have completely different implications and may result in conflict (see Box 7.1 and 7.2).

The famous question, *"Is the glass half-full or half-empty?"* is representative of this dilemma, to which the comedian George Carlin responded, "All I care about is who owns the glass." L-Ns must be adept at recognizing and using frames (Figure 7.3).

TABLE 7.1 Common Frames in Business Environments

Common frames	Subcategories
Economic	Markets, market forces, economic cycles, budgets, etc.
Political	Interest groups, power, policy, etc.
Human resources	Law, equality, rules, equity, etc.
Environmental	Living and evolving systems, etc.
Legal	Power, penalties, etc.
Sociological	Group behavior, crowd behavior, political party affiliation, etc.
Psychological	Individual behavior
Executive	Change represents an opportunity for future growth, for the whole organization, not necessarily for the interests of individual employees
Production	Change represents a risk of job security and should be resisted

Box 7.1 Is the Glass One-Half Empty or One-Half Full?

Consider a glass of water. Four people are viewing the glass of water. Each person comments on the glass from his/her frame:

- An economist wants to know, "Who owns the glass?"
- A politician sees a water shortage; therefore, water rates should be increased.
- An entrepreneur sees the need to market smaller glasses.
- A negotiator sees a glass that could be divided into several more equitable glasses of water.

Box 7.2 An Imaginary Trip

Allow your imagination to transport Gandhi from both the time in which he lived and the geographical context in which he lived. Transport Gandhi forward in time to the 1940s. Now situate him inside the context of World War II's Germany under the command of Adolph Hitler. Reasoning from the historical knowledge of that moment in time, think about what could have happened to Gandhi's philosophy under Hitler's dictatorship? It is a projection that Gandhi's name might not be the household name we recognize today. Why? Most likely, Gandhi would have vanished from the streets of Germany, nowhere to be found and without reference to his teachings.

FIGURE 7.3 Eye glasses and the glass half-full.

THE AWESOME POWER OF THE LISTENING EAR: SIX FRAMES THAT FILTER INFORMATION

The first step of effective leadership is not action; the first step is understanding. **The question then is—to understand what?**

This section introduces the concept of filters and sorting information that influences problem-solving, decision-making, selecting effective action, building competent teams, and crafting strategy. The six filters are given below:

1. The risk-opportunity filter (away vs toward)
2. The information filter (similar vs difference)
3. The relevance filter (global vs specific)
4. The persuasion filter (see, hear, experience)
5. The motivation filter (possibility vs necessity)
6. The problem-solving filter (rules vs guidelines)

The Power of Habits Tend to Override Knowledge

Under pressure and stress, our habits control our thinking. Knowledge must be transformed into effective habits if it is to be useful under conditions of stress. In addition to L-Ns learning their unique patterns of **sorting**, it is equally important to recognize others' patterns. In order to build competent teams, each team member's unique sorting preferences need to be identified and respected. It has been my experience that people excel when their sorting skills are respected and utilized. An L-N's sorting preference reveals the way he or she thinks and crafts strategies. Being aware of one's own and others' sorting preferences protects L-Ns from being locked into a "cul-de-sac" that reinforces status quo thinking; a sorting preference for maintaining the status quo blocks out potential perspectives as if they do not exist.

FIGURE 7.4 Risk-opportunity filter.

Others will not move in the direction we desire them to move until we understand their point of view. Conflict tends to be arguments about how people sort; often positioning one party as "right" and the other "wrong." Most perspectives are legitimate; however, some are more relevant to the context than others. In 45 years, I have never listened to a person whose perspective is "wrong"; however, I also have not listened to a perspective that has been complete. In other words, the opposite of a "right"–"wrong" argument is another point of view.

Following are explanations of six prevalent sorting filters, or frames that influence the direction of negotiated outcomes.

The Risk-Opportunity Filter

The way L-Ns sort information influences the direction of a negotiated outcome. The risk-opportunity filter (Figure 7.4) identifies if one's sorting pattern may lead them *toward* opportunity ("risk-inclined") or *away* from risk (risk-reluctant).

- Risk-inclination is an opportunity pattern, whereby L-Ns tend to take calculated risks. Risk-inclined L-Ns tend to tolerate ambiguity and uncertainty. They are not afraid to pursue possibilities in the face of potential loss.
- Risk-reluctance is an avoidance pattern that is characterized by a mind-set that is hesitant and prefers safety and assurances. Risk-reluctant L-Ns need guarantees against potential and actual loss and become cautious and guarded as risk increases.

Risk maybe classified into six general categories:

1. Financial risk—the loss of resources, the high cost of maintenance, or cheaper alternatives.
2. Performance risk—how dependent one is on others to get work done; the implications of a task not being completed on time, or as expected.
3. Physical risk—unsafe or injurious outcomes.
4. Psychological risk—something disagreeable with one's mind-set, values, or reputation.

5. Social risk—something that could or will have an adverse effect on the way others think about you.
6. Time risk—lost time can cause inconvenience because plans must be adjusted within previously established time frames; an opportunity may cease being available at a point in time.

The amount of risk an L-N accepts is unique to each person and each situation as risk-opportunity varies as situations vary. The amount of risk one is willing to accept is not an objective process; otherwise, it would not be a "risk." The criterion that one uses to accept risk is related to particular payoffs or benefits that may or may not happen. Negotiations are not guaranteed to work out as anticipated. The L-N with the most flexible thinking maximizes their opportunity for success. Risk is a normal human experience. However, if "normal" implies thinking patterns that narrow ones' point of view, the L-N must work to disarm these patterns.

- One-dimensional thinking limits one's powers of observation and often results in preferring safer alternatives.
- Diminished insight leads to the inability to understand the nature of complex situations.
- Limited creativity exposes one's resistance to the power of imagination to develop new and original ideas, problem-solving, and decision-making.

Balance of Risk-Opportunity and Risk-Reluctance

L-Ns must recognize that both risk and opportunity will be present during the negotiation process, and they must realize that their tendency toward risk-opportunity or risk-reluctance will influence their problem-solving and decision-making. Most often, however, people tend to stay with familiar, status quo blueprints and obey previous behavior patterns despite the need to change. For example, avoiding risk may be a deeply embedded instinctive reflex. Frequently, the behavior of someone who is risk-reluctant or risk-avoidant is characterized by the desire to eliminate one's own internal tension and/or the pressure she or he experiences with risk in general. In a sense, people may try to eliminate risk with the purpose of easing their anxiety, stress, conflict, and worry. They may not actually resist what is being proposed; rather, they mostly dislike taking risks. Regardless, risk-avoidance can limit potential opportunities. It is critical for the L-N to distinguish whether the resistance point is a resistance related to the proposal or is related to their conditioning to resist risk—any risk.

Success does not favor the L-N who is perfect or flawless, as this mindset tends to promote risk-avoidance. It is my viewpoint that **perfectionism** is destructive and not possible to achieve. Therefore, accepting the shortcoming of human imperfection, recovery from oversights, miscalculations, and failures is one of the most mature skills that an L-N can develop.

Remember:

- If an opportunity or a risk is not perceived then in a sense, it might as well not exist. There are also risky outcomes to preferring an opportunity

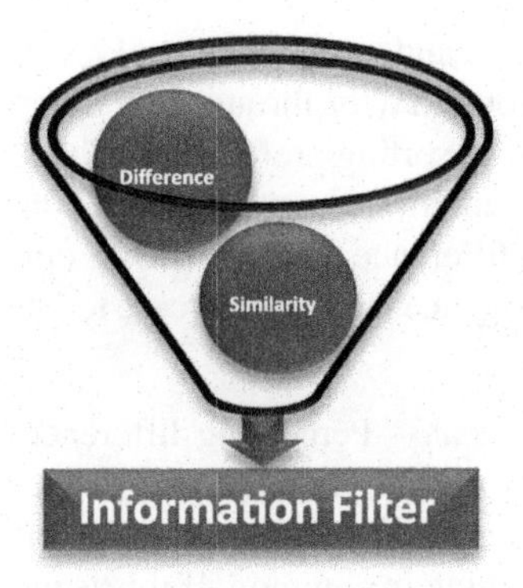

FIGURE 7.5 Information filter.

while not recognizing potential risks. Risk-taking may involve choosing to avoid a more serious or greater risk presently or in the future. This implies that the best choice may involve a "balanced-tension" stuck between an imperfect risk and a defective opportunity. This requires judgment among trade-offs.

- Success doesn't favor the L-N who is perfect or error free, as this encourages risk-avoidance. Successful negotiation is not about perfection, it is often about *recovery.

The Information Filter

The information filter (Figure 7.5) explains how people interpret their first impressions. The information filter is described from two conditions: similarity and difference.

- When people first look at information through a "similarity filter," they tend to make sense of people, tasks, and situations in terms of their likeness or common characteristics.
- When people look at information using the "difference filter," they tend to make sense of people, tasks, and situations in terms of their dissimilarity and unique distinctions.

This is how people look at the same information and come up with different conclusions.

All negotiations are context-dependent. **Context** explains a circumstance or event that imparts meaning and frames action. Context influences L-Ns' alternatives. Similarity is valuable in that it identifies common ground. Common ground helps achieve agreement by offering the possibility that you have more in common than nothing in common or of interest. Considering only differences magnifies dissimilarities and makes things seem less negotiable than they might actually be. Difference may harden resistant attitudes between people and promote polarized thinking. Recognizing *both* similarity and difference assumes that there is more than one way to look at a situation.

A barrier to cooperation and agreement involves the tendency to judge and evaluate statements and/or behavior through the filter of one's deeply embedded and mostly unconscious sorting preferences. The tendency to disapprove of other's ideas increases as emotions intensify. Often, one's preference for seeing only similarity or only difference arouses strong emotions. When emotional intensity heightens, intelligence tends to decrease to 'shoe size' which can sabotage productive outcomes.

- *Considering only difference*—Perceiving difference may result in concluding that neither party have nothing in common. This could be disadvantageous if it results in no incentive to continue negotiating. There are situations where people have nothing in common. If this is the case, cease negotiation. Considering only differences, however, may intensify an impasse or stalemate and escalate conflict due to misunderstanding and disagreement. A focus on difference may emphasize how far each party is apart. This perceived distance may reinforce that an agreement is not possible. It is important to recognize that having nothing in common with others should be based on the fact Insert - that you have nothing in common, not upon a preference for only sorting from a difference filter. The L-N must insist on exploring both Similarity and Difference.
- *Considering only similarity*—Considering only similarity may result in not recognizing legitimate differences. This has been termed the "halo effect" which is the tendency to consider something as being totally good because one aspect of the agreement is advantageous. Similarity is the common-ground denominator and the momentum needed to bridge obstacles and differences. If there is enough common ground, it may motivate others to perceive that it is possible to reconcile their differences. Downplaying difference on the other hand and emphasizing only similarity may neglect legitimate, incompatible issues. Rejecting an offer that is not in your best interest is as strategic as accepting an advantageous offer. The point being that one's 'sorting' preferences need to include both similarity and difference, not just one or the other.

Understanding others' points of view is a very mature human skill as it requires LN's to control their sorting preference so that they can strategically listen to other divergent points of view without rejecting an alternative point of view because it is different than one's habitual sorting preference controlling one's emotions. This may sound simple, but understanding is not automatically mutual. Controlling one's emotions requires self-control and depersonalization.

Remember:

1. People are more willing to be disagreed with when they know they have been accurately listened to. People tend to get upset when misunderstanding is combined with also being disagreed with.
2. A preference should remain a preference. Once a preference becomes an absolute position it usually generates unresolvable conflict, as it becomes

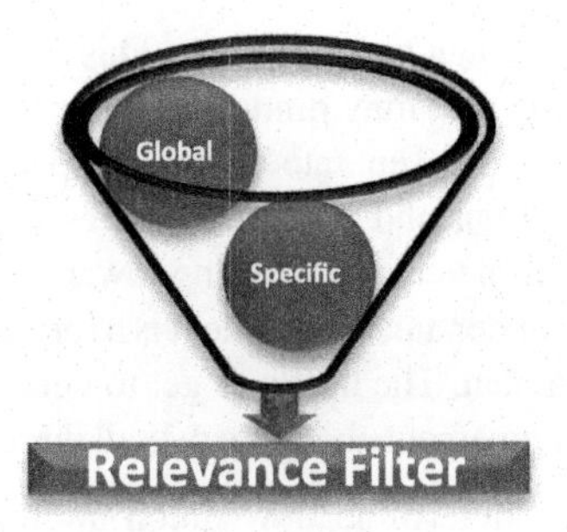

FIGURE 7.6 Relevance filter.

almost impossible to negotiate because there is no room for concessions, compromise, or mutual common ground. A common cause of lost opportunity and increased conflict includes viewing one's thinking as being 'absolutely' correct - often referred to as "exceptionalism."

The Relevance Filter

The relevance filter (Figure 7.6) refers to how people determine if information is valuable or not valuable. This is described by two conditions: global and specific.

- The "global filter" prefers comprehensive, broad, and all-inclusive information—the grand. This filter prefers contextual information first. In fact, unless the global context is first understood, facts and details are considered irrelevant.
- The "specific filter" prefers detailed, meticulous, and thorough information. In fact, unless the details are presented first, efforts to explain the "big-picture" is considered irrelevant.

People with specific filters make sense of their world by concentrating on details. Those who prefer specificity may experience resistance and *impatience* when listening to global information—until they first know all the details. They often ask questions regarding how, when, why, where, who, and what in order to secure the details.

People with global filters have difficulty understanding the importance of details until they first understand the global **context**. Generally, those with global filter preferences may display resistance and impatience and seem fatigued when listening to details without first knowing the larger global context.

Typically, when people with opposite relevance filter preferences are communicating with each other, they may be predisposed to be impatient and annoyed. People with opposite filter preferences frequently interrupt each other to ask questions about the global and/or specific relevance of each other's filters. Two kinds of failure are related to global and specific filters:

Failure #1: Specific details are separated from the global context.

Context influences how details are interpreted as relevant or irrelevant. If the context is not articulated it permits people to interpret the context from their own point of view. This is an invitation for conflict, misunderstanding, and may hinder plan implementation.

Failure #2: Global context is separated from the specific details.

Under time limitations and performance pressures, people often hustle to get the details hammered out. Rushing toward getting the details without slowing down to understand the context is a formula for setbacks that delay the progress of a plan. The hustle to get to get agreement often results in the facade of an agreement about the overall direction or purpose of a plan.

The pressures of time determine how much attention one can allocate to issues such as context and/or detail. It is problematic when communication gaps remain open for interpretation; people tend to interpret communication gaps with whatever they think is reasonable. However, a reasonable interpretation is frequently misunderstood or is out of context given the differences among each person's sorting filters. Global overviews are helpful, but may permit others to implement plans at the detail level using their unique filter perspectives. Gap filling is best allowed when the risks of failure are insignificant.

As a final point, when time is limited and an action must be taken immediately, and if you are working with knowledgeable people who have demonstrated high levels of reliable judgment in ambiguous situations, you can move forward and trust your team to make everything hit the target. If none of the above exists, some level of unwanted failure usually results. Detailed analysis is best implemented when time deadlines are reasonable, and risk depends upon meticulousness execution of the plan. A detailed analysis is recommended when the workforce is inexperienced and needs to be *told* what to do, when to do it, how to do it, etc.

Suggestions:

1. Time deadline pressures usually determine how much thoughtfulness can be given to contextual overview or how deeply details can be considered. When time is limited, there is a tendency to provide a global overview. However, you can expect people to fill in the gaps between global and detail with their own schemes. A common disruption to excellent plan execution can be traced back to too much gap filling during the planning phase. Conflict related to non-specific, global sorting tends to show up deep into the implementation phase. Often, this can undermine the best of plan intentions.
2. Time constraint is organizational reality. A technique to quickly and efficiently communicate both details and global context involves asking each person to write and not verbalize their issues on a whiteboard. They will then have 30 minutes or some reasonable amount of time to explain their agenda thinking.
3. If time crisis happens endlessly, then it is an indication that the organization is in a crisis mode, which is not an effective format for long-term success. However, this is not always within everyone's control. Control what you can and work at repairing a crisis type culture. However, there is often not enough time to repair a system related problem when one is in the middle of a crisis. This is when an LN must cope with imperfection.

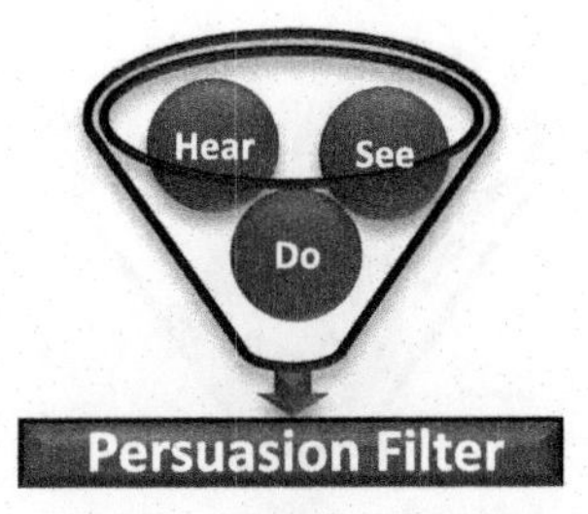

FIGURE 7.7 Persuasion filter.

4. If people need to deepen their understanding of context or detail, ask them to meet outside the group meeting. This technique eliminates thinking out loud at everyone else's time expense. It is very difficult to write out thoughts that are intuitive, belief centered, and/or experienced based. Writing forces people to quickly *get to it.* Writing usually saves time because most people can read faster than listening to others speak. Moreover, most people can read with better comprehension than they can listen because they can review written information.

Remember, there are no answers, formulas, or techniques that resolve problems related to time limitations other than building competent teams who are prepared to perform without the advantage of time.

The Persuasion Filter

Persuasion filter (Figure 7.7) involves how people are influenced to agree. The persuasion filter is described from three conditions:

- Seeing—The tendency to prefer visual observation of an idea; to read it; visibly see it.
- Hearing—The tendency to prefer to listen to an idea; to talk about it with others.
- Experiencing—The tendency to prefer a hands-on approach.

How are people persuaded to do or not do something? People are mostly influenced by what they "see," "hear," and/or "experience." Most people can "see"—but we all "see" or perceive differently. Most people can "hear" but we all "hear" (perceive) differently. Most people can "experience" but we all "experience" (perceive) differently.

People are often a combination of all three persuasion filters. However, most people have a preference for one or two filters. Thus, some people will read this document (visual) and enjoy reading it. Others will prefer to hear about it (auditory). Yet, others will prefer to experience (do) this information. If a person is given information outside their preference, they may not respond to it because of how their brain prefers to receive information. Historians have concluded that Michael Angelo was one of the brightest of the human race because his mind was wide open to all three filters—all the time.

FIGURE 7.8 Motivation filter.

The Motivation Filter

The motivation filter (Figure 7.8) refers to a preference to work at certain tasks and not others. Generally, this filter is described from two conditions:

- Possibility refers to something that people are motivated to do because of the possibilities. Possibility thinkers often use words like—might, likely, maybe, could.
- Necessity refers to something that people feel that has to be done because it is necessary. Necessity thinkers often use words like—need to, must, should, have to.

For example, some people work because it is a necessity for survival; while others work to create possibilities for life.

Remember:

1. The concept of human motivation is complex, and what is known about the theory of motivation is modest indeed. Be aware that there is much yet to be learned about the concept of human motivation. Most motivation theories do not resolve the absence of motivation. Understanding motivation is a work in progress.
2. Motivation is not a one-time pattern of behavior. Human beings tend to change over time, experience, and context.
3. Not all people can be motivated via persuasion techniques. The key here is to recognize what you can influence and what you cannot. The science of influence is not a science, it is an art.
4. Accepting responsibility for others' motivation is a formula for dysfunction. There is an old proverb that says, "Never do for others what they can do for themselves."
5. A simple formula is to retain your motivated people and find ways to purge the unmotivated. This is more easily said than done.

Note: L-Ns must accept responsibility for motivating themselves and to protect themselves against allowing others to demotivate.

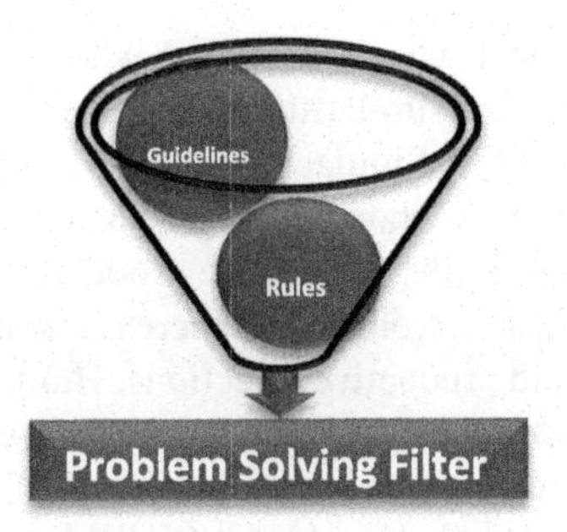

FIGURE 7.9 Problem-solving filter.

The Problem-Solving Filter

The problem-solving filter (Figure 7.9) involves describing how people prefer to do things the way they do. Generally, these two filters are described from two conditions:

- Guidelines are guiding principles regarding how to do a task. Guidelines thinkers take more of a divergent, creative, and flexible approach. They lead with explanations about why they did what they did (i.e., justify) and tend to prefer being given alternatives that they can explore, rather than being told what to do. Guidelines thinkers also often prefer to find ways to bend the rules.
- Rules are time-proven principles set forth from previous knowledge and conventional ways of solving problems. Rules thinkers are motivated to continuously improve processes, methods, or procedures. They lead with descriptions about how they did what they did. They receive satisfaction doing things the "right" and "correct" way. They may have a strong need and/or desire to complete tasks, exhibit an almost a compulsive inclination toward achievement, and—they may tend to be perfectionistic.

Remember:

1. There are situations when people must be told what to do, how to do it, and when it needs to be done. Telling people what to do generally stems from situations where there are time constraints and lack of expertise among workers and no time to train them.
2. There are situations that require ambiguous guidelines with the expectation that teams can "figure it out" as they go along. This includes situations when circumstances are continuously changing and where geographical distance requires local judgment.

Summary of the Six Sorting Filters

These six sorting filters are what L-Ns depend upon to organize and make sense of their world. By recognizing these filters in yourself and others, you increase your potential to communicate effectively. The sorting filters should not be used to create an argument about who is right and who is wrong. They are about understanding differences and similarities. Differences tend to emotionally distance people from one another. Similarities tend to bring people closer because they prefer to work with those whom they agree and like. This can enhance job performance and make work-life much more productive.

Sorting filters have been introduced to increase awareness of how to manage ourselves and others in productive directions. Human filter preferences can vary over time and context; moreover, the six filters are not the only filters we possess. Remember, no two human beings are identical. Our unique sorting filters shape our set of interests, habits, likes and dislikes, and rules for behavior. Filters shape each person's "model of the world"—which in some way *will be different* from others' models of the world. These differences can either become bridges of communication or walls of conflict and resistance. The choice is ours.

EVERYTHING IS CONTEXT-DEPENDENT

An Imaginary Trip

Mohandas K. Gandhi, the famous leader from India is known throughout the world for his teachings on passive resistance and civil disobedience. Negotiation books and articles repeatedly imply that Gandhi's tactic of civil disobedience is the only tactic for all negotiations. However, the underlying assumption that Gandhi's method is the "only" tactical approach should be questioned. Let me emphasize that what is being challenged is neither Gandhi nor his civil disobedience philosophy. Rather, the challenge is directed to those who suggest that Gandhi's approach is the "best" and/or "only" negotiation tactic. See Box 7.2—An Imaginary Trip.

Now, return to the historical Gandhi that we are knowledgeable about. A critical and overlooked dynamic in Gandhi's success in India was the British. Remember,

Frames are where expectations are developed.

What if Gandhi and Britain were switched to Gandhi and Hitler?

Gandhi might be unknown.

Gandhi was a bright man. And this illustration *does not* imply that Gandhi would not have adjusted his strategy. In fact, our imaginary trip is not a statement about Gandhi at all. Rather, it questions the frame within which Gandhi negotiated. However, the point is not Gandhi, the British, or—even Hitler. The point is the British dealt with resistance differently than Hitler did. The point is that the *contextual frame* of a negotiation significantly influences how we draw conclusions about the use of strategy and tactics. *All negotiations are context-dependent!*

Framing and reframing aka "I went to the store to buy an apple. How did I return home with an apple orchard?" Take a look at the DVD Story (Box 7.3).

SHIFTING FRAMES

A frame, or **reframe**, is able to influence the focus point of a negotiation. That is, it directs the viewer to consider certain features and ignore others. The

Box 7.3 A DVD Player Story

A buyer (Jim) enters an electronics store to buy a DVD player. Jim explains to a salesperson that his objective is to decide to either buy a DVD player or to not buy a DVD player. The salesperson asks Jim if he has considered a TV with a built-in DVD. A "cinema package?" (Jim's frame has just been reframed from a DVD player to a TV-cinema package.) The salesperson then reinforces the reframe by showing Jim several computers that can do *similar* functions. Jim's original frame was to buy either a DVD player or not. The *reframe* shifted Jim's decision-making objective to:

- Should he buy a DVD player?
- Should he buy a cinema package?
- Should he buy a computer?

Once Jim's original objective was reframed, how could Jim argue that a DVD player alone is better than cinema package? The reframe has been achieved. Jim buys the "best alternative." The salesperson increases his sale.

psychological frame, for example, encourages the observer to attend to a feature that is preferred and disregard other features. Frames happen in both verbal and nonverbal ways, as well as in combination. The following examples of how to reframe are easy to understand. You may read them and think of a situation you have been in or anticipate being in, where reframing a frame to solve a problem or make a decision may result in changing the outcome of a decision.

FOUR FRAMES AND REFRAMES

The Defiant Client

A physical rehabilitation group was increasingly frustrated by clients' low compliance rates. For some reason, patients were not following the physical exercise routines recommended by therapists. When the therapists changed the office décor, patient compliance increased 30%.

- The reframe involved placing their professional credentials up on the wall. This increased the patient's perception that they were talking to "authoritative experts."
- Point of example: The client's frame that physical therapists were not expert professionals was changed by posting symbols (a nonverbal frame) of their education (authority). This shifted 30% of the patients' resistance from not following their therapists' programs to respecting and doing what the therapists advised.

Stop Looting!

NATO (North Atlantic Treaty Organization) convoys in Somalia were frequently looted. To reduce looting, military commanders broadcasted authoritarian commands to stop looting! It had little to no effect. However, when the broadcasters reframed their message away from threats, the looting almost completely stopped.

- The re-frame involved military commanders adding phrases that influenced the looters' self-concept, self-worth, and intelligence. Why was this effective? Because the looters had to be consistent with their self-image (i.e., reduce cognitive dissonance).
- Point of example: The original frame was directed at stopping unwanted behavior. When this proved ineffective, broadcasters reframed their message to appeal to the looters' higher values—their self-esteem.

I Do Not Like Your Music!

Owners of a chain of convenience stores had problems with teenagers hanging out in their parking lots. The stores wanted the teens' business, but not the fights and drug-dealing that sometimes accompanied late-night loitering. The problem had grown worse over a 2-year period of time. An observation was made that the chain stores played music in the parking lot speaker system that attracted high school students. The owners decided to reframe the style of music broadcast. Upon hearing the new music, the teenagers voluntarily left and stayed away from the parking lot. The music did not, however, affect sales to teenager.

- The reframe? A change in music to—Frank Sinatra!
- Point of example: The store's owners solved their loitering problem without offending their customers. They took time to examine the motivation for teenagers hanging out. It was determined that teenagers hung out because the genre of music played was appealing. A change of music genre' solved the owner's problem. Note: Solving this problem was not as transparent as it appears. It took *months* for the owners to recognize that music drew the teenagers like a moth is drawn to a light bulb. The reframe involved playing music that was undesirable to teenagers. This is not a comment about Frank Sinatra and his music; rather, it is about a particular audience's frame preference.

"House for Sale by Owner"

A house for sale is advertised for $170,000. The buyer opens with an offer of $155,000. The seller counters with $164,000. At that point the buyer, a bit frustrated by the "negotiation dance," offers to split the difference at $160,500. The seller rejects the offer, countering with a demand of $163,000.

Let's enter the negotiation at this point.

- *Buyer*="So, did the seller accept my offer?"
- *Seller's agent*="No, I'm sorry. The seller countered with $164,000."
- *Buyer*="$164,000!? I can't believe she rejected my offer. Is she crazy? I made a *very fair* offer to split the difference. What's going on?"

FIGURE 7.10 Elephant and little man with telescope.

- *Seller's Agent*="Let me explain what I think is going on. The seller paid over $200,000 for the property. He knows that he can't sell the house for that much. But still every dollar really counts. On the other hand, the two of you are only $2500 apart. He probably figures that an extra $2500 to you is just another $19.56 per month for a 30-year mortgage at 8.5% interest."
- *Buyer*="It's true that $2500 is just an extra $19.56 per month. But $2500 is still *two thousand five hundred dollars*! Are you trying to tell me that $2500 isn't a lot of money! Think of all the extra furniture I can buy for that much money. And if I pay an extra $2500 now, that's an extra $2500 I need to get back when I sell the house."

Each of the four examples above reveals that there are frames at the core of all negotiation transactions. The issues on the "negotiation table" symbolize those frames. It is critical that as negotiation issues and positions develop that we take note of the frames generating those issues and positions. If negotiations are at an impasse, reframing an issue frequently advances the negotiation. If an effort to clarify each party's understanding of the facts and issues fails to advance the negotiation, then reframing it is your best next step.

Note: Clarifying issues does not guarantee negotiation progress. Clarifying may perhaps result in each party accurately understanding the issues and that the negotiation should cease, or pause (Figure 7.10).

RARELY IS A SINGLE FRAME ADEQUATE FOR SOLVING COMPLEX PROBLEMS

It is important to note in the above "House for Sale by Owner" example that price has become the single and only frame in this transaction. A single frame often impedes progress because it eliminates other important considerations.

- Put yourself in the shoes of the buyer. What frame explains his or her decisions, ambitions, and aspirations?
- Put yourself in the shoes of the seller. What frame explains their decisions, ambitions, and aspirations?

  What does each party need and want?

- The house could be a symbol of a need that is separate from the sale and/or purchase.

Box 7.4 Purchasing My Home aka "I Like Your Flowers, but What Is the Sale Price of Your Home?"

My wife and I were shopping for a home. We located a home in a desirable location for work and other interests. We made an appointment with the sellers who were selling the home themselves. After a brief handshake and greeting I was prepared to enter the house for a thorough inspection, primarily searching for our likes and possible concessionary dislikes. Before we could enter the sellers' house, the wife began a tour through her sizable garden, showing us her flowers—literally thousands of flowers and trees and plants. She referred to the flowers as her "babies." She made it clear that whoever purchased their home must protect and care for her garden. We explained that we would enjoy caring for her garden. After about an hour touring the garden, we began an inspection of the house. My wife and I agreed that this was a house we wanted to buy. We thanked them for showing their home and said we would talk it over and get back to them. Upon returning home (about 30 min later) a message from the wife was on our answering machine. She offered to drop the price of their home by $10,000 because of our caring for her garden "babies." We returned her call and thanked her for the offer, but needed to talk about it. She immediately offered to drop the price another $2500. The next morning before leaving for work the wife called our home and again offered to drop the price another $2500. We said that we would come over to their home and talk with them following work that evening. We purchased the home. It turned out to be a great place for us to live. Point of the story: I approached this negotiation prepared to negotiate down the asking price by finding fault with certain features of the seller's house (an economic frame). It took me several minutes to recognize that I had assumed a frame that was inappropriate to the sellers' frame. The negotiation frame was significantly influenced by the care of her flower garden. The price of the home dropped $15,000 on recognizing the sellers' frame. End of the story: The seller's wife dropped by often, happy that we kept our word about caring for "her" garden. However, 10,000 flowers, 35 fir trees, and 750 plants occasionally made me rethink my commitment. We now live in a home with three trees and almost no flowers.

- How are offers and counteroffers being framed or reframed? How effective is each party counterframing these tactics?
- How are the real estate agents compensated in this transaction? Does their compensation influence the negotiation? Do the real estate agents have an agenda?
- Is each party locked into pursuing only their values and concessions? If the answer is "yes," then this becomes the foundation for an impasse. How would you reframe this?

As you recall, frames involve how we make sense of our world. When others do not understand the world as we do, it usually does not mean that they are crazy. Rather, it means that their "sense-making frames" are different from ours. This often explains why different people can observe identical experiences and yet interpret it differently. See the example in Box 7.4—Purchasing

FIGURE 7.11 Elephant and little man.

My Home aka "I Like Your Flowers, but What Is the Sale Price of Your Home?"(Figure 7.11).

REVIEW: ONE-SIZE DOES NOT FIT ALL

There is no single frame that will make sense of every situation; L-Ns need different "lenses" that can be applied to different situations.

- Skillfully used, frames can influence and alter others' perceptions.
- It is important that a frame matches the relevant context; in other words, an offer must be relevant to the other party in order to be applicable to that party's needs and interests.
- Reframing influences others to be aware of different perspectives. Preferably, your perspective.
- Frames are frequently at the core of a negotiation conflict. Each party may understand the data and the issues, but could be "out of frame" with each other. For example, one party views the situation as a risk frame, and the other party views the exact same data and issues from the opportunity frame. Pending recognition that there are two different frames, they likely will experience an impasse. Note: Reexamining the data for the purpose of clarifying misunderstanding will not solve a frame-related impasse. If parties do not understand each other's frames, reexamination of the data and information may widen the impasse.
- Frames contribute to each party believing that their position is best. Consequently, each party interprets their behavior in favorable terms while interpreting the other party's behavior in negative terms.

To summarize, effective L-Ns skillfully influence the other side's perception with regard to the risks, limits, or mixture of possible outcomes. When skillfully used, frames and reframes significantly change the other side's perception of a position and as a result, changes what they can expect to be a reasonable offer. Frames involve concerns such as human needs, future hopes and expectations, the fear of losing, the psychological need to win, and the fear of success. Each of these influences the negotiation outcome. Preparation is your best defense and offense in framing your mind to successfully negotiate. How to prepare for a negotiation is covered in Chapter 8.

RETURN TO KANSAS

Let's go back to Kansas for a moment.

We all make certain assumptions when we enter into any situation, whether it's a marriage, a new job, a social event, or a business negotiation. The problem is, we are often unaware of our assumptions and/or they are out of context, leading us down a path to a less-desired outcome.

Consider Dorothy in *The Wizard of Oz*. She was told that if she paid a visit to the great and powerful Wizard, she would soon be on her way back to home and farm—presumably just outside Small-Dot, Kansas. As a trusting Kansas girl, Dorothy assumed that those who told her about the Wizard were correct. She shared her assumptions with the Scarecrow, the Lion and the Tin Woodsman—all of whom bought into those assumptions—and off they went down the Yellow Brick Road.

Every character they met on their journey enhanced the assumption that the Wizard was all powerful and could definitely help them. Even their adversary, the Wicked Witch of the West, supported their assumption by doing everything possible to prevent them from reaching their goal. It could be that she bought into the assumption of the great and powerful Wizard herself. At times our heroes could have used bulletproof (or fireproof!) vests to thwart the witches' vile onslaughts.

After the foursome finally overcame the Wicked Witch along with other frightening obstacles and arrived in the Emerald City, they paid a visit to the Wizard's Palace. They were ushered into a huge room where they came face-to-face with the intimidating presence of a huge being. But Toto, a dog with few assumptions, pulled on a curtain and thereby revealed that the Wizard was a small, timid man with a big microphone—and not a huge powerful being.

Fortunately, despite the errors in their assumptions, Dorothy and her friends got what they came for, even if it was more of their own doing than the Wizard's.

Things do not always end so neatly for L-Ns. *Operating under the wrong set of assumptions can lead to disaster*. How could Dorothy have better approached her situation? I have no desire to ruin her compelling story, but she could have started by asking better questions.

Did she ever ask, "Why should I believe that?" (no).

Did she ever question whether or not the Yellow Brick Road would, in fact, lead to the Emerald City? (no).

Did she ever question the plausibility of a Wizard being able to grant a brain to a Scarecrow or a heart to a man made of tin? (no).

Chapters 4 and 5 described EQ. EQ would have been a strategic advantage for Dorothy and her friends. Now, let's walk together down the (Yellow Brick) EQ road into Chapter 8: Strategies.

Chapter 8

Perspectives on Strategy

THE BULLETPROOF LEADER-NEGOTIATOR

A **negotiation** can be viewed as a problem-solving process in which parties communicate their differences and attempt to reach an agreement. Negotiations occur on a continuum spanning contractual and routine resource allocation to negotiating major organizational change. Negotiation is inherently a way of redefining relationships between people, resources, and structures. The process of redefinition acknowledges the redistribution of power and/or a change in values that often results in some level of conflict.

Taking a close look, the purpose of negotiation, very simply stated, is to gain something you need but do not have, by exchanging something you do have in order to obtain it. The objective of negotiation is to complete the exchange under terms that are most advantageous to your interests. The outcome of the negotiation can either be a Win–Lose, a Win–Win or, a decision to suspend or end negotiations. Negotiation, therefore, can either be a wall that prevents you from meeting your needs and interests or a bridge that helps you meet your needs and interests.

The philosophies of collaboration and competition have been described in previous chapters, but to fully understand them, we have to look at how they evolved in our culture and how they impact our society today. While we may wish for collaborative relationships, competition is in our DNA. It's a part of America's national heritage and is firmly entrenched in most Western institutions. That's why we are so often forced to wear 'bulletproof vests'. Think about this for a moment. This nation was not born out of collaboration with the British. It came into being as a result of a bloody war— the ultimate expression of a Win–Lose competition. The Revolutionaries won, the British lost. Net result, the United States of America.

In political races, the two (or more) candidates don't decide "You take the first half of the term and I'll take the last half." It's not permitted by law, for one thing. But the fact is that both candidates want to win; neither wants to lose.

From the first moment a child can pick up a ball, we learn that sports are competitive. The last thing we want to do is lose. The second last thing is to tie. Professional athletes are paid huge amounts of money because the team owners and coaches believe that highly skilled, highly paid athletes can help their teams win. If it were just a fun game, they'd play for free. No, every sporting match has a winner and one or more losers.

In the educational system, teachers and professors are often asked to sign contracts in which they specifically agree that their students will be graded on the bell curve. Students' performances on tests will be judged in comparison to one another. The top performers will be awarded A's. The bottom students will receive D's or F's, and all the rest will be lumped in the B and C categories. The class is divided into winners and losers, even if the entire class scores 90% or above. And other school structures—clubs, social groups, sports teams, the election of homecoming royalty—are no less Win–Lose. Children are being conditioned and taught to compete at every level, all through life.

Is it any wonder, then, that when we grow up and enter the world of business, we instinctively know that we have to compete to survive? That's why, frankly, most businesses find themselves in "Chicago" more than "Kansas." (See Chapter 6 for a complete description of the "Chicago" and "Kansas" negotiation philosophies.)

Every Chicago-style negotiator—whether a professional or someone assigned the challenging task at the last minute—enters the negotiation wanting to win, and often not caring how much the other side has to lose. They realize that in this bottom-line-driven corporate culture of ours, failure in the negotiation arena isn't tolerated for very long. Positive results are anticipated, expected, even demanded. Management, workers and stockholders, though seldom in agreement, all join together to insist on nothing less than success. Raises, bonuses, job security, profit sharing, dividends, and future growth are often tied to the outcome of a single negotiation.

Kansas-style negotiators, on the other hand, have trusting feelings about the people on the opposite side of the table. "I'm sure we can work this out so everyone is happy," they say. As a result, Kansas-style negotiators are often weeded out of the process because they can't accept the ugly truth that one party is probably going to lose or, at least win less than the other party.

Ironically, the Win–Win person or party often ends up losing more than would have been lost had a competitive mind-set ruled their actions, and the Win–Lose person or party unwittingly leaves unexplored opportunities on the table and poisons the water for future negotiations. The result is they often obtain much less that what could have been gained had the negotiations been approached from a collaborative mind-set.

SO WHAT MAKES FOR A SUCCESSFUL LEADER-NEGOTIATOR?

The key is to know when to be competitive and when to be collaborative, and to understand that the stance of each party can shift several times within a negotiation as line items are individually considered and resolved. Collaboration and competition are highly fluid concepts. It is virtually impossible to be "bulletproof" and complete successful negotiations by being consistently collaborative or consistently competitive. L-Ns have to be both.

WHAT IS STRATEGY?

Strategy is a simplification of reality. Therefore, to some degree, it distorts or misrepresents reality. Strategies and theories are not reality, only symbolic representations of reality in peoples' minds. **Strategic thinking** is the art of outdoing an adversary, and knowing that the adversary is trying to do the same. The art is the ability to apply an appropriate strategy to an infinitely diverse set of contexts. Ever-changing circumstances are the common element in strategy making. *What is the purpose of strategy?* Strategy provides a framework within which to make decisions and to measure progress. Strategy is a set of assumptions that are relevant for a specific and limited period of time. One of the prominent ambiguities of using the term **strategic planning** involves the fact that everything gets to be called strategy. Therefore, the information in Box 8.1 is provided to clear up the confusion.

THREE NEGOTIATION STRATEGIES

While there are numerous negotiation tactics, there are only three strategies. The three strategies are: (1) **Diplomacy** (2) **Psychological Fear**, and (3) **War**. It is probable that L-Ns will move back and forth among these three strategies in the normal course of a negotiation. This implies versatility.

- Diplomacy relates to the Kansas-style Win–Win strategy.
- Psychological Fear relates to a transitional strategy between "Kansas" and "Chicago."
- War relates to the Chicago-style Win–Lose strategy.

You may have heard someone say something like, *Our strategy is to gain market share. Gaining market share* is not, technically speaking, a strategy. Rather, it is more precise to say that it is an objective. When the objective is to gain market share, the question is, will gaining market share be achieved via a Diplomatic strategy, a Psychological Fear strategy, or a War strategy? This all depends on the context of the negotiation.

Diplomacy Strategy

An expansive range of interpretations comprise Diplomacy Strategy. Diplomacy, separated from its context, is not easily understood. Diplomacy approaches the

Box 8.1 Origins and Meaning of the Word "Strategy"

The term "strategy" is from the Greek *strategos,* which means a general overall conceptual idea or vision. Vision is seeing a desired future situation. Jean-Paul Sartre defined vision as the ability to think of what is not. Strategy is a future possibility. Once a strategy has been articulated, it is then (and only then) that tactics (how to achieve strategy), policy (the principles that govern strategy), and resources (the assets to achieve strategy) come into the discussion.

negotiation process from an influence strategy. Diplomacy actively pursues agreements that are beneficial for *each party*. Diplomatic characteristics are as follows:

1. *Soft power*: Soft power relates to the potential attractiveness of the negotiation. This approach promotes or offers advantageous reasons for negotiation.
2. *Long-term opportunity*: Long-term opportunity emphasizes the negotiation in terms of the advantages of the long-term gain, more than the short-term gain.

The core objective of the Diplomacy is collaboration demonstrated by the mutual search for opportunities such as common and mutual:

- *alliances*
- *enemies*
- *interests*
- *gains*
- *advantages*
- *efficiencies*
- *opportunities*

Diplomatic skill should lead each party to conclude that there is *more to gain than lose*. There must be something "attractive" and advantageous for each party to invest time and energy exploring common and mutual opportunities.

Psychological Fear Strategy

The primary focus of Psychological Fear is to influence the other party to consider the implications and consequences of not negotiating.

The Psychological Fear strategy is twofold:

- First, to reframe the negotiation toward a Diplomatic course of action by using questions to surface realistic and probable unintended consequences and the potential losses related to not negotiating. Asking questions involves exploring overlooked, disregarded, ignored, or unnoticed opportunities. Primarily, this is done by using E-Questions that *contrast* certainty versus uncertainty. (See Chapters 4 and 5 for more on Effective Questioning (EQ)).
- If exhaustive efforts at reframing the negotiation toward Diplomacy fail, the second objective could involve accelerating toward War strategy. The choice to go to "war" should be painstakingly thought out. Resist all imprudent, unthinking reactions when considering this strategy. Give yourself and the other party time to cool down and reconsider the implications of war. War never goes as planned. It never does. It never will.

War Strategy

War should be considered when all diplomatic and transitional strategies have been exhausted. Fatigue and anger are not acceptable rationales for war. A few of the characteristics of a War strategy are as follows:

- War is a total commitment to the Win–Lose philosophy; the winner takes all. Domination via power is the objective.
- Communication, as a rule, is in the form of action and not words.
- Vital resources are controlled to the disadvantage of the other party's interests.
- Opponents' weakness are maximized at the most inopportune time, while maximizing your strength to the other party's greatest point of vulnerability.

A War objective is twofold:

1. The first objective could be to reposition the negotiation toward returning to Diplomacy.
2. The second objective is to take advantage of the War situation.

Note: In Sun Tzu's book, *The Art of War*, the following negotiation guidelines are prioritized:

- A Diplomatic outcome is the highest demonstration of victory. This exhibits a superior form of human intellect and behavior.
- Human history is a problematic record revealing that War is too often humanity's first and only choice for settling disagreements.
- War requires a negotiator to practice considerable restraint, self-control, a passion for diplomacy, but a realistic mind-set to *know when to abandon idealism*. This requires wise judgment together with skill.

OVERVIEW OF NEGOTIATION PLANNING

"Effective leaders must learn how to manage numerous negotiation dynamics, all at the same time."

Ken Sylvester

Strategy is the framework for planning. There are seven steps of the planning process (Box 8.2).

In each of the steps, E-Questioning is encouraged to avoid getting trapped in pursuing arguments based on incomplete, oversimplified, or distorted information. The planning steps and examples of questions to ask in each step are in Table 8.1—Collection of Relevant Information—and in Table 8.2—Strategic Arrangement of Information. The sequence of steps and information provided in each column in the tables below may or may not be in the order that is needed. However, all of the information needs to be considered. An assumption imbedded in all planning processes is that you have time to prepare. My observation has been, however, that business increasingly does not have time to think or prepare.

Box 8.2 Seven Steps of the Planning Process

Step 1: What is the Purpose of the Negotiation?
Step 2: What is the Objective?
Step 3: Separate Facts from Assumptions
Step 4: Agenda
Step 5: Position
Step 6: Needs
Step 7: Strategy and Tactics

TABLE 8.1 Collection of Relevant Information

Step 1	Step 2	Step 3
Purpose	**Objective**	**Facts and assumptions**
What is the context? What is your goal or interest? Precisely define the conflict. What is the cause of the conflict or disagreement? What is the other party's perception of your position? Rules versus guidelines? What is your range of responsibility, authority, and power? Theirs? What laws or ethics need to be observed?	Is your objective what you want or need? What are the short-range and long-range advantages and/or disadvantages? What facts do you know? Are there consequences to getting what you want? Do you anticipate a shift of power?	How have the facts been classified? As a problem? An opportunity? A symptom? Which of the following could be used to achieve an agreement? Verified by Science Authority Logic Uses Intuition Emotive Belief Sense Experience
Use EQ to—	**Use EQ to—**	**Use EQ to—**
• Define the problem and symptoms • Look beyond symptoms to cause and effect	• Consider diverse explanations • Question everything at first; do not draw conclusions too quickly	• Challenge evidence presented as opinions and assumptions • Listen for biases • Identify your own assumptions to avoid self-entrapment

TABLE 8.2 Strategic Arrangement of Information

Step 4	Step 5	Step 6	Step 7
Agenda	**Position**	**Needs**	**Strategy and tactics**
Determine if the agenda should be mutually designed. How will you and the other party agree on a course of action? Agree on the course of action. If you can't agree, alternate agenda items.	Analyze the audience. Determine what the other party wants and how much they want it. What are they willing to concede to get what they want? Concede nothing without thought about future consequences and implications. Consider options when concession-making.	Avoid reasoning from your own needs only; understand the needs of the other party. Are the needs measurable? How will you test the acceptability of your proposal? Allow for irrational behavior in the stress of weighty decisions.	Will the strategy or tactic selected help you achieve what you want? Will it result in a competitive advantage *over time*? Will it contribute to a competitive or collaborative outcome? Be prepared for conflict (Chapters 11 and 12).
Use EQ to—	**Use EQ to—**	**Use EQ to—**	**Use EQ to—**
• Tolerate uncertainty and ambiguity • Avoid over-simplification and stereo-types	• Avoid emotional reasoning • Consider others' perspectives and interpreta-tions	• Listen and sort information through the six frames (Chapter 7) • Put a question mark at the end of statements	• Assess the use of tactics and strategies • Determine the nature of the conflict

Collection of Relevant Information (Steps 1–3)

Note: Steps 1–3 should be done first because they determine what you do in steps 4–7.

Strategic Arrangement of Information (Steps 4–7)

Remember, what happens is not as important as how you interpret what happens. Your ability to interpret what happens is directly related to your ability to maintain self-control and emotional maturity, depersonalize conflict, manage failure, and cope with imperfection.

STRATEGIC ADVANTAGES, DISADVANTAGES, AND CONTRADICTIONS

Advantages

1. Strategy sets the direction of a negotiation and establishes limitations in order to make the best use of an organization's strengths and assets.
2. Strategy establishes predetermined options in order to defend itself against its' own weaknesses.
3. Strategy focuses an organization's collective energy on a precise objective(s).
4. Strategy clearly defines the organization's distinctive niche.
5. Strategy creates order and meaning out of disorder.
6. Strategy fosters the efficient and effective use of resources.
7. Strategy makes clear the purpose for certain actions and values and similarly makes clear the necessity to not perform other actions and values.

Disadvantages

1. Strategy can become so inflexible that it could function as a straitjacket or set of strategic "blinders"—a "psychological cul-de-sac."
2. Strategy can promote groupthink, the tendency for all members of the group to think alike and suppress dissent. Groupthink occurs when a group's need for total agreement overwhelms its need to make the best decision and when the need to be accepted overwhelms the ability to disagree with a decision.
3. Strategy can promote the oversimplification of ideas, often expressed as overgeneralizations, either-or thinking, anecdotes and metaphors, stereotypes and labels, etc.
4. Strategy can interfere with valuable feedback and constructive criticism.

Contradictions

1. If strategy is viewed as *a model* it may distort reality to some degree. These distortions may appear to be, or may be, contradictory to certain realities. This is a normal, but often unavoidable side effect.
2. If strategy is viewed as imperfect because it tends to describe *an ideal outcome*, adjustments to the difference between the idealized expectation and reality should be expected.
3. If strategy is operative within *a particular context* and limited to a specific period of time, as contexts change over time and competitors counter your strategy by "imitating" it, the organization must adapt if it intends to stay in a competitive market position.
4. If strategy is developed in the medium of *imperfect information*, as information improves so should the sophistication and refinement of the strategy.

5. If strategy is fashioned out of previous knowledge, L-Ns are depending upon what has been learned from their past to adequately guide them into the future. Their perceptions and information, though, may be inadequate for future challenges.
6. For every problem that a strategy answers and for each opportunity that it promises to achieve, plans frequently result in new and *unexpected problems and unintended consequences*. All strategy demands continuous modification and adjustment if the future that it desired is to be achieved.

> *"There are no 'perfect' strategies. There is no strategy for all time. Rather, strategy succeeds for only a relatively brief moment in time and then has to be recreated or re-strategized."*
>
> Ken Sylvester

MULTITASKING

Negotiation is not a single event. To the contrary, it is numerous subprocesses that play out with each other to achieve a favorable outcome. L-Ns must be adept at **multitasking**; the ability to manage a lot of things simultaneously. Typically, the L-N is simultaneously addressing a multiplicity of issues: solving problems, making decisions, working out conflicts, managing present–future opportunities, communicating throughout the organization, satisfying Board issues, dealing with interpersonal problems, handling the paper flood, attending meetings, making presentations, uncovering hidden agendas, planning, approving financial resource allocation, delegating, building team competence, keeping the "troops" motivated, dealing with problem people, improving one's own effectiveness, paying attention to fair employment practices/avoiding lawsuits, assessing performance, dealing with turnover, and so forth.

Negotiation can be viewed as a problem-solving process in which interested parties identify their differences and attempt to reach an agreement. In a sense, an effective negotiation depends upon all that is going on around "it" (the context) and what is going on among the negotiating parties. This is called "contextual intelligence" (referred to in Chapter 4). One reason for negotiation failure involves not positioning one's ideas within the relevant context. Effective L-Ns must consider numerous, simultaneous, and conflicting dynamics within the relevant point of reference.

RELEVANT CONTEXT

> *"Success is thinking within the relevant context."*
>
> Ken Sylvester

Box 8.3 The $100 Dollar Bill Tactic

Frequently, we hear about strategies that have been successful in particular contexts. Such is the "$100 Dollar Bill" tactic told to me by a former client. This client told me that he was going down to a specific auto dealer to make a cash offer. When I asked him about his approach to making this offer, he said he heard that if you just "lay down" (on the hood of the car) what you are willing to pay for the car in $100 bills, the salespeople would give the car to you for your asking price—due to seeing the cash. The next day he reported that he was unsuccessful buying the car. Further discussion revealed that the tactic he used to buy the car was not relevant to the salesperson because the dealership had a 6-month waiting list of people who had put deposits down to buy that particular car model. It was after the fact that he realized that the "$100 Dollar Bill" tactic was not relevant within a seller's market.

Point to this story: This negotiation approach was not successful because it was not connected to the relevant context. There is no such thing as a tactic or a strategy for all situations or for all time. Our approach must match the situation. End of this story: The client purchased his car at a premium price.

Imagine that you seek a doctor's help for a health condition. As the doctor enters your examination room he or she says, "Hello, let me write you a prescription." Your response may be, "But you haven't even talked with me and you don't know why I am here to see you!" If the doctor says, "Don't be concerned. I wrote this same prescription for the last 25 patients and it worked great!" In this situation, the doctors' *prescription* is likely to not be **relevant** to your context. Thinking in a prescriptive manner is not adequate. In patient–health care provider interactions, as in other forms of negotiation, success depends upon thinking within the relevant context.

I am often asked, "What is the best buyer's tactic to get the seller's price down on the purchase of such things as a home or a car?" Working from the principle that *success is thinking within the relevant context,* the answer is, *It depends upon whether or not you are in a buyers or a seller's market.* If you are a buyer in a seller's market, it is probable that you cannot negotiate the price down because there would be potential buyers prepared to pay more than the seller's asking price. This requires exploring negotiation alternatives other than price. However, if you are a buyer in a buyer's market, then negotiating the price down is contextually relevant.

To summarize, strategy is contingent upon the context. In the examples above, context determines the L-Ns' approach and, therefore, the relevance of an offer.

THERE ARE NO TACTICS OR STRATEGIES FOR ALL TIME

"All negotiation strategies have shelf life."

Ken Sylvester

TWELVE CONDITIONS FOR EFFECTIVE NEGOTIATIONS

There are 12 conditions that increase the *probability* that a negotiation will be effective. Each party

1. is willing to participate
2. needs to reach an agreement
3. needs something from each other
4. is prepared with relevant knowledge and information
5. recognizes areas of common ground upon which to build an agreement
6. possesses the expertise to organize an agreement
7. possesses the necessary resources to support a decision
8. possesses the authority to make decisions
9. believes that the best alternative is a negotiated agreement, not an impasse or rejection
10. considers problems to be reconcilable
11. recognizes that making concessions is rational within the negotiation process
12. is in a contextual situation or business cycle that favors agreement

The more these 12 conditions characterize a negotiation, the more potential exists that the negotiation will reach agreement. It is possible though, that all 12 conditions could exist in a negotiation and yet, an ill-timed venture or an unfavorable context could impede, prolong, delay, or prevent parties from achieving an agreement.

THE THREE DECISIONS—"AIR"

All L-Ns come to a decision point in the negotiation process. The question is "What are my decision alternatives?" Three alternatives exist. They are:

Decision One: Accept the Offer—When you accept the other party's offer, terms, request for concessions, and/or conditions, it means the negotiation is complete and your position is to abide by or accept these terms.

Decision Two: Improve the Offer—When you desire to improve the other party's offer, terms, request for concessions, and/or conditions, you are communicating that there is an opportunity for expanding the alternatives. At this point, you must position what you want and need. Some would advise that you tell the other party that their offer is not acceptable, but you would be open if they offered better options. See the example in Box 8.4.

Decision Three: Reject the Offer—When you reject the other party's offer, it signals that the negotiation process is at a stage of termination. Terminating a negotiation should be cautiously thought out. Once terminated, requesting negotiations at a later date can place the L-N at a significant disadvantage. Rejection communicates that there will be no further negotiation. To repeat, think this over very carefully! A negotiation myth is that negotiators need only tactical power to negotiate. This is an oversimplification. Moreover, it is false.

Box 8.4 The Back and Forth

Henry Kissinger employed many understudies who assisted him in his state department obligations. Mr Kissinger would routinely send his assistants the following written request, "You can do better than this." After Mr Kissinger sent these requests, the assistants would always return their proposals to him with improvements. This "Back and Forth" would occur numerous times. Mr Kissinger, however, never indicated how they were to be improved. This was left up to the imagination of the sender. Lesson learned: There is always opportunity for improvement.

THE RELATIONSHIP AMONG STRATEGY, POLICY, AND RESOURCES

Strategy is related to policy and resources.

- Strategy involves answering the questions, "Why are we going there and what is our purpose for going there?"
- Policy involves answering the question, "How do we organize and control?"
- Resources involve answering the question, "With what?"

Strategy is characterized by a combination of inputs, processes, and outcomes. Strategy development *selects* from alternative courses of action, *matches* that with the available resources, and *combines* these in a way that will most effectively achieve the objective.

It is the complexity of strategy formation that gives strategy its *nonlinear* nature. Linear thinking is a two-dimensional way of thinking and assumes that that a single line of thought will work in a three-dimensional world. Simplicity is desirable; however, there are three inseparable factors that must be considered when charting ones strategy.

Strategy must

1. be able to be implemented (put into action)
2. be selected based on the pros and cons of *unintended consequences* as well as adverse consequences (future *probabilities*, not possibilities)
3. be adaptable to change, making sure that the three organizational zones in your company are organized and matched to complement the external environment

Strategy involves charting the probable variables from many *simultaneous* directions. The advantage of doing the hard work of variable-strategy development is that it enables L-Ns to realistically manage unintended obstacles.

Policy is what the company does and where it does it. Policy allows management to communicate the corporate purpose and objectives. Policy spells out the corporation's core values and beliefs, and/or defines the company's position on a specific issue. This involves operational policies (rules, regulations, guidelines, or contractual standards) that govern conduct.

Resources—The purpose of resources is to supply the assets that are the energy of an organization. This involves human and physical resources, both tangible and intangible.

Strategy is a triangulation of three factors:

1. Strategy: The purpose for going where we are going
2. Policy: The standards and guidelines that establish boundaries
3. Resources: The material that allows the strategy to be realized.

Keeping these three words and concepts clear is important in the strategic planning process.

REALITY CHECK

Unpublished Research: 26 Years, 30,000 People, and 8 Countries

People talk about Win–Win all the time. In practice, however, Win–Lose most often trumps talk of Win–Win. The research indicates about 99% of the time.

The Mossey Rock Exercise

The Mossey Rock Negotiation Simulation is described in detail in Appendix C. Its purpose is to establish a baseline experience of negotiation and to provide a structural model for the negotiation process. The real-world negotiation issues that are addressed by this exercise are: (1) The need to manage trust while minimizing threat and (2) The relationship between time and pressure. The simulation creates a situation in which two autonomous groups make independent decisions about how to manage their two separate businesses. For sake of this exercise, the two businesses are: the Country Store and the Corner Market. Basically, there are financial rewards and penalties associated with each of three decision-making alternatives that must occur within a limited period of time, on the telephone. Decisions included the choice to: (1) Stay open, (2) Close, or (3) use the "Arson Card" which implies burning down the other store.

For 26 years, I have conducted research on negotiations and negotiation skill development throughout the United States, South America, Latin America, Mexico, Europe, Canada, China, and Japan using this simulation. The results are that:

- 29,917 (99%) of executives, managers, and business students lacked negotiation skills to achieve desired negotiation outcomes. Similarly, they ended up with different outcomes than expected.
- 29,917 (99%) of executives, managers, and business students desired different negotiation outcomes than they expected; and yet, they did not know how or why they ended up other than expected.
- 29,917 (99%) of executives, managers, and business students were unfamiliar with the negotiation skills required to be effective flanked by the Kansas and Chicago ways of thinking.

- 29,917 (99%) of executives, managers, and business students used the "Arson Card."
- 29,917 (99%) of executives, managers, and business students were confident that *their* failed negotiation effort was out of the ordinary.

This research studied more than 30,000 peoples' ability to think about how to negotiate. The results suggested that the participants had been educated and conditioned reflexively to follow rote answers, formulas, and techniques (AFT's). However, 99% did not understand how *to think* about negotiation.

Without a specific or implied threat, there is no negotiation. Let me say that again. A threat is a part of every negotiation. The threat in this exercise as the "Arson Card." Think of it this way. In every negotiation, you are dealt a certain hand, a certain number of cards with which you play the game, so to speak. Among the cards may be price, performance date, cancellation clauses, strikes, and so on. Any one of your cards can become your "Arson Card"—your threat that can end negotiations or make it desirable for the opposing party to see things your way. The "Arson Card" is, in effect, your opportunity to take advantage of your opponent. When none of the parties wishes to compromise and the negotiation enters the hostile phase, your "Arson Card" may be the only way to move things forward. However, by playing your "Arson Card," you expose your greatest threat. It seems logical, therefore, that the party with the most threatening "Arson Cards" is likely to be the victor. The word and/or concept of "Arson" had to be modified when in certain cultures because that word/concept does not exist in that culture.

Box 8.5 provides an example.

This brings us back to being a fish in water. We live in a culture that is saturated with Win–Lose competitive messages. People are willing to practice the Win–Win as long as they believe they are going to win. However, as soon as they think they might lose, they reflexively adopt the "Arson Card" mentality and the entire philosophical environment of the negotiation is shifted toward "Chicago." The point is this may be completely perceptual or actual, either way it puts both parties into a position to defend themselves. See Figure 8.1 Synthesis: The Mossey Rock Simulation-45 Assumptions

"One of the greatest powers a L-N possesses is the ability to generate alternatives."

Ken Sylvester

Box 8.5 Playing the "Arson Card"

In 1981, the Reagan Administration was engaged in intense negotiations with the nation's air traffic controllers. Talks deteriorated to the point where the controllers decided to play their "Arson Card." They went on strike. They played this card even though President Reagan had already revealed his Arson Card—he threatened that if they went on strike, he would fire them.

"He'll never play that card," they must have reasoned. *We're too important—too vital to the nation. Air traffic flow will be severely impeded without us. The public would be in too much danger.* Nonetheless, Reagan played his Arson Card and every controller who observed the picket lines was suddenly out of a job.

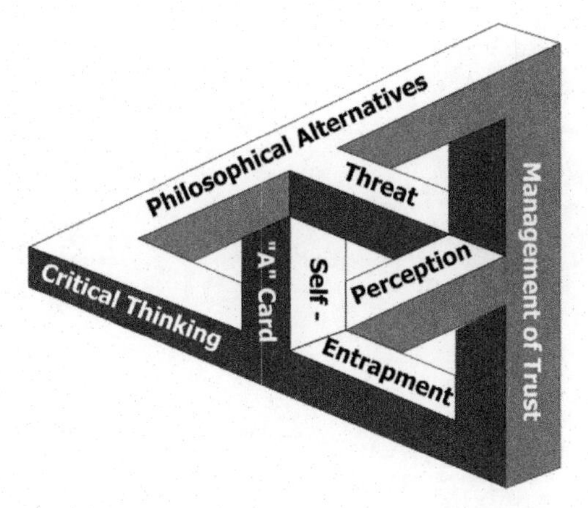

FIGURE 8.1 Synthesis: The Mossey Rock simulation.

One of the options that the Mossey Rock simulation allows, but was infrequently selected, was to request more time. In 26 years, no one asked for more time (one of the most valuable assets in a negotiation and more than 30,000 participants). The more or less time one has to negotiate influences whether you are in a "Kansas" or "Chicago" negotiation. A second option was to request disarmament of the "Arson Card." Again, only 1% of the 30,000 participants exercised this alternative. Time and threats influence the L-N's philosophy. In the real world, the two issues of time and threat remain constant. Not understanding the thinking behind the negotiation process and a reliance on using AFTs is why so few people recognized time and threat issues. The focus needs to be on the thinking of the L-N, the role of EQ to uncover assumptions, and the application of frames to the negotiation process, not AFTs.

Chapter 9 describes necessary criteria for selecting tactics. Thirty (30) common tactics are described.

Chapter 9

Perspectives on the Use of Tactics-Refer to Appendix D: Thirty Tactics

A WORD OF CAUTION ABOUT SELECTING TACTICS

Seldom does a secret forever remain a secret and, remember, time has a way of relaxing people's oath of secrecy. If you are considering using tactics to gain advantage over another party, odds are that in time your tactics will be revealed. As a predictable rule, when a person realizes that another party has intentionally used a tactic to gain advantage, they may never forget and may never again trust you. It is also not uncommon that once they realize that they have been tactically manipulated, they may pursue a course of retribution. Make sure that you are prepared to accept the consequences of using tactics—the potential permanency of losing trust.

SELECTING AND USING TACTICS: SIX IMPORTANT CONSIDERATIONS

Tactical Consideration #1: Tactics are tools to accomplish a plan, but one tool is not adequate for all jobs. As the Russian proverb states, "A hammer breaks glass and forges steel." Wisdom involves selecting the proper tool to accomplish one's objectives. Tactics are context dependent, meaning, they may be advantageous within a particular business context but not in another. The use of tactics is unacceptable to some people and yet completely within acceptable limits to others.

Tactical Consideration #2: Tactics can be effective if used appropriately. This requires judgment, wisdom, and a precise understanding as to why a particular tactic would work within a given situation. Lack of experience influences judgment in selecting tactics. The fact that someone knows a tactic and wants to try it out is not an advantageous business practice.

Tactical Consideration #3: Think long term when considering the use of tactics. You must evaluate the gain of a single transaction versus the potential opportunity of a long-term relationship, as there is usually damage control required from an adversarial relationship. Think from the other party's point of view—they may view tactical use as manipulative and wrong. In addition, consider that your choice to not use tactics is not a reason to assume that others would not use tactics. Remember the Chicago–Kansas equation.

Tactical Consideration #4: Sufficient experience and insight into human behavior is required to the facades people develop to disguise their true negotiation agenda/s. Much of human behavior is subconscious, meaning that ironically, often a person or party you are negotiating with does not know their own agenda. At other times, the other party is deliberate. Remember, tactics in and of themselves are amoral; they are neither good nor bad. They are simply human behaviors that have been observed over time and then classified as a tactic.

Tactical Consideration #5: Tactics depend upon proper execution to succeed. It is advised that you *do not* use a tactic that you have not practiced or do not fully understand. The fact that you are familiar with a tactic is not the same as being proficient at employing it. Tactics can be challenging to learn. Selecting the right tactic is dependent on the situation and your ability to execute it. There is no such thing as a tactic for all situations. Tactics, by definition, are limited and restricted to particular situations. Further, once a tactic has been used, it is probable that you will not be able to use that tactic again with those people.

It is difficult to select the right tactic for a given situation because often, we have "cognitive **blind spots**"—we fail to see all the probable options and alternatives of a negotiation. Most decisions are made based upon imperfect and incomplete information. Stress (emotional, physical, political, time deadlines, aspirations, etc.) usually limits our perception. Assume that you may have overlooked significant information. Lack of impartiality also limits human objectivity. Misjudging others' intent is common. Underestimating the intelligence of others and, overestimating our own intelligence can further set us up for failure in selecting the right tactic.

TIME intensifies negotiation and imposes either real or self-imposed pressure. The two great dimensions of time are deadlines and the passage of time. Clearly, the passage of time is a powerful factor in most negotiations because the passage of time allows each party to get past seeing only their position and understanding the other party's position. Real-time assessment requires judgment and experience, not just tactical knowledge.

Reliance on the same tactic may develop because certain tactics may have previously succeeded. Success reinforces the repetition of behavior; however, habit interferes with tactical outcomes. Whether or not a particular tactic is advantageous in a given situation depends on many factors (personality of each party, importance of the situation, urgency of the matter, long- and/or short-term relationship goals, relative power, etc.). There are no perfect tactics and—no one tactic is best.

Tactical Consideration #6: What are the risks of any given tactic? Wisdom suggests that we do not use an elephant gun to kill an ant. Make sure the tactic fits the context. Consider possible reactions from the other party. Who might deal themselves into your negotiation? When assessing a problem, assign a time component to it: (1) immediate response, (2) no response, or (3) a delayed response (at times *ignoring* certain situations is an appropriate tactic).

To assess tactical appropriateness, you must understand traditions encompassing the culture in which the negotiation takes place. What do other people expect? Remember–traditions die slowly. Read the volatility of the situation. How sensitive is it? Explosive? Then take care to defuse conflict. Consider, "What is the potential fall-out if this tactic is not effective?" The significance of the situation will dictate how confident you are of the information you have. When in doubt, verify information sources; check out their reliability and validity. Few things will make you look as incompetent as acting confidently on bad information.

Personal Characteristics

The wisdom of using one tactic rather than another depends on the characteristics of *the people* involved and the context of the situation. Following are 13 topics that require careful consideration:

- *Personality—Your* personality will allow you to use certain tactics, and preclude you from using others. Personality traits of those involved should influence the tactics selected. Tactical selection depends on whether yours and others' basic disposition is compliant or belligerent, stable or unpredictable.
- *Power*—Perceptions of power can lead to overestimating one's own power and/or underestimating the power of others. You may have power to affect everyday activities but not have power to alter an organization's structure. Be clear about where your power begins and ends.
- *Values*—The use of tactics can lead to asserting your values to the exclusion of others' values. This preference of one's values having a higher priority over others' promotes conflict, encourages a competitive Win–Lose environment, intensifies distrust, reduces constructive communication, polarizes each party into only seeing their point of view, and frequently results in substandard agreements.
- *Abilities and skills*—An old proverb states, "Others may, you may not!" Do not use tactics that require skills you do not have. Do what you do best. Find others who do what they do best, and let them do it. Lead with your strengths.
- *Resources*—What are the resources of all the parties involved? Money, time, no need for money, not afraid to lose, nothing to lose, etc.
- *Motivation*—Make sure you are able to finish what you start. In addition, do not start things you did not plan to start. This process begins with assessing the task's difficulty in relation to your level of motivation and time to overcome challenges.
- *Allies*—Make a careful assessment of who will be on your side and who will not. Remember that allies can change based on politics changing. Find a way to "lock" your allies into their commitment to be an ally in such a way

that they must perform their agreed-upon actions. Either there must be some benefit from an allied relationship or, fear about consequences of not being your ally.

- *Future relationships*—How you treat long-term relationships is often much different than short-term or one-time relationships. Will you need the other party in the future? Will they need you? Bear in mind, people have an unexpected way of reappearing in your future.
- *Legal position*—If your legal position is strong, you can use strong direct tactics. However, if your legal position is tentative or vulnerable to judicial interpretation, then you should consider a covert approach. One's legal position unfortunately, is difficult to predict with certainty.
- *History of relationship and past negotiations*—Digging into past negotiations may help you discover clues that will help you with the selection of effective tactics. A word of advice: If a tactic was used in the past, DO NOT make use of it again. Why? Because the other party may expect its repeated use and be more prepared to counter it than the last time it was used.
- *Interests*—Understand the interests of all parties. Conflict of interest is the cause for most disputes. If you are preparing to threaten an interest of others, expect a passionate reaction and defense in return.
- *Vulnerability to Retaliation*—Know your vulnerabilities. Reprisal often occurs due to an unexamined weakness. Look past the tactic. Do you have the necessary power to carry out the proposed tactic and withstand possible retaliation? Consider several courses of action that the other party could pursue and anticipate what you will do in each situation. Success favors the prepared.
- *Ethics*—Your values (your ethical code) will govern the use of particular tactics. If your values are known to others, they may count on your ethics preventing you from taking a particular action in certain situations. In addition, your values may be in direct conflict with others' values. Know your values. Then, ask how others could take advantage of your values. This critical thinking exercise is not easy; however, it is very beneficial. Remember, *Anyone can fly an arrow. However, no one can bring the arrow back once released.*

Despite the discussion about careful consideration of the use of tactics, 30 tactics are described in Appendix D. Knowing what these tactics are, identifying and naming them, even if you do not intend to use them, will help you protect and disarm the other party's use of tactics.

EVALUATING THE USE OF TACTICS

Consider the following when selecting a tactic for use:

- *How easy is it to use the tactic?*—This relates to its simplicity. Complicated tactics require major skill and often some luck to execute. However, complicated situations demand complicated tactics. Do not get caught into thinking that direct, straightforward tactics are always best. At times, indirect, flanking tactics are very effective.

- *How much support do you need from others to use a particular tactic?*—If you can do it yourself, do not ask for help. The more people involved, the more complicated its usage. The greater number of people required to execute a tactic, the greater the risk of failure.
- *If there is a cost, are you able and willing to absorb that loss?*—Money, time, reputation, etc.
- *What is the likelihood of success?*—Be harshly realistic with yourself on this point. Do not let enthusiasm carry you into a failure.
- *What is your previous experience with the tactic?*—Effectiveness and productivity often are related to experience in using previously used tactics and not merely one's knowledge of a particular tactic.

There is no limitation to the variations of using tactics. The intent of this chapter is to increase awareness of tactics and their selection. Tactical behavior is not a set of formulaic actions and behaviors. Each tactical application requires some degree of modification and/or tailoring to the context. Keep in mind that the objective of tactics is to not win the battle and lose the war.

THREE TACTICS TO OVERCOME GRIDLOCK

1. **Mutual Synergy**—Explore common goals through which everyone can share the result proportionately. Each party benefits in a way that would be unattainable if they did not work together. Frequently, synergy involves combining each party's differences and uniqueness into new and innovative formations.
2. **Shared Goals**—Is there a shared goal through which each party works toward a common end but benefits differently? Each party receives different rewards but each party gains advantages by working together on a mutual goal.
3. **Joint Goals**—If each party has different goals, explore the possibility to combine their goals for one common goal. In the final analysis, it must be each party's intent to collaborate, rather than to compete, which allows this approach to succeed. In other words, both parties need to be intrinsically committed to a goal that benefits all parties rather than only their own needs. However, one note of caution. Being motivated to help others reach collaboration agreements does not infer that you should take responsibility for satisfying the other party's needs and outcomes. *If the Joint Goal involves combining forces against a common enemy, be cautious—as soon as the goal has been achieved—the unity of this joint goal might rapidly change direction in opposition toward you. As a rule, the enemy protects the spirit of collaboration. Once the goal has been achieved, collaboration can end in a "heartbeat."

TWENTY-FIVE ALTERNATIVES TO AN IMPASSE

1. **Recess**—a break can help relieve tension and assist through an impasse.
2. **Recap or Summarize**—review progress and agreements to the point of the impasse.
3. **Doomsday Tactic**—explaining the direct consequences of not reaching an agreement can often shock the other party into agreement or continuation.
4. **Express Feelings**—clearing the air may further progress.
5. **Introduce Another Issue**—particularly one that may get you back on track again.
6. **Agree in Principle**—get agreement, even on minor issues, to build momentum.
7. **Disclose Something**—revealing sensitive information can help.
8. **Hypothetical Situation**—can increase creativity in problem-solving ("What if…" or "Suppose we thought about it this way…").
9. **Empathy**—particularly effective when relationship is important.
10. **Quick Close Tactic**—throw in a bonus when the other party is close to agreement.
11. **Appeal to an Ally**—someone on their team with whom you can deal easily or a third-party mutual acquaintance.
12. **Use Humor**—humor can loosen up a tight situation. Do not use humor if you are not funny.
13. **Summarize**—put facts, agreements, and differences in writing. This helps all parties think more clearly. In addition, writing removes intuition, emotion, and ambiguity from verbal conversation.
14. **Conditional Concession**—give up something, but with a condition that they also give something.
15. **Change Locations**—a change of site can stimulate a sense of new beginning.
16. **Change the Shape of the Money**—changing payment schedules, interest rates, amount of down payment, etc., often fosters overcoming an impasse.
17. **Change Specifications**—rearrange the specifications or terms of the agreement can often provide a fresh starting point for negotiation.
18. **Change Negotiator**—a new team member can supply a restored approach or trust.
19. **Provide a Guarantee**—guarantee something that the opponent considers a risk.
20. **Bring in an Expert**—new ideas plus the power of an expert add momentum toward agreement.
21. **Change Levels**—negotiate up or down one organizational level may help.
22. **Refer to Impartial Sources**—keep negotiation open with added input from neutral people.
23. **Use a Mediator**—a mutually agreed upon third party can be of great assistance.
24. **Add Options**—options often provide great incentives in negotiations.

25. **Postpone or Delay**—postponing indefinitely leaves the door open to continue future negotiation. Completely terminating the negotiation leaves little to no opportunity to revisit the negotiation. Time is a powerful tool in changing positions.

FIVE TACTICAL METHODS

Each of the following methods is designed to deal with five different types of negotiation situations. Each method works best when there is a concern for:

- **Problem-Solving** involves a concern for each party's mutual outcome
- **Competing** involves concern about only one party's outcome
- **Concession-Making** involves concern about only the other party's outcome
- **Repositioning** involves concern about only your position
- **Inaction** involves concern about neither party's outcome

1. **Problem-Solving**—Problem-solving involves using a mutually accepted method or approach to work out each party's interest among those goals. Four common approaches to problem-solving are:
   a. expanding the resources (the pie) that is either perceived to be scarce or is in fact limited;
   b. cost reduction which involves scaling back one's expectations or scope of outcome;
   c. prioritizing concessionary alternatives which involves yielding on selected priorities for trade-offs regarding other priorities; and,
   d. creative generation of new alternatives that satisfy each party's goals.

Higher risk problem-solving techniques involve making concessions with the expectation that the other party will offer reciprocal concessions. The idea is that once a concession has been made, the other party may feel obligated to reciprocate. If they do, it may place you in a vulnerable position.

Revealing potential concessions as discussion points depends upon the willingness of the other party to reveal their concessionary interests. The risk is that if you conceded first, they may not be willing to offer their concessionary possibilities. Further risk can develop if the other party perceives your talking points as firm proposals, as a threat to reveal their concessions, or uses your openness as a basis to threaten you based upon knowledge of your interests. Revealing one's interests, goals, and values to the other party with the expectation that they also will reveal their interests is risky due to the possibility that the other party will take advantage of your openness and honesty.

The techniques of problem-solving are of less importance than the two conditions that contribute to effective problem-solving. When the following two sets of conditions exist, it improves the probability that problem-solving will result in an agreement.

- *The first condition* is that there is a strong probability that the negotiation pie can be expanded, that costs can be sensibly reduced, that making concessions will not cut too deeply into each party's opportunity, and that alternatives for achieving each party's goals are flexible.
- *The second condition* occurs when each party maintains high expectations that they will be able to achieve their needs. The challenge is to explore possibilities that will help each party mutually achieve their goals. One implication of this condition is the additional time required for this negotiation approach. If each party is under rigid time limitations, the time-related stress may decrease tolerance for a problem-solving course of action. The problem-solving process may require each party to revisit their self-interests as well as reevaluate previously agreed upon proposals. Reassessment of a previously agreed upon solution may require additional time.

2. **Competing**—Competing asserts the Win–Lose philosophy. The basic Win–Lose approach involves forcing the other party to accept alternatives that benefit only one side's interests while disregarding the needs of the other party. Classically, competitive tactics use the following positions to achieve their desired outcome:

- Asserting demands that exceed the limitations of the other party
- Demanding commitments to rigid, inflexible positions that do not allow for realistic implementation of the contract requirements
- Insisting on concessions that damage or harm the other party
- Making threats that coerce the other party to make concessions that have adverse consequences
- Threatening withdrawal from the negotiation or punish the other party for not agreeing to make concessions that are not in their best interest
- Demanding deadlines that are beyond the control of the other party
- Information sharing that is one sided
- Concealing or omitting information about their own position so that the other party cannot use it against them, while at the same time using your information against you.

3. **Concession-making**—Concession-making involves persuading the other party to accept other alternatives and/or solutions as a trade-off to achieving some but not all of their priorities. Making concessions is the practicality of negotiation. It is idealistic to approach a negotiation thinking that you will not make concessions. Concession-making should be done slowly and at a gradual pace. Not fast, and too much too fast. The general scheme involves giving a concession or waiting for the other party to offer a concession; then, holding firm until a comparable concession is offered from the other party. This continues at a slow and reluctant pace.
4. **Repositioning**—Repositioning involves altering or changing one's original negotiation position. It takes place as new understanding and previously unknown information are discovered. Repositioning should occur when one

learns that either the original goal is no longer valid (as first expected), or pursuit of the original goal is no longer pragmatic given newly acquired information.

5. **Inaction**—Inaction is a passive, delaying tactic. It is used to confirm a lack of interest and/or indifference. Inaction is a carefully selected decision to adjourn or reschedule, but not terminate, the negotiation process. This tactic can be used to de-escalate situations that are emotionally intense and the act of separation would provide both time and distance for each party to calm down. In addition, it is employed to put distance into the decision-making process in order to enhance objectivity. In addition, it can be used to give the other party time to think before a decision is made that could potentially lead to an impasse.

Chapter 10 introduces Troubleshooting the Collaborative Process.

Chapter 10

Troubleshooting the Collaborative Process

INTRODUCTION: FACILITATING THE COLLABORATIVE PROCESS

If a Leader-Negotiator's (L-N's) objective is to build the most successful and resilient organization possible, he or she must convert their organization's culture from a competitive environment to a collaborative environment. **Collaborative negotiation** is the process of identifying a cooperative blueprint and a course of action to realize it. It is an approach wherein people understand their obstacles as mutual problems, which therefore need to be mutually resolved. However, people do not always perceive obstacles as a mutual opportunity. This often results in conflict, and conflict can result in a competitive Win–Lose organizational culture. L-Ns tightrope a delicate balance between a climate that motivates through competition but does not succumb to Win–Lose outcomes. The formula for organizational success is, and continues to be, intense internal collaboration with an externally competitive mind-set (Table 10.1).

This chapter will focus on ways to build competent teams that in turn will build collaborative organizations.

ENHANCING COLLABORATION

1. **Avoid arguing over positions**—Behind all the infinite variety of human behavior lies the pressure of a few basic and universal needs. Avoid disagreements over positions. Rather, pursue the interest behind the position. An understanding of negotiation behavior must begin with understanding those needs. A problem is that most negotiators may not know what they need. Yes, they assertively present their positions as if they know; and, the problem is that they genuinely think they know. However, most negotiators attempt to satisfy their needs without understanding them.
2. **Be willing to see the other parties' perspective**—So, the point is to actually define and understand the problem. One of the greatest powers that an L-N possesses is the mind-set to generate alternatives. Collaboration requires that both parties persist and promote objective criteria that promote collaboration. Arguing over positions generally

TABLE 10.1 Five Insights That Enhance Collaboration

1	Avoid arguing over positions
2	Be willing to see the other parties' perspective
3	Define problems in the smallest and most precise way possible
4	Separate people from the problem; do not label, accuse, or insult others
5	Allow for an environment of open dialogue; focus on similarities, manage differences

results in dysfunctional competition, imprudent outcomes, and an inefficient use of energy that compromises an organization's competitive edge. Once a one-dimensional position has been taken, a typical mind-set is to defend it instead of challenging it. This means the primary objective is to not be open to improvements. Defending one's position often leads to promoting the status quo.

3. **Define problems in the smallest and most precise way possible**—One method for managing conflict is to describe the problem or the conflict in the smallest and most precise way possible. The smaller and more precise the definition of a conflict, the easier it will be to resolve. The more general and ambiguous the definition of a conflict, the more difficult it will be to resolve.
4. **Separate people from the problem; do not label, accuse, or insult others**—Within the context of collaboration, do not label, accuse, or insult others. People do not like to be labeled. Rather, describe their actions. Focus on behavior, not personality. If a conflict defined as a problem to be solved, it is much easier to resolve constructively than is a conflict positioned in Win–Lose terms. This approach works best when conflict is reframed toward a new rationale in which the conflict can be viewed as an opportunity.
5. **Allow for an environment of open dialogue**—However, an open, full disclosure of information needs to be cautiously pursued. Recognize areas of difference while seek points of similarity. Do not allow difference to become the dominating focus. Search for agreement that represent everyone's goals and objectives. This takes time and a tough firmness of mind to not be sidetracked by lesser issues.

PERSPECTIVES ON HOW TO FACILITATE SYNERGISTIC OPPORTUNITIES

In a competitive environment, our information about others is typically limited to their weaknesses or vulnerabilities. However, in a collaborative process we should consider mutual strengths so that we can consider synergistic opportunities. There are six perspectives that help us reach synergistic opportunity.

Perspective #1: In understanding another party's positions, we should consider what is of great interest to them. It is important to remember that efforts to change an organization improve when assumptions have been clearly outlined.
Perspective #2: One of the paradoxical qualities of conflict is that it helps L-Ns become familiar with conflict-related issues. However, this requires objectivity and self-control of one's emotional maturity during conflict. Collaboration involves the complex process of observing the consequences of our own actions as regards the behavior of others, the impact we are having on the negotiation, and accepting the demands made on us in the process.
Perspective #3: Effective Questioning is a process for testing one's assumptions. It takes strong intellectual discipline to maintain a mind-set that is willing to challenge one's own assumptions.
Perspective #4: L-Ns need to know that their understanding of the whole organization is accurate in order to build synergy. Synergy implies something beyond what presently exists; something greater than the immediate context. People often are "tolerant" of present problems if their hope in the future is believable and achievable.
Perspective #5: Collaboration, when viewed from a holistic viewpoint, requires that L-Ns pursue the highest common denominator. However, seldom is the highest common denominator known before its pursuit. Collaboration begins as a pursuit, not as a known outcome. This requires persistence in the face of ambiguity and uncertainty.
Perspective #6: Generally conflict involves two or more people seeking their self-interest. Achieving collaboration requires understanding self-interest. This involves the process of finding common ground which at times can seem disorderly, nonlinear, and ambiguous. Differences cannot be ignored or set aside. It is very difficult to achieve a common vision without taking a hard look at the issues that could potentially block the vision from becoming a reality. Vision can create possibility and hope. Vision engages parties in a large enough perspective that everyone can find a place in it and, it is inspired by possibilities. Possibility is stimulated by asking What iF questions. A collaborative philosophy moves each party into and toward a new form of relationship and reframes conflict toward an opportunity that is more promising than previously envisioned.

ESTABLISHING COMMON GROUND

Common Ground provides the motivation and the context for engaging in collaboration. Collaboration requires that the parties reconceptualize themselves, their relationship to one another, and the nature and purpose of their interdependent actions. To accomplish this they must embrace a way of perceiving both of their worlds and focusing on a shared horizon. They must learn to *see together*. This involves establishing a future destination. Collaboration puts us on a different course by plotting a *new* goal, one that is interdependent rather than mutually exclusive.

Future opportunity must be sufficiently challenging, urgent, and compelling to redirect the parties' unproductive or aggressive positions with each other toward some mutually beneficial outcome. Focusing on future opportunity shifts attention to the future and away from the present or past.

Collaboration often has its motivation not in aspiration or inspiration, but in a shared animosity toward some person, entity, or principle. Shared animosity is a powerful binding agent. Collaboration based on animosity toward a common enemy lasts only as long as the enemy is a threat to both parties. Once the common enemy no longer binds them together, old conflicts among temporary allies may reappear. "Politics makes strange bedfellows" refers to this type of temporary arrangement and not to a more permanent alliance.

BALANCED POWER

Collaboration implies a different attitude about power. Most forms of conflict management involve the use of power and control. Most conflict is about the fear of powerlessness Collaboration requires power but it is power to achieve rather than power to control. Collaboration means that power is equitable and in equilibrium among the parties. The advantage of collaborative power is in its influential, positive (but not unrealistic) future direction and destination.

Why shouldn't we impose our will and power on others? Why should we collaborate? Isn't it a dog-eat-dog world? The answers are found in the relationship between power and wisdom. The fact of the matter is that having power does not mean we understand its best use. One assumption of collaboration is that the potential of working together is significantly expanded beyond what one party can realize working alone.

The Restraint of Power—Power is usually an illusion. Few people actually have as much power as they think they have. Most negotiations overexaggerate the amount of power the other party actually possesses. It is sometimes necessary to not use power in order to initiate or sustain collaboration.

The Maturity of Relational Thinking—Relational Thinking is the discipline through which we view ourselves as part of the whole. Relational thinking requires us to simultaneously observe two areas of influence:

Influence area #1: Ourselves, Others, and the Overall context of which we are a part

We need to both stand our ground while simultaneously finding common ground. This means that we stop thinking against each other. Instead, we must think for ourselves and about others. The kinds of questions representative of Relational Thinking are:

- What exactly do I want?
- Why do I want it?
- What will I get?
- What do I have to give?

- What am I willing to do to get what I want?
- What will I refuse to do?
- Who have I been in the past in relation to this issue?
- In what ways am I willing to change in order to achieve my goals?
- Where do I want to be when this is over?
- In what ways am I open to being influenced by others? In what ways do I resist being influenced?

  In short: How well do I know myself and, how well do I know what I want and don't want?

Influence area #2: Synergistic opportunity

Collaboration is not a matter of simple arithmetic. Cooperation will allow each of us to use the other to get what we want, but collaboration expects more of us. It pushes us beyond our private aspirations to a larger vision. In collaboration, 1 + 1 = 3 or 4 because collaboration is synergistic; it increases the size and idea of the pie. Conflict, on the other hand, promotes self-interest and self-occupation. Human beings can gravitate toward thinking of themselves as the center of the universe. In fact, one of the great attractions of conflict is that it is so easy to justify the extreme self-concern it generates. Collaboration is seldom possible when thinking only about one party's needs. Collaboration involves putting the interests of the group ahead of self-interest.

THE DILEMMA OF TRUST, HONESTY, AND OPENNESS

An essential phase of reaching an agreement involves developing and maintaining trust. To the extent that L-Ns know what others want, they will be able to develop an effective negotiation outcome. The interdependence required of collaborative negotiations, however, represents two dilemmas:

1. The Problem of Trust—Trust involves how much L-Ns can believe the validity of others communication. To trust the other negotiator is to risk potential exploitation. To distrust the other negotiator means greatly decreasing the possibility that a productive agreement can be reached.
2. The Problem of Honesty and Openness—Honesty and openness involves the risk of either being exploited for disclosing too much too quickly or seriously damaging the negotiation relationship by seeming to be deceitful or distrusting.

Is Trust Important? Trust is a necessary condition in securing cooperation and effective communication. People will more openly express their thoughts, feelings, reactions, opinions, information, and ideas when the trust level is secure. When the trust level is unsure, people will employ behaviors such as being evasive and dishonest, will fear being taken advantage of, tell half-truths, and become noncommunicative.

What Is Trust? Trust, or the lack of it, is both simple and complex. Trust involves the belief that one's choices can lead to a win rather than a loss. This usually depends upon the trustworthy behavior of the both parties and that a potential gain will be greater than a potential loss. Trust is ultimately associated with listening to one's actions, not one's words. In other words, agreements should be based upon action and not rhetoric. There is no universally accepted definition of trust except in books. The meaning and interpretation of what trust is, is uniquely peculiar with each person or party. The accumulated conditioning of our life's experiences influences how we understand trust. This is why the concept of trust is "tricky" and "risky."

Is Trust Simple? Trust either exists or it does not exist. The reasons for this are complex. The actual reasons for trust or the lack of trust are concealed within the complexity of the human mind and in the context of the negotiation. In the final moment of a negotiation, trust is a matter of faith that the other party is who they say they are and will do what they say they will do.

FIVE APPROACHES THAT HELP PROMOTE TRUST

1. **Clearly define problems**—Defining the problem should occur before trying to solve the problem. The problem must be identified in a way that it is mutually understood and accepted by all parties. All too often, the rush to reach an agreement skips this step. Skipping this step is a mistake. Insist that the problem is clearly defined using E-Questions.
2. **Simplify the problem** down to its core concerns, while downplaying secondary issues.
3. **Identify barriers or obstacles to reaching a solution**—In my opinion, it is better to know these barriers or obstacles upfront than to realize them after the agreement.
4. **Describe the agreement in writing**—Do not accept the other party's "word or promise" that they will fulfill a specific part of the agreement.
5. **In the event that solutions to a problem are not readily available, encourage brainstorming**—Possible alternative solutions are best understood via a written (not verbal) list of possible alternatives. Groups are often better problem-solvers than individuals. Groups usually provide a greater number of perspectives on problems that hence results in greater quantity as well as quality of alternatives. This increases the probability of reaching an agreement. However, there are problems to which individuals not groups are better suited. This usually depends upon the context of the conflict and the level of expertise and specialization needed to solve complicated issues.

Section V Chapter 11 describes the Context of Conflict.

Section IV

Managing Conflict

Chapter 11

The Context of Conflict

INTRODUCTION TO THE CONTEXT OF CONFLICT

History is the story of human conflict. Conflict is a part of everyday business and life. Managed effectively, conflict can enrich individual, group, and organizational effectiveness. Managed poorly, conflict can downgrade the potential for success, contributing to dysfunctional work teams that can undermine well-planned efforts.

The ability to manage conflict is built on the assumption that we understand conflict as a system, rather than only a specific, singular incident or event. Conflict systematically invades human relationships, consumes corporate energy, and undermines potential opportunities. We learn how about conflict from the culture we are born into, our families, educational institutions, etc.

It is assumed that the primary interest of a business is to achieve tasks that support its mission to survive and grow within a competitive environment. This author assumes that an organization needs to focus first on task competence and secondly, on relational cooperation. Poor morale, unsuccessfully managed conflict, and resistance to change will obstruct an organization from implementing its principal concern—to get the job done efficiently, effectively, and profitably. This is not to say that relationships should be considered a secondary priority. Rather, it is to say that a business that has magnificent relationships but cannot fulfill its task responsibilities will almost certainly not survive a competitive environment.

I am frequently asked, 'What do you mean by context?' My answer may be best described by a story located in Box 11.1—The Farm Family Story.

Understanding conflict is complex. We must widen our perspective to include recognizing forces that cause conflict outside our immediate control, otherwise we may error by blaming ourselves and personalizing the conflict that is situation dependent.

WHAT CAUSES CONFLICT?

Another frequently asked question I receive is, 'What causes conflict?' There is no definitive answer. The causes of conflict are one of the most profoundly difficult human puzzles to understand. However, there are a few observations I have made and perspectives I have formed over the years that tend to help Leader-Negotiators (L-Ns) better understand how to manage and resolve the complexity of conflict.

Box 11.1 The Farm Family Story

During the 1970s, a friend moved to the Midwestern part of the United States to become a farmer. He explained that his family history involved farming and he wanted to continue the three generations of that family tradition. A year or so passed when I received a phone call from my new farmer friend. He was very distressed because he was on the edge of financially going under and losing the farm. The overall gist of the conversation focused on personalizing the failing farm as his fault. He asked questions that implied, 'What have I done wrong?' In the end, the family farm went bankrupt. At this point, let me insert the larger context of this story.

During the 1970s, the Federal Government was reorganizing their long-standing farm subsidies program away from small farmers to large farms. My friend's farm was small compared to other huge farm operations. The government's shift in policy jeopardized many small farm operations, rendering them uncompetitive with other larger operations. In context, my friend's three generations of family farming developed when the government's policy favored subsidizing the small independent farmer. The point is, my friend (along with many small farm operations) went out of business because they could not compete with the government's policy of promoting larger farm operations. My friend was caught within a *contextual shift*. The family farm could not survive no matter what my friend did. At first, he blamed himself for the farm's failure. He eventually recovered. He went on to become a politician and has done very well.

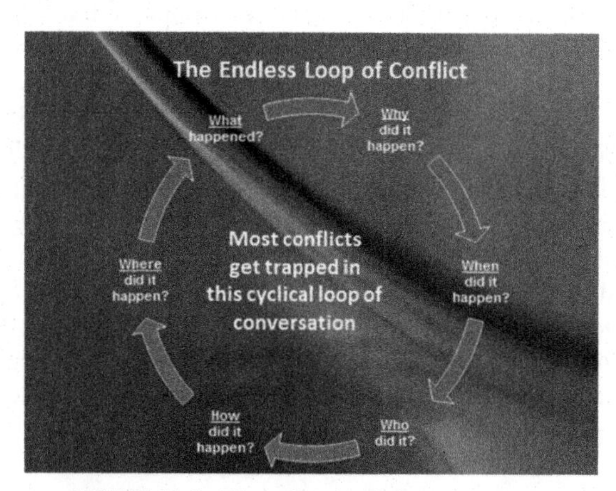

FIGURE 11.1 The endless loop of questions cycle.

First, most conflicts get trapped in the endless loop of the questions cycle (Figure 11.1).

This endless loop is often described as The Six Basic Questions. It is important to note that these six questions are quite valuable. However, they have limitations. One limitation is that they are rational and analytical.

They are not designed to surface the assumptions that often lie beneath rationale analysis (The nine assumptions described in Chapter 5). The six basic questions are very useful—but ONLY when the underlying assumption(s) are first identified.

JABs—JUDGMENTS, ATTRIBUTES, AND BLAME

Conflict is cognitive, psychological, and contextual; and, JABs—Judgments, Attributes, and Blame are the delivery system for how conflict is learned.

- **Judgments**: Negative or positive values attached to our sense of self, our character
- **Attributes**: Characteristics attached to our self-esteem, self-worth, and efficacy of mind
- **Blame**: Accusations directed in ways such as fault-finding, criticism, disapproval, 'pointing the finger,' and so on.

JABs happen everywhere and almost all the time. We live in a culture of judgment, attributes, and blame. In such a culture, it is not uncommon for JABs to influence our self-image, self-worth, and self-efficacy. If we allow our actions, and others' perceptions of them, to become attached to who we are, then we may interpret a less-than-desirable assessment of our actions as criticism, misunderstanding, and/or disagreement. In personalizing JABs, we "attach" these attributes to who we are rather than on our task performance.

Case in point, have you ever spilled a glass of milk? (Figure 11.2)
Read the story in Box 11.2—Spilled Milk.

FIGURE 11.2 Have you ever spilled a glass of milk?

Box 11.2 Spilled Milk

As children, we likely spilled a glass of milk. The reaction from those at the kitchen table was most likely, "What you have done?" and, "Why are you so careless?" These comments are not really questions being asked by parents to inform children about what has happened and why it happened. These questions, with accompanying voice tone, pitch, and points of emphasis rather dispense judgment, attributes, and, blame (JABs), inferring clumsiness and/or carelessness. The actual intention of the adults' comments was to infer that you had disrupted a warm meal and family gathering. This is a JAB can carry on for the rest of your life. When years pass and you are an adult and spill a glass of milk or some other kind of liquid, your first reaction may be to say "I'm sorry," indicating that your training as a child has manifested itself into your adult self-image.

REASONS FOR CONFLICT

Understanding conflict involves the fitting together of numerous fragments of perhaps several peoples' accounts of the conflict that reflect their fractional awareness of the conflict. This is referred to as "insight." Insight involves understanding a conflict beyond only the facts and biased interpretations used to identify the cause(s) of a conflict. It is the process of working through the layers of biased perceptions that help restructure thinking and therefore, enhance conflict management. Take a look at Figure 11.3.

In the picture above, it is predictable for people to perceive:

- a goblet
- two people face-to-face
- a face looking directly at you with two eyes on each side of the face.

FIGURE 11.3 The goblet.

There are more than three perceptions. It is thinking about the way that we have been influenced to see the goblet or, the two faces, as "correct" and others' views as "wrong" that initiates a conflict. Our preferences should remain preferences and not become absolutes.

The 10 Reasons for Conflict described below are intended to offer explanations about how conflict is created. I am not proposing that these reasons are the only 10 reasons for conflict. Rather, the 10 reasons are describing what regularly and repeatedly occur in most organizations within which I have worked.

1. *Misunderstanding*—People tend to judge themselves by their intentions and judge others by their actions. Misunderstanding often occurs when one person interprets the behavior or words of another differently than intended.
2. *Dishonesty*—The aim of a dishonest person is to mislead others. Dishonesty occurs when people do not speak the truth or when they communicate only partial or half-truths, when they eliminate significant facts that influence how the context is understood, or when they interpret the context of what was said inaccurately. Not all dishonesty is motivated by a desire to harm or mislead others.
3. *Interdependencies*—Most everyone depends upon others to help them achieve their work-related goals. How we interpret unkept promises and commitments is the source of interdependent conflict. Our response to such situations is likely based upon how we have been conditioned to interpret interdependencies. However, holding people accountable for what they promise and do not deliver does not have to be resolved with anger.
4. *Intentional Wrongdoing*—Intentional wrongdoings occur when one party deliberately does something to harm another party. Intentional wrongdoings are often part of the Win–Lose negotiation philosophy. The Win–Win philosophy, however, assumes that negotiations will not intentionally hurt others. The phrase, "I can't believe somebody did that" reflects a Win–Win expectation.
5. *Self-interest*—Self-interest, the tendency to take care of oneself and one's interests without regard for another's interests or needs, is prevalent in negotiations. In fact, self-interest tends to trump almost all values.
6. *Boundary Crossings*—Individuals in organizations are assigned job responsibilities that frequently *cross over* into other employees' job functions. Each job represents a potentially susceptible conflict because such organizational boundaries are often ambiguous. Boundaries are similar to invisible electric fences that are the dividing lines between an organization and its external environment. Intraorganizational boundaries (also invisible electric fences) are dividing lines among and between various internal organizational divisions. Referring to the phrase, No one can serve two masters at the same time we will now discuss the matrix organization in Box 11.3, which has "two masters."

Box 11.3 Matrix Organizations

Matrix organizations are temporary organizations. They likely will intensify both individual and system conflict. The source of conflict in a matrix organization is *the absence of authority*. An assumption of the matrix approach is that everybody involved in the matrix should be able to freely cross over boundaries to get their job functions completed. Therein is the source of the conflict. The nature of the Project Manager's job requires that he/she continually cross the boundaries of other departments, such as research, development, engineering, production, marketing, and sales; in addition to coordinating activities with people from outside the organization. Conflict tends to be caused by a Divisional Manager in a division being threatened by a Project Manager who has a job description that requires him/her to cross over that manager's boundary. Neither the Project Manager nor the Divisional Manager has authority over one another. They are expected to collaborate. In my experience, the expectation of a collaborative effort conflicts with the Divisional Manager's prerequisite to control his or her assigned area.

7. *Task Relations*—Task relationships refer to the activities or processes that interdependent groups perform and the way these processes conflict. Task relations fall into two categories:
   a. Independent: One group's task can be done without any relationship to others' tasks.
   b. Interdependent: One group's task completion is dependent upon another group's task completion.

   Organizational groups with independent tasks have much less conflict because they are not dependent upon others to achieve their goals. Interdependent organizational groups have much more conflict due to each group's perceived differences in task priorities. Same group members tend to view their goals, time, and group cohesion in similar ways. Different groups may have dissimilar views of goals, time, and cohesion. These differences may influence the way that each group interprets other's actions.

   What are the implications of each group's differences in interpreting goals and time? Differences may promote a competitive Win–Lose mind-set. A competitive, Win–Lose mind-set promotes having a negative attitude toward tasks, a distrust of others, a dislike for other group members, and actions without regard or respect for others. A collaborative, Win–Win group, in contrast, encourages trust, mutual respect, coordination of effort, and acceptance of differences among group members.
8. *Fear*—Fear is the primary (but not the only) motivating characteristic behind dishonesty. Fear underlies a concern about losing something that is very important to us. Feeling "unsafe" or fearful can be motivated by uncertainty, thinking others will become angry or might reject us. A challenge to our

belief system/s can be viewed as a personal attack and a threat to our self-identity. If we have become deeply invested in and attached to our own belief systems, we may be fearful that our belief system will be perceived as wrong or inadequate. Fear usually promotes defensiveness in order to protect oneself and, defensive positioning increases conflict.

9. *Counterfeit Teamwork*—If in your organization everyone in a face-to-face meeting smiles, nods, and agrees on courses of action but nothing gets done between teams without repetitive follow-ups and/or badgering, something is amiss. Hidden agendas occur when one party has an undisclosed intention. If meetings take place "after the meeting" to promote personal or selected team agendas, then teamwork and communication is not effectual. In fact, this is an indicator that meetings are both an energy leak and a form of silent warfare. Energy is wasted either arguing about whose priorities should take priority; or worse, not arguing at all because people have lost interest and don't care.
10. *Psychological Need to Win*—A psychological need to win is a deeply embedded *need* to triumph and save face at any cost. Winning is more important that obtaining a positive outcome. People may be willing to put the organization at risk in order to psychologically win. This results in a dysfunctional and highly antagonistic climate.

(Note: Perspectives on managing these 10 reasons for conflict are provided in Chapter 12 Table 12.2.)

THREE OBSERVATIONS

Three observations follow. Note that these observations have been limited to *the context of Westernized countries.*

Observation 1: People Routinely Disagree with One Another Regardless of the Topic Being Discussed

The point of this thought-provoking observation is that there appears to be no added value contributed *when people agree with one another*. In fact, the primary way to add value seems to be by means of disagreement. See the example in Box 11.4—Neighborly Relations.

Disagreements are seldom about the topic being discussed, rather, it is about proving one's self-worth and self-efficacy. If a person's sense of value has been depreciated they may feel *obligated* to disagree with almost anything that is communicated.

One possible contributor to self-deprecation is the 24-7 technology addicted culture in which we live. This paradigm seems to have influenced how people assert their value during everyday conversation and communication exchanges. People increasingly defer to computer-accessed information that is outside themselves. They appear to no longer trust their own thinking

Box 11.4 Neighborly Relations

Upon moving into a new neighborhood, I ventured out to mow my lawn. My neighbor was also mowing his lawn. We waved at each other and so we idled down our lawnmowers and made our way to the fence. Shaking hands, I said, "It looks like we have a beautiful day to mow our lawns." His response was, "I don't think so. It most likely will cloud up and rain today."

I interpreted this conversation to be a symbol of his need to assert his personal value via disagreeing with me about the weather. I could have intensified the situation by countering his disagreement, by asserting *my* value by reporting that the local weather station indicated that it was going to be a cloudless, sunny day. Instead, I said to him, "That's a good point. We had better get our lawns mowed before the rain starts."

We went back to our idling lawnmowers. By recognizing that his disagreeing with me about the weather was not what was really going on, I avoided a pointless argument about weather. He was making a case about his value. This is an example that there is no value in agreement—only in disagreement.

and sense-making. It is conceivable that this deference and dependency on technology contributes to a depreciation of one's self-efficacy and personal value. If this is accurate, then it may stimulate conflict to debate one's point of view about any topic of discussion because this may only intensify a person's *need* to assert his or her value via disagreement in order to feel good about themselves.

Observation 2: People Live in a Talking Culture, Not a Listening Culture

Have you ever been in an argument? Usually, the answer is 100% **yes**. The next question is, do you know how you got into that argument? After asking countless number of people and many audiences these two questions, the widely held answer is, "NO, we do not know how we got into an argument!"

The rejoinder to the question about how most arguments *happen* is—because the majority of people make statements and don't ask questions. Making statements is an invitation for others to disagree or argue. So what's the point? The point is, that people who need to assert their self-worth often do so via disagreement. I suggest that you *change a disagreement* into a mutual conversation by asking questions instead of making statements. However, it's possible that if a question is not well constructed, others will argue about the inadequacy of the question.

Observation 3: People Personalize Conflict

About 80% of job-related conflict occurs from the organization's *disorganization*. Note: If you personalize or individualize a system, it could dysfunctionalize you from the inside out. See the example in Box 11.5—Getting Fired.

Box 11.5 Getting Fired

I was consulting with a large international manufacturer. The VP of Operations asked to discuss why the hiring and firing rate was so high in one particular job division. He explained that in that one area, five employees had been fired within the past year. He asked if I would look into it and provide a recommendation regarding how to not hire such incompetent people. I studied the situation. What I learned was that these five people personalized their firing. They had given it their best, but were told they were inadequate. The high turnover rate within this area, however, was related to poorly designed job descriptions. It did not matter who held a job; if they did their job description, they would fail and then get fired.

For example, if you had been one of the five people working in the job description situation above, it is important to recognize that the continual failure to perform your job function would not have been about *you*. This does not diminish the conflict of being terminated—particularly if you adequately performed your job description. But, if you had interpreted getting fired personally, it is possible that it could have damaged your self-worth, self-esteem, and self-efficacy. Your preference may be that others recognize your personal value and self-efficacy; but then again, if your preference becomes a *need* and therefore you expect others to respect your worth, to listen to you, and to accept your ideas without criticism, you will be trying to get your needs met instead of pursuing the best possible negotiated outcome.

"The art of managing conflict involves maintaining a disposition of depersonalization; not allowing your personal needs to be at odds with achieving your objective."

Ken Sylvester

FIGURE 11.4 The Gordian Knot: Artist Unknown Following Extensive Search.

1. What Is The Gordian Knot?

The Gordian Knot originated its name as a proverbial term for solving complex problems. In 333 BC, Alexander the Great, on his march through Anatolia, reached Gordian, the capital of Phrygia. There Alexander was shown a Chariot which honored the ancient founder of the city, Gordius. A rope had been secured to the Chariot's yoke by means of an intricate knot with its end hidden. According to tradition, whoever untied this knot would become the Ruler of Gordian. Numerous challengers were unable to untie the Gordian Knot. In this popular account, Alexander studied the problem and then sliced through the Gordian Knot with his sword. The phrase *cutting the Gordian Knot* thus came to signify finding a solution to a complicated problem. (Figure 11.4).

What's the point of the Gordian Knot in Figure 11.4? It is that L-Ns must know how to lead highly complex systems, metaphorically speaking—Gordian Knots. Gordian Knots are difficult because a problem needing to be solved in one area is likely related to problems that need to be solved in another area. In other words, there is no simple path to a solution. Every solution is the next problem.

Every business, government, and educational system with whom I've worked has faced the dilemma of resolving their Gordian Knots. Management books propose that the primary way to untie Gordian Knots is to do so through the process of *reorganization*. However, reorganizing Gordian Knots is a complex process that requires a knowledgeable understanding of how and why the knots were originally formed; and, how it's many bonds and loops interconnect with other Knots among and within an organization. Untying the Knots involves understanding how untying the Gordian Knot will benefit the organization; and, more importantly, knowing the consequences and implications if it is untied. There are consequences and implications to every decision.

Every organization has Gordian Knots. Each organization's Gordian Knots are not the same, but are similar in concept. The purpose of Chapter 4 on Effective Questioning outlines a process about how to question the assumptions that underlie an organization's Gordian Knots. Gordian Knots come in many types. Some of those types are things such as—legal agreements that cannot just be "untied." In fact, some Knots are legal agreements that could take years to be untied or if untied, would incur penalties.

- During the **early stages of an organization's development and growth**, knots are less tight, not entrapped with tradition, and therefore more easily untied and retied in order to reorganize.
- When organizations are in the **middle stages of development**, growth and increased complexity cause Gordian Knots to grow tighter. Untying them becomes more difficult due to the desire leadership has to stabilize organizational operations.
- When organizations have **grown into mature structures**, Gordian Knots become problematic and strongly resistant to change. Every solution becomes the next problem. Some knot problems are long-standing; knots such as—legal contracts, financial reports to shareholders, taxes, unions, licenses, grants, bonds, leases, commissions, HR employment policies, laws and by-laws,

edicts, rulings, statutes, regulations, conflicting international standards and legal ethics, political agendas, preexisting and binding agreements that cannot be discontinued without huge financial penalties and the resulting loss of trust, legal obligations for Boards to operate, government regulations, political alliances, traditions, technological limitations and dysfunctions, and mergers and acquisitions that pull the strings of the knot tighter.

It is significant for L-Ns to note that no matter what strings you pull, you cannot avoid the consequences that occur as Knots are pulled tighter. The challenge for L-Ns is, the tighter the Gordian Knots, the more complicated it is to lead and negotiate. This brings up the old adages of "Work smarter, not harder" and "Measure twice; cut once." President Franklin D. Roosevelt said, "It has always seemed to me that the best symbol of common sense was a bridge, not a wall." The wisdom here is Roosevelt's understanding of the use of power to manage Gordian Knots.

SEVEN POSITIVE OUTCOMES OF CONFLICT

Despite the complexity of conflict, there *can be* positive outcomes (Figure 11.5).

FIGURE 11.5 Positive outcomes of conflict.

1. Better ideas are produced if conflict is viewed as complementary and not negative.
2. People are compelled to search for new approaches if they desire to reach an agreement.
3. Solutions can be considered from multiple viewpoints.
4. People are required or motivated to clarify their ideas.
5. Positive tension can provoke awareness and stimulate creativity.
6. A person's potential can be activated.
7. Relationships can become stronger and trust might increase.

DYSFUNCTIONAL OUTCOMES OF CONFLICT

There are, however, dysfunctional outcomes of conflict (Figure 11.6).

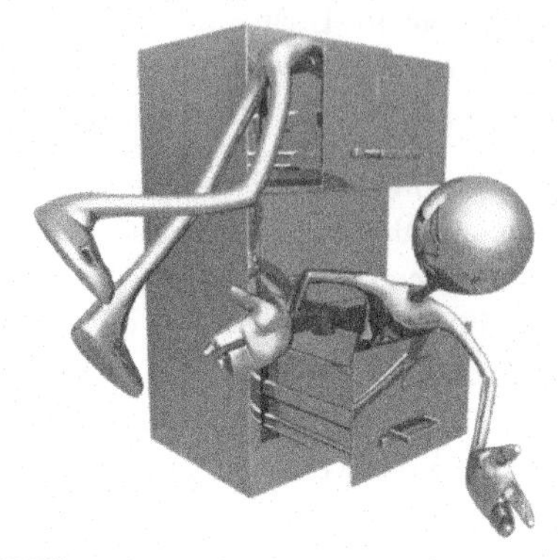

FIGURE 11.6 Dysfunctional outcomes of conflict.

1. If people feel conquered and defeated, they tend to withdraw. This can neutralize potential contributions, for example, inhibit the potential for intellectual capital.
2. Distance (psychological, interpersonal, political, etc.) among people may increase. This can obstruct and/or slow the strategic flow of necessary resources such as information, knowledge, data, decision-making, and collective synergy. Distance can decrease organizational effectiveness.
3. A climate of distrust, suspicion, pessimism, cynicism, and skepticism might develop. If this climate permeates an organization's culture, then the organization may become weak and therefore vulnerable to external competitive threat. In such a culture, when cooperation is required, there may be withdrawal and defensiveness instead of strategic cooperation. Conflict that neutralizes cooperation can be more than just troublesome; it can be translated into the cost ($) of doing business.
4. Resistance to teamwork might develop. If so, obstruction to progress follows and teams become organizational silos where they are closed off to everything but themselves. Attempts toward progress are organizationally difficult, expensive, and often ineffective.
5. Too much conflict can cause people to be AWOL (absent without leaving) with regard to organizational objectives. This means people may become indifferent and/or passively resistant to change.

THE ESCALATION OF CONFLICT

Under conditions of mistrust, suspicion, heightened emotional passion, and anger, the appearance of cooperation might be viewed by others as a ploy or trick to lure them into a false sense of trust. As conflict escalates, the following six characteristics are typical of an environment that hinders leadership initiatives and effective negotiation outcomes.

1. **Hostility, frustration, suspicion, and mistrust** increase within an environment when no one listens to each other. If one party is overtalking another party, this is a symptom of not wanting to listen to anyone else's viewpoint but one's own (Figure 11.7).

FIGURE 11.7 Hostility, frustration, suspicion, and mistrust.

2. **Communication lines become closed or unresponsive**—One mainstay of a successful negotiation is the capacity to communicate. Without exception, communication is the most significant resource available to achieve a positive outcome. When communication breaks down, so does trust. Passion usually reduces objectivity. Self-control and emotional maturity are valuable assets that help disarm conflict (Figure 11.8).

FIGURE 11.8 Communication lines become closed or unresponsive.

3. **The Original purpose for the negotiation has become ambiguous**—Additional issues are unexpectedly introduced that alter the original intent for the negotiation; or, the original purpose for the negotiation was never accurately determined at the outset. This may be interpreted as unfair and aggressive, as well as disadvantageous (Figure 11.9).

FIGURE 11.9 The original purpose for the negotiation has become ambiguous.

At this point, it is recommended that you suggest returning to the original purpose of the negotiation by requesting a review of the original agenda. Once the agenda has been clarified and if it has been agreed to in writing, continue negotiating unless the newly entered agenda items are unreasonable or to your disadvantage.

4. **The focal point is upon differences, not common interests**—An overemphasis on difference hinders achieving an agreement by highlighting obstacles and problems rather than possibilities and solutions. The more that differences take parties away from what you have in common, the more difficult it becomes to reach an acceptable outcome. Note: obstacles should not be minimized or ignored. There are nonnegotiable issues. If there are legitimate differences, then the differences should not be set aside as this will raise their importance in the future. Better to deal with them now (Figure 11.10).

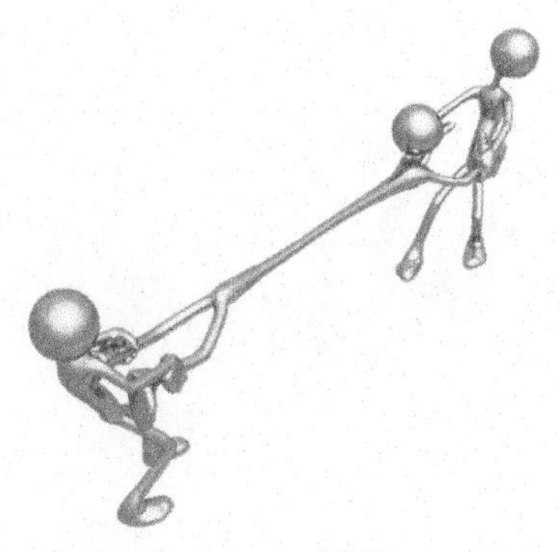

FIGURE 11.10 The focal point is upon differences, not common interests.

5. **L-Ns have become totally locked into their position**—Positional lockdown may result in the increased use of competitive tools, such as tactics, threats, distortion of communication, exaggerated or animated behavior, overdependence on power, inequitable offers, and overuse of coercion. Taking a firm position does not imply escalating a conflict via competitive approaches. Rather, just assert your position (Figure 11.11).

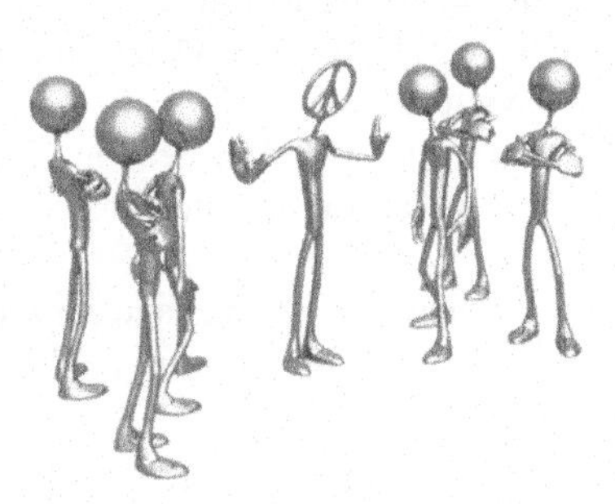

FIGURE 11.11 Negotiators become locked into their negotiation position.

6. **Each side becomes internally agreeable with itself, often resulting in Groupthink**—Groupthink demands group conformity. When parties form "dogmatic" forms of inner-group consensus, the group's disposition about considering alternatives becomes limited and the group becomes defensive rather than objective. If possible, using E-Questions may help ease the tendency toward and power of Groupthink. However, be cautious because Groupthink can result in removing a dissenter from the negotiation; even costing one their job (Figure 11.12).

FIGURE 11.12 Each side becomes internally agreeable, often resulting in groupthink.

CONCLUDING STATEMENT ABOUT THE COMPLEXITY OF CONFLICT

This chapter began with the suggestion that conflict is not simple, but complex. Resolving conflict is similar to trying to figure out where a perfectly drawn circle begins. This is, of course, not possible. Management of conflict acknowledges that we cannot always understand where the perfect circle begins; but then again we should not be in pursuit of perfection. To be more precise, we should attempt management of a conflict, not perfectionistic aspirations to resolve human affairs.

Chapter 12 covers how to diagnose and manage conflict. Conflict is seldom logical. At times, it makes no sense at all. Onward to Chapter 12.

Chapter 12

Diagnosing and Managing Conflict

INTRODUCTION

Whenever people work as a group, conflict is one of the predictable outcomes. Most managers spend upward of 25–60% of their working time dealing with conflicts or fallout from people-related problems. Mismanaged conflict results in inefficiencies such as—misdirected workforce energy, malfunctioning lines of communication, mistakes that must be corrected, lost opportunities, and increased turnover rates. It is difficult to calculate the losses related to organizational conflict.

The purpose of this chapter is to provide methods for effectively diagnosing and managing conflict. An overview of the assumptions that undergird six conflict theories is presented (Table 12.1). In addition, a new approach to understanding conflict, referred to as Personal Attachment Theory P.A.T., is described. PAT is the author's theory on how conflict is generated and reinforced in business systems. Additional resources that provide an in-depth treatment of conflict management are listed in the Resource Section.

OVERVIEW OF SIX CONFLICT THEORIES

Conflict is complex because at minimum, it involves the interaction of cognitive, psychological, physiological, and contextual dynamics. Most conflict theories take only a psychological and/or an economic approach to understanding and managing conflict. Following is a concise overview of assumptions that undergird six prevalent conflict theories. The intent of the following theories is to reduce or resolve conflict among individuals and groups. However, what is missing from these theories is that conflict resolution must occur within the contexts of bureaucracies.

Conflict occurs especially within large bureaucratic organizations. Bureaucracies have the following characteristics: (1) Each employee has specified and official areas of responsibility that are defined and controlled by rules—rules that have little or no exceptions; (2) There is a clearly ordered system of supervision and subordination, which allows appeals from a lower to a higher authority in regulated protocols; and (3) Written documents are required and maintained as a means of managing everything and everyone.

TABLE 12.1 Review: Six Conflict Theories

1	Self-Interest	Satisfying only individual and/or group needs
2	Interest-based	Satisfying both parties mutual interests
3	Boundary-crossing	Protecting one's rules and borders
4	Procedural	Following procedures has a higher priority than resolving conflict
5	Loss of trust	Blaming others rather than focusing on the resolving the conflict
6	Styles	Recognizing human patterns of behavior in order to reduce or resolve the causes of conflict

The above bureaucratic characteristics offer a secure, unchanging work environment by knowing how everything and everybody *should* work. Secondarily, bureaucracies contribute to structural conflict. When attempts are made to apply a psychological or an economic solution to a bureaucratic system, efforts to manage conflict are likely frustrating—at best.

1. **Self-interest theories** consider the interactions among peoples' different needs, wants, desires, and hopes. Pursuing one's self-interest is not right or wrong. However, it does not foster group collaboration. Rather, the pursuit of self-interests in a bureaucratic system classically promotes a Win–Lose negotiation mind-set. When one party seeks only their self-interests, it tends to stimulate increased self-interest among other parties—referred to as *adverse reciprocity*. Routinely, people approach negotiation by using words that imply a *Win–Win* approach. However, as soon as one party believes that they might lose, they often change their negotiation philosophy from Win–Win to Win–Lose. As a general rule, *self-interest tends to trump almost all known values.*
2. **Interest-based theories** suggest that to resolve conflict you first need to identify mutually substantive (practical, concrete, and tangible) interests that are in conflict among each party followed by an interest-based *process* that should facilitate resolution of differences. This theory assumes that Leader-Negotiators (L-Ns) have *time* to engage in what might be considered a psychologist's sphere of influence; that L-Ns understand the cognitive, psychological, and contextual dynamics that contributed to the conflict; and, that each party's interests are able to be identified and are therefore resolvable. However, bureaucracies are complicated to diagnose. Causes are often buried with the root cause often being the nature of a bureaucracy itself.
3. **Boundary-crossing theories** assume that conflict occurs when parties cross boundaries that "should be" known and, that outsiders should be aware of these boundaries. However, most organizational boundaries are like invisible

electric fences. Boundary-crossings occur everywhere and conflict often develops from unwritten or unarticulated boundary assumptions. Following are a sample of conventional tools used to establish and enforce boundaries: formalized behavioral standards, legitimate authority, a set of laws, norms, customs and traditions, policies, stated rules, governmental controls, etc. Boundary-Crossing Theory stipulates that conflict is resolved by means of these tools. Bureaucracy is a form of impersonal conflict management. Conflict is viewed as a "systems adjustment"—not a personal issue. In most bureaucracies, leaders do not exercise individual judgment. Instead, L-Ns are informed what the rules are; they don't create the rules and, they do not have the authority to make exceptions to those rules.

4. **Procedural conflict theories** address and resolve conflict by adhering to a formal process. In fact, adhering to the process often takes precedence over resolving the source of the conflict. For example, case in point: Legal procedure often trumps breaking the law. In the legal profession, police are required by law to read to suspects their Miranda rights. If this procedure is not followed to the letter of the law, allegations against the suspect may be dismissed and the suspect goes free. A procedural approach is characteristic of bureaucracies that emphasize an impersonal compliance to a system of rules. This approach tends to prioritize *organizational structure over personal relationship.* The assumption is that by removing personal biases and prejudices from organizational decisions, productivity will be protected. Procedural Conflict Theories attempt to pursue mutual areas of *common ground.* However, within a bureaucratic context, *the concept and definition of common ground* is not relevant to individual conflict; rather, common ground is connected to the organization. Again, a bureaucratic structure uses rules and policies to control conflict—not individuals. As such, bureaucratic organizations are characterized by a passive form of "low-grade anger" that cannot be resolved.
5. **Loss of trust conflict theories** ascribes conflict as the fault of poor management, incompetent leadership, and anyone and everything else—even your dog. Realistically, there are trust-related conflicts and losses that cannot or will not be improved, resolved, or restored. If a conflict is severe enough that people can no longer work together, then L-Ns may have no other alternative than to separate or isolate the conflict parties. Distrust often makes communication guarded. When people trust each other, their communication tends to be more accurate and open. When people distrust each other, they are more likely to be secretive or hesitant about talking openly. As a side note, communication problems related to loss of trust are most acute when organizational members conduct employee evaluations such as performance reviews. Perceptual distortions and inaccurate attributions often dominate such situations. When L-Ns are aware that organizational conflict exists, they should first examine how effective the communication process is. Communication problems often

show up as symptoms of amotivation, lack of leadership, dysfunctional group dynamics, and ambiguous organizational change, etc.

6. **Styles theories** focus on a leaders' personality and behavior characteristics. Popular styles inventories include: the Myers-Briggs, the DISC, Types A & B, and the MBIT, among others. Research indicates, however, that there are no styles or behavioral characteristics that can accurately predict leadership success. In other words, a leader's style will not substitute for the need to be competent at performing the five essential leadership skills of: (1) solving problems, (2) making decisions, (3) taking effective action, (4) building competent teams, and (5) crafting strategy. These five skills should be completed in one's unique style. The concept of styles is a set of assumptions about human behavior—which usually exists consciously or unconsciously inside a person's head. Styles are not a managerial philosophy; not a management style; not the property of an organization or a management system; not a set of external managerial behaviors or strategies or tactics. Styles Theory assumes an *inner set of assumptions* from which L-Ns express their behavior. It is from these deeply embedded styles-related preferences that conflicts occur among others who have different embedded style preferences. To further complicate matters, it is often difficult to explain what has "stylistically" acquired over a long period of time.

The most prominent conflict characteristic within bureaucracies is that there is no person or persons who can authorize exceptions to bureaucratic procedures. Overall, bureaucracies function by rules and procedures, not by its leader's human judgment and discretion. A bureaucratic leader's responsibility involves reviewing and clarifying rules and procedures for organizational members. The L-Ns who manage bureaucratic conflict do so by referring conflict parties to impersonal policies and procedures. Bureaucracies endeavor to properly organize tasks and relationships—but are, at best, systems of contradictions and inconsistencies. In my experience, it is not possible to effectively control the infinitely diverse versions of human behavior.

Hierarchical organizations contribute to communication conflicts as a result of how they centralize authority. Centralization gives some organizational members access to more information than others; or, some subunits receive very different information than other subunits. Nevertheless, they are expected to efficiently work together. Since some people know more information or different information than others, centralization (which discourages shared information) increases the potential for misunderstandings and therefore conflict among the various subunits. The best I can offer is that bureaucratic conflict is to be expected. All the best!

DIAGNOSING CONFLICT IS BOTH A SCIENCE AND AN ART

Everyone practices conflict every day. However, diagnosing conflict is not only a science; it is an "art." A common assumption is that we understand the reasons for conflict and therefore its resolution. However, many conflicts may not be understandable and therefore are not resolvable. There are no secret formulas that will resolve all conflicts. The aim of every conflict resolution practice (similar to the practice of medicine, law, engineering, etc.) is to first diagnose the cause of the conflict and then resolve the problems it creates.

Conflict theories guide one's diagnoses; and, diagnosis informs our solutions and remedies. However, theories alone are inadequate for effective diagnosis. In general, theoretical knowledge functions as a framework, but *application* of those theories requires specific knowledge, experience associated with that knowledge, and tools that match solving specific problems. You cannot fix all problems with one tool, or one theory.

Everyone has a limited point of view. In a sense, everyone is correct, fair-minded, truthful, and honest in his or her point of view; yet, everyone is equally incomplete and limited in their ability to understand. Strong feelings often interfere with human reason and objectivity. Recall that 85% of all conflict has nothing to do with the people involved in the conflict. As a general rule, most conflict is the result of the system. Depersonalizing conflict is hard work. However, it is the starting point for a conflict to be effectively managed.

PERSONAL ATTACHMENT THEORY

A review of the six conflict theories prompts me to assert an additional conflict theory that usually influences the effectiveness of a negotiated outcome. I refer to my theory as, the **Personal Attachment (Conflict) Theory (PAT)**. What I mean here by *personal attachment* is that when a person's self-worth, self-image, and/or efficacy of mind (who they are) become attached to *what they do*, then their task performance becomes attached to their self-value. Consider the following example:

What if at <u>your</u> job <u>you</u> are in a meeting. <u>Your</u> manager expresses that they have reviewed a proposal that <u>you</u> have worked on, but <u>your</u> manager does not think that <u>you</u> have done a good enough job on <u>your</u> proposal. <u>Your</u> manager's feedback is a simple, task-related statement. In spite of this, if <u>you</u> have attached <u>your</u> personal self-worth and efficacy of mind to <u>your</u> proposal, feedback of any kind may be perceived and interpreted as a criticism of <u>your</u> self-worth and efficacy of mind. In other words, <u>your</u> manager's impersonal feedback has now been interpreted as an offensive attack on <u>your</u> personal worth and intelligence. <u>Your</u> proposal and <u>your</u> manager's feedback are now two issues: (1) <u>your</u> manager's impersonal feedback, and (2) <u>your</u> personalization of <u>your</u> manager's feedback, making it an attack rather than a task-related improvement.

As you return to the top of this example, reread how many pronouns have been used that personalize this example. You will find 19 pronouns by my count. A symptom of personal attachment to performance is the continuous repetition of pronouns such as "me"—"ours"—"your"—and so forth, gradually attaching what you *do* to who <u>you</u> *are*. This does not suggest that you should not be committed to your job. Rather, it suggests that you should be cautious not attach your personal worth to your commitments. For instance, I may *fail* at performing a task today but that does not mean that *who I am* is a failure.

Let's begin with am assumption that a person has attached who they are to defending their department's boundaries. If this person has attached his or her personal value to their organizational boundaries, anyone who crosses that boundary has provoked a personal conflict that is not just a clarification about where one's responsibilities start and end. The problem of personal boundary crossings has now become two discussions: (1) one involves an objective, impartial discussion about where one's boundaries begin and end (not intended to be personal); (2) the second discussion involves how a boundary crossing has been personally interpreted, which likely has been perceived as a personal attack or threatening act of disrespect; in other words, the crossing has become attached to this person's self-esteem, self-worth, and efficacy of mind. The act of crossing into personally guarded organizational territory often results in a reaction that is completely out of proportion to what happened. Diagnosing the situation as "personal attachment" is essential to managing this conflict.

The six conflict theories do not address personal attachment. In Chapter 11, the concept of JABs (Judgments, Attributes, and Blame) was described. If we accept others' JABs toward our actions and we allow those JABs to become attached to who we are, then we will likely interpret issues such as feedback as personal criticisms, impolite misunderstandings, and/or insulting comments. Personalizing JABs implies that we have relinquished control of our personal worth to others. Sooner or later, this results in no longer trusting ourselves. Hence, we become what others perceive us to be. This is damaging to one's personal and professional development.

SEVEN REASONS CONFLICT AND SUGGESTED ACTIONS

Conflict resolution begins by first diagnosing context.

Ken Sylvester

Recognizing the reasons for conflict improves one's conflict diagnostic skills. Conflict is always context dependent. There are no effective conflict solutions without understanding context. This is why conflict resolution begins by first diagnosing the context. Once a diagnostic investigation has been conducted, we begin exploring potential remedies that may help resolve the conflict. This assumes that a conflict has some logical, rational explanation. Conflict is frequently not logical or rational. Personal Attachment Theory complements the other six conflict theories, effectively strengthening their effort to diagnose and manage conflict by understanding the context of most conflict—personal attachment.

The reasons for conflict described in Chapter 11 are actually symptoms, not causes, of conflict. L-Ns must recognize conflict symptoms as symptoms and not confuse them with causes. Table 12.2 below lists seven reasons for (or symptoms of) conflict. Additionally, it offers seven perspectives or actions that may help manage conflict. I am not proposing that there are *only* seven reasons

TABLE 12.2 Seven Reasons (or Symptoms) of Conflict and Suggested Actions

	Seven Reasons for Conflict	Suggested Actions
1	**Misunderstanding**	One way to disarm misunderstanding is for one party to acknowledge that they do not understand if and how they contributed to the conflict. At that point, listen to how the other party interpreted your words, your actions, and/or your silence. Remember to not take this personally. Likely, the interpretation is not about you; rather, it is about how the other party has learned to interpret.
2	**Interdependencies**	Anger over unkept promises and commitments, in effect, tends to draw action and emotion together, confusing what was promised and did not happen with how you have been conditioned to interpret disappointment. My counsel is to separate others' failure from *your* expectations. First, manage yourself; then, deal with others.
3	**Self-interest**	Self-interest frames issues as right and wrong, to diffuse such positioning, L-Ns must employ E-Questions to all vaguely used numbers and words. Do not accept percentages, approximations, future projections, or nonspecific words. ALWAYS get the actual numbers from which the percentages are drawn; and *always* request the specific meaning of words.
4	**Boundary crossing**	Conflict resolution requires managers to discuss how they will handle the intersections of their job functions. All matrix personnel need to recognize that conflict is an inherent part of this organizational design. No one can serve two masters at the same time. To prevent and/or resolve conflict, Project Manager and the Divisional Managers need frequent meetings.
5	**Task Relations**	Reducing conflict among groups requires the L-N to impose integration and collaborative rules, rewards, and penalties to reinforce task relations. Collaboration MUST be rewarded. The reward system of an organization strongly influences what people will do to get the reward. If an organization's reward system is based on individual incentives, then the L-N will have a very difficult time motivating groups to work together.
6	**Counterfeit Teamwork**	If there is a pattern of counterfeit teamwork in your organization, you must focus meetings on *results* and *accountability*. Results are your *only* measure of progress; therefore, require that written documentation be maintained, identifying what department and/or what person is responsible for doing what has agreed upon. Routinely send a cc on routine e-mails updating a higher authority about the meeting's direction and progress. Such e-mails should be delivered to the highest shared executive who can *enforce* teamwork. Without *enforceable* accountability, you may have a polite social atmosphere but, in fact, the organization's effectiveness is slowly deteriorating with products and services underperforming along with diminishing morale.
7	**Psychological need to win**	The psychological *need* to win requires a higher authority to intervene; one who can dictate what direction is best for the organization.

for conflict and only six potential actions. Rather, my intent is to briefly describe what regularly and repeatedly occurs in the organizations where I have worked.

METHODS AND SKILLS FOR MANAGING CONFLICT

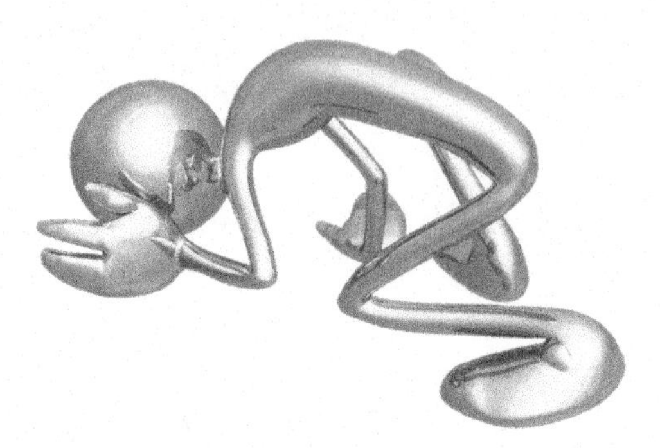

FIGURE 12.1 Listening.

Conflict cannot be resolved if L-Ns do not first understand the causes of conflict. Only when a diagnosis develops into concrete terms, you will be able to propose alternate solutions. The following methods and skills will improve one's understanding about how to manage conflict.

Ask E-Questions then, LISTEN—Listening to others express their issues usually helps release pressure so that the negotiation can proceed (Figure 12.1). Following are five suggestions to help improve listening skills:

1. Paraphrase accurately and in a nonjudgmental way your interpretation of the content and the perspective of each negotiator's position. Understanding should precede interpretation.
2. Request verbal and/or written responses from each person indicating agreement or disagreement, and specify in writing what needs to be clarified. The written word is preferred over the spoken word because this method helps separate the emotional elements from the tangible components. Clarify until there is acceptance regarding agreement or disagreement about the meaning of the words. This process may lead to an agreement, or it may lead to the profound understanding that you have come to a critical impasse. Understanding what others have communicated does not mean that you agree with them. It means you understand them.
3. Find ways, if possible, to integrate your position with your opponents' position. Integration assumes an understanding of the other party's needs.
4. Satisfying both parties' needs may be achieved through concession. Concessions have to be meaningful—that is, they must be relevant and able to be achieved in order to satisfy both parties' needs. The quality of your position will not be better than your understanding of how your opponent's position differs from yours and/or agrees with yours. You will know these differences only if you ask E-Questions and then listen to the other party's response.

Note: The United States of America is not a listening culture. It is primarily a culture that makes statements of position. However, track the following logic: Question: "Is knowledge considered a source of power?" If you said "yes," then the next question is: "What is talking?" Answer: Talking is giving away power. The primary objective of a strategic negotiation is not to tell others what you know. That is giving away power. The primary objective is to *understand what you do not know.* This involves asking questions and then authentically listening to the answers.

Listening requires intellectual humility. Intellectual humility assumes that we realize that no one person can know everything, see everything, understand everything, etc. That is why we should ask questions more than making statements.

Graduated Concessions—During the negotiation, slow down and take one-step at a time. Begin with a small concession that each negotiator could take that would be a gesture of both sides' good faith, which represents a desire to manage the conflict so as to reach agreement. The gesture should be large enough so that it can be interpreted as a desire to negotiate.The gesture should also be small enough that if only one side follows through, it would not make the other side weak or vulnerable. The concession being offered should be exact, specific, and explicit in communicating a reduction in conflict (Figure 12.2).

FIGURE 12.2 Graduated concessions.

- If possible, publicly declare that the concession is deliberately being offered to lessen discord.
- Select a specific time or schedule when the concession will be completed.
- Invite the other side to reciprocate in some specified form at the same time, schedule, or deadline.
- Each side should act on giving their concession without expecting the other side to reciprocate.

THREE KEYS TO UNDERSTANDING OTHER'S PERSPECTIVES AND THEIR POSITIONS

Key #1: It is common to misunderstand the motivations behind an opponent's actions. This is because *we tend to judge ourselves by our intentions and judge others by their actions.* This usually results in a conflict where people are not clear about what the conflict is about. A common error is to assume that we know others' intentions. We cannot know this because intentions are invisible and unique to each person (Figure 12.3).

Key #2: Others' resistance to our ideas is often a complete mystery. In order to understand an opponent's position, we must attempt to understand the conflict from his/her perspective. This requires that you be detached (nondefensive

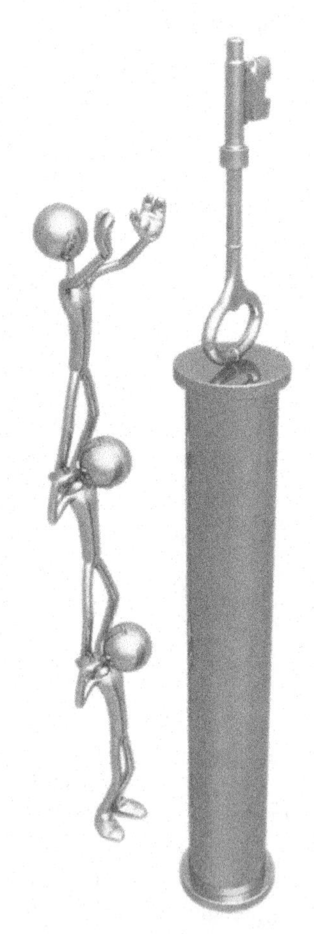

FIGURE 12.3 Three keys to understanding.

and impartial) from your efforts to understand the conflict. Try arguing for your opponent's side of the issue. Communicate what you are doing so they understand and persuade them to take a comparable perspective (to argue your side of the issue). One note of warning: viewing the negotiation from another's viewpoint may result in changing your position!

Key #3: Conflict management—an assessment of both parties' similar *and* different interests. It requires conceding some of the conflicting interests so that the parties can build common benefits, concerns, advantages, and needs. This is easier to think about than it is to do because impartially it requires self-control and emotional maturity.

SUGGESTIONS FOR DISARMING DISAGREEMENTS: ASK E-QUESTIONS

Most conflict is not caused by a persons' desire to provoke conflict. Rather, most people are unaware that what they have said and/or done, or not said and did not do, could have in any way contributed to the conflict. The fact that we unintentionally contribute to a conflict is one reason that we quarrel. Discovering that others have interpreted our words and actions differently than what we intended is usually a complete surprise to us. What this means is that we did not understand the assumptions behind questions and/or statements that have been made. The incentive for asking E-Questions is to clarify misunderstandings. Clarification should be pursued with the purpose to win.

The skill of asking questions includes: knowing when to use open-ended questions (exploring) versus closed questions (controlling). Using questions is a risk reduction strategy. When someone is emotively stimulated into a conflict disposition, asking them questions is one approach that helps them calm down; and once calmed, be able to listen. When we talk too much in an atmosphere of conflict, it frequently results in arousing further disagreement.

After asking E-Questions, listen with the purpose of understanding the other party's point of view. The purpose for listening includes clarifying issues and identifying differences among positions. Listening may help determine whether you are in a Kansas or a Chicago environment. The challenge of effective listening is suspending the impulse to defend ourselves when others may be accusing you of things you did not intend. Emotions are not based on reason. It is common to be emotionally inconsistent. In spite of this, understanding does not imply agreement. One challenge of effective listening is to understand the rationale of someone while you are in the conflict situation. This involves: knowing how to listen to the meaning behind one's words, knowing what to listen to, and not merely paraphrasing their words back to them. Here are three suggestions.

1. **Preface a statement with a question so as to not stimulate an argument**—For example, say, I want to ask you a question, but first I want to get my thoughts out, and then I would like to hear your viewpoint. Is that

acceptable? This phrase lets a person know that you want to hear their added value. It also asserts that they please "hold their comments" until you get your thoughts out.

2. **Disarm the impulse to disagree or interrupt**—*What is the meaning of an interruption?* Interruptions are signals that a person may be so value deficit that they are compelled to interrupt you in order to assert their value. It may also be that they are afraid they are going to forget what they want to say.
   - **a.** This happens, ask them to hold their question or statement and write it down.
   - **b.** If you perceive that they are experiencing impatience or a value deficit, then assertively repeat your question as a statement. For example, "I thought you agreed to let me get my thoughts out first, and then I would listen to your thoughts. Is that correct?" If they agree, you continue. If they do not agree and/or cannot control their interruptions, you may need to delay the conversation or take a break. This may not be advantageous if this is your supervisor.
   - **c.** Another method to disarm the impulse to disagree or interrupt is to precede what you are going to say with this simple phrase, *as you know*—and then make your statement. By using this phrase, you are crediting the other person with already knowing what you are going to say and most often this disarms their need to interrupt. In addition, this phrase may increase others' willingness to listen to you.
3. **Clarify Each Party's Position in Writing**—Most people judge themselves by their intentions and judge others by their actions; yet, most conflicts are contributed to by both parties. However, in the heat of the moment most people insist that they had *nothing to do* with contributing to the conflict. They might even *swear* that they did not contribute to the conflict as much as the other party. Defensiveness will not resolve a conflict. Clarifying each party's conflict story involves communicating in specific written statements. Their written comments should focus on how each party would prefer to come to a decision about resolving the situation. *Why in writing?* Writing forces intense conflict to be less emotional, more specific, and logical. If the atmosphere becomes intense, you should write *their* story as you understand it; and, while writing, ask the other party to slow down, pause for a moment, and write their thoughts. Writing lets everyone let go of trying to remember what has been said in order to retrieve it later; and, it allows you to control the escalation of conflict. People are more careful about what they say when they realize you are writing it down. Another effective strategy is to write on a whiteboard. This improves collective memory and eliminates repetitions that can become points of frustration. Last, make sure you are accurate when you write things down. To do so you may say, "Would you please repeat what you said so I can write this down accurately?" This results in making the respondent become more mindful of what they are saying while simultaneously checking for understanding (Box 12.1).

Box 12.1 Three Exercises That Help Diagnose Conflict

1. **Role Reversal**—an opportunity to experience walking in another person's shoes. It is useful in understanding specific misinterpretations. This process is most successful when, coupled with the data and information, an emotive understanding of the other person's position is attained. Switching positions with your opponent can do this. Spend a specified period presenting their position as if you were them, and have the opponent spend a specified period presenting your position, as if they were you. Temporarily argue your opponent's position. This may result in insight into your opponents' perspective, and change your understanding about the issues being negotiated. However, it is important to state that this process will not automatically result in an agreement. It may improve the recognition that the two positions they are advocating are actually incompatible. Role reversal may in fact sharpen the areas of incompatibility.
2. **Perception Exchange**—perception is difficult to objectify. One method of objectifying issues is through each side writing out their positions and exchanging written documents. Following is a recommended six-step written procedure. Each negotiator is asked to separately respond in writing to each of the following questions:
   a. Describe how they see their own position, and themselves.
   b. Describe how the other side appears from their position.
   c. State how they think the other side would describe them.
   d. State how they think the other party sees themselves.
   e. After writing, each side exchanges their written information.
   f. Discussion then centers on what is similar, and what differences require clarification and understanding. This often saves time, money, and helps preserve the relationship.
3. **Looking Glass**—This process involves the use of a third party. Use the same questions as described in the above Perception Exchange. Establish an oral interview setting where both parties talk with each other in the presence of a third party. The success indicator for this format is that the third party must maintain control of the environment, and encourage each side to listen to each other. If this kind of control cannot be achieved, then this technique will not succeed.

CLOSURE

You need to know where you are in the conflict process. The idea is that people are less able or willing to resolve conflict at the beginning stages of conflict than at its closure.

Three Stages of the Grieving Process

Readiness to resolve conflict is often attached to one of three phases of the grieving process:

1. Denial re: something you have invested so much in—ending
2. Anger re: confusion and/or distress over unresolved conflict
3. Acceptance—of a new beginning.

Conflict has a beginning and a closing. Conflict management involves knowing when, and when not to, engage in discussing a conflict.

Three Predispositions for Closure

The three predispositions for closure may be a need or not be a need, depending upon how one has been conditioned to resolve closure to some kinds of conflict. In reality, some people *do not need* to engage in closure. For example, in the ending of a relationship, or a nonclosure person, the relationship is over and there is no need to talk it over or say good-bye. They just end it. On the other hand, some people need closure. In the example of ending a relationship, if they are a "need for closure" person, they need to talk it out and have formal moment where both parties say good-bye. In these two examples, one person (say the no need for closure person) experiences a "satisfying" closure to the relationship by ending it. In contrast, the other person (the need for closure person) experiences a very dissatisfying end to the relationship. In fact, they may never be able to get closure without a formal ending.

Following are three predispositions related to Closure. Each is a predisposition because it is a need. For people in constant conflict, it is suggested that they undo their need for closure and reframe it as a *preference*—the view that all three closures are able to be selected based upon the context of the conflict (e.g., an alternative rather than a basic human "need").

1. *Satisfactory Closure*, which means conflict is resolvable. In other words, a conflict doesn't interrupt the ability of people who have had a conflict to get their job done. Therefore, intervention needs to be conducted (Figure 12.4).

FIGURE 12.4 Satisfactory closure.

2. *Dissatisfactory Closure*, which means an effort is made to resolve a conflict, but there is a "hangover" effect. Usually, a "hangover" effect continues in passive-aggressive behaviors. Such behaviors look like *periodic reminders* of another person's previous "offensive actions." A competitive *cold-war* attitude remains that keeps the conflict "open" but not "hot" (Figure 12.5).

FIGURE 12.5 Dissatisfactory closure.

3. *NonClosure*, which means a conflict is not (and may never be) resolved. This is the most difficult of all conflict issues. The most frequently offered advice is to learn to let go. This is easier to say that it is to achieve. Why is it so difficult? A few reasons are: (1) closure requires the passage of time. It has been said, but I do not by whom, "that *time heals all wounds*." However, if friends, colleagues, and family frequently ask you, "how are you doing"—in reference to a conflict—then, caringly without being aware, they continually reset the clock *backwards*. This may cause you to *reexperience* that particular conflict. This caring inquiry often prolongs the closure of that conflict (Figure 12.6). For example, see Box 12.2.

FIGURE 12.6 Nonclosure.

Box 12.2 Sometimes There Are No Words

A friend's spouse died in an automobile accident. I went to comfort him during this deeply grieving time. I sat for hours and said nothing. Months later, he said to me, "Thank you for being with me during my grieving about my wife's death. I can't tell you how much that meant to me." I never said a word because this was during the first stage of grieving. There are no words at this stage. I was just there. However, about a year following my friend's loss, he was ready to hear words of perspective. The important point here is that timing is everything during the grieving process.

When I am trying to bring closure to a serious conflict, I respectfully ask friends and family and concerned inquirers to not ask me about that particular conflict for about 1–2 months. This provides me time to let go. I know what you might be saying to yourself, "But, I wake up in the middle of my sleep thinking about the loss or the conflict." Our minds will incessantly run the conflict scenario through our brains again and again if we let it. If we persist in actively repeating those conflict conversations, we allow our mind to believe that it is beneficial to keep the conflict fresh and alive via repeated conversations.

My experience is that in time this will decline. However, it will likely decline more quickly if you do not talk about the conflict for 1–2 months. Desensitizing our thinking patterns requires the discipline to not relive past conflict. How do I do this? At times, I say just say "*NO*" to my mind's habit pattern to reexperience the conflict (sometimes the continuous obsession of reliving something is referred to as *perseverating*). The best advice I can offer you is to "*stop it!*"

Section V

Hidden Traps

Chapter 13

Closing Words: Hidden Traps

The greatest vulnerability is to think we are not vulnerable.

Ken Sylvester

Organizations that do not change, do not survive. If an organization is to survive, it's strategy must be integrated into a fluent and synchronized focus. It is the act of collaborative integrations that causes strategy to be advantageous. Fragmentation causes organizations to fail. Simply put, the way an organization's leadership thinks reflects its success or failure.

In business, there are no broad-spectrum answers, formulas, or techniques (AFTs) to answer the many questions and challenges that arise. A Leader-Negotiator (L-N) is not effective if their source of leadership advice is everyone else and not themselves. Why not? Because, if strategy were a simple search for AFTs, it would apply to all competitors. If this were true, then every company would have the same strategic advantage, which implies no strategic advantage at all. Strategy is the relevant factor in achieving effective outcomes. Yet, how leaders reason is often overlooked when assessing leadership competence.

There are numerous ways to think. However, context determines whether or not one's thinking is advantageous or disadvantageous—relevant. Strategic advantage involves selecting a strategy that is most favorable given the context. No single strategy is adequate in all situations. Alternate ways to think are essential to success if one seeks freedom of choice. No choice, no freedom.

A person is not free to do that which they cannot imagine. Effective Questioning is a reasoning tool that helps stimulate an L-N's imagination; it helps protect L-Ns from getting caught in many of the following 10 traps.

This book is about enhancing L-N reasoning, therefore, the following information identifies 10 common leadership traps that can act like a wall around one's mind. The problem is, they are often invisible. Effective leader must break through walls to build bridges in order to craft strategy.

TEN TRAPS THAT INFLUENCE AN L-N'S THINKING

1. **Anchoring**: Giving disproportionate weight to information we receive first, while ignoring relevant information that surfaces over time

Negotiating in the Leadership Zone.

2. **Framing**: The mental box used when we first frame a problem, which then determines the resultant decision-making process
3. **Rationalization**: Seeking out information supporting an existing position and discounting opposing information
4. **Overconfidence**: Overestimating the accuracy of forecasts and subsequent plans
5. **Generalization**: Specific experiences that become generalized to make them universally true apart from their particular, original context
6. **Tradition**: Biases that favor maintaining the status quo, even when better alternatives exist
7. **aRousal**: Leads us to give undue weight to dramatic, emotional, exciting events
8. **Abstract Comparison**: Any idea that suggests a comparison against some invisible yardstick
9. **Psychological Cul-de-sac**: Inclines us to perpetuate the failures or successes of the past by continually repeating the reasoning habits of the past
10. **Playing it safe**: Overcautious and risk-adverse when making estimates about uncertain events.

(An Acronymic Memory Device for the 10 Traps: **A-FROG-TRAPP**)

TRAP #1: Anchoring

Placing disproportionate weight on the first information received. Initial first impressions, assessments, or known facts can anchor all subsequent thoughts and judgments to one's first impression. Once Anchored, the mind will resist considering other possibilities or viewpoints. It closes down the mind's exploration for alternate viewpoints. For example, when you hear the words, "I cannot think of any other way to do this," you are observing the Anchoring effect. Once Anchored, the mind literally does not seek additional options.

> *A great many people think they are thinking when they are merely rearranging their prejudices.*
>
> William James

Anchors range from very simple to highly complex. Anchors link memory and thinking into habitual reasoning patterns. Most Anchors develop slowly over time without a person's conscious awareness. Most of these Anchors are firmly established by early adulthood (2–5 years of age). Once a person's mind accepts a particular Anchor, they can become doggedly locked into a kind of "thought box" (Box 13.1).

TRAP #2: Framing

Mental reference points influence our reasoning. The way a problem is framed (the act of conceptualizing an issue so that it is defined and understood within a

Box 13.1 Counters to the Anchoring Trap

1. **Consider other interpretations:** Think about the problem from diverse perspectives. Leaders should be careful not to eliminate alternative explanations too soon. Generate as many interpretations of the evidence as possible before settling on the most likely one.
2. **Buy time:** Think about the problem so that you avoid being anchored by others' ideas. Buying time to think is invaluable.
3. **Be careful to avoid being anchored by your own source of counsel:** Before you tell others your ideas, estimates, and/or strategies, ask them what they think. If you dominate the conversation or disclose too much, your thoughts may eliminate potential opportunities or solutions generated by your team.
4. **Be open-minded:** Seek information and opinions from a variety of people to expand your thinking. Although we all benefit from supportive colleagues, we also benefit from communication with adversaries and even enemies who will express their thoughts without any consideration of your relationship and/or position.
5. **Think through your position:** Know what you want so as not to be unduly anchored by others' initial suggestions. At the same time, look for opportunities to use anchors to your own advantage. Make sure your position gets you want.

desired context) can profoundly influence the way a problem is understood. The kinds of things that typically capture our attention are the unusual, the odd, the exceptional, the spectacular, or the dramatic. The kind of things that rarely get our attention are the routine, the obvious, the ordinary, the cultural modus operandi that are so much a part of everyday life that they evade our notice. Culturally conditioned reflexes that produce "knee-jerk" reactions. A knee-jerk reaction is the opposite of contextual intelligence (Box 13.2).

A person is not free to do that which they cannot imagine.

Box 13.2 Counters to the Framing Trap

1. **First, recognize the frames exist; then try to reframe the problem in multiple ways:** Look for the opposite side of a frame (e.g., risk-avoidance is the opposite of risk-seeking). If someone says, this is "right," you need to consider what would make it "wrong." See the substantive issues from multiple perspectives.
2. **Write out or record your thinking:** Writing requires that you clarify your thinking. Writing clarifies ones thinking, emotions, and intuition. Write how your thinking might change if the frame changed. This requires the discipline to stop verbalizing and to write.
3. **Examine the way the problem has been framed:** When others recommend decisions, challenge them with opposite frames. These are often "what if" statements that question the opposite point of view.

TRAP #3: Rationalizing

The psychological need to win, to be right, and/or the fear of losing leads people to seek information that supports their existing point of view, while avoiding and resisting information that contradicts it.

> *I believe it to be true.*
> *Therefore, it must be true.*
> *Wouldn't you agree?*

When seeking counsel from others, they give us their particular viewpoint about a particular situation. What else could they do? Biases give too much credibility to supporting information and too little to conflicting information.

There are two cognitive forces at work in this trap: (1) our tendency to subconsciously decide what we want to do before we figure out if it is the best thing to do, and (2) our inclination to be more engaged by things we like than by things we dislike. As a result, we are often drawn to information that supports our preferences (Box 13.3).

Box 13.3 Counters to the Rationalizing Trap

1. **Check to see whether you are examining all the evidence with equal rigor**: Avoid the tendency to accept confirming evidence without question.
2. **Select someone you respect to play the devil's advocate**: Ask them to argue against the decision you are contemplating. Do this until the decision becomes obvious, then stop.
3. **Ask yourself if there is another alternate viewpoint**: Consider this question with an open mind.
4. **Be candid with yourself about your motives**: Are you gathering information to help you make an intelligent choice? Alternatively, are you just looking for evidence that confirms what you think you'd like to do?
5. **Don't ask leading questions**: Seek the advice of others without inviting confirming evidence. In addition, if you find that an adviser always seems to support your point of view, find a new adviser. Don't surround yourself with "yes-people." "Yes-people" seem helpful until their advice goes bad.

TRAP #4: Overconfidence

Most people are skilled at making estimates about things that are certain. Years of practice condition our minds to become comfortable with making judgments about circumstances that are certain. However, making estimates about uncertain events requires different reasoning. Our minds are not as finely calibrated for making estimates in the face of uncertainty.

> *There is no question that I will win.*

Although most L-Ns estimate and/or make judgments about events daily, we tend to be overconfident about our level of accuracy. Overconfidence can lead to errors in judgment, and in turn, result in negative outcomes. Counters for the overconfidence trap are included under TRAP #7.

TRAP #5: Generalization

Generalizations become a trap when you take specific experiences and oversimplify them. In so doing, you probably delete important information or alter the context. Deletions occur where details and context have been omitted. Distortions occur when we selectively take details out of the context and make them appear to be the whole story. Both deletions and distortions lead to misleading generalizations.

There are times when it is important to generalize. Generalized statements consist of words such as—no one, everyone, never, always, all, and nothing. These kinds of words generalize specific experiences to make them true in all circumstances. One way of countering generalizations is to use their generalizations as a mirror back to them by asking questions such as: "Always?" "No one?"

Mirroring challenges the communicator with the ownership of their statement. This can generate conflict if the person does not want to take ownership of their statement. One danger of this trap is that once a generalization is accepted as a universal truth, it prevents exploration of other alternative viewpoints. This can undermine the integrity of an outcome.

TRAP #6: Tradition

Frequently, L-Ns believe that they make enlightened and wise decisions. However, research has revealed that the biases that all people acquire influence the decisions. For as much as people talk about change and the need for change, people demonstrate a strong bias toward maintaining the status quo.

> *One of the great powers that a leader possesses is the ability to see the same thing from multiple perspectives.*

The Tradition Trap is powerful because it falsely preserves the illusion of security and delays the anxiety associated with change. Therefore, people who avoid or resist taking action because they have a habit of maintaining the status quo, frame changes in terms of how to prevent change rather than how to support change. In a world where change is essential for survival, traditional reasoning may become a postponement of the inevitable (Box 13.4).

Box 13.4 Counters to the Tradition Trap

1. **Do not pick Tradition just because it is the easier choice**: The easier choice can be a formula for short-term security and long-term failure.
2. **Remind yourself of your objectives**: Examine how the organization would be advanced by the status quo. You may find that traditional values act as barriers to your goals.
3. **Do not allow Tradition to become your only alternative**: Identify other options and use them as counters, carefully evaluating all the advantages and disadvantages. Is there only one way to do what you need to do? If the answer is "yes," then you have a deficit in creativity.
4. **Ask yourself these kinds of questions**: Would you choose the current alternative if, in fact, it weren't the status quo? Are you fearful of the consequences of change? Are you afraid of the effort and amount of energy it would take to change? ("Fatigue makes cowards of us all."—Vince Lombardi).
5. **Avoid exaggerations**: There can be a tendency to overstate the effort or cost involved in switching from the status quo to a new position. I cannot overstate this enough!
6. **Remember that the desirability of the status quo will change over time**: When comparing alternatives, always evaluate them in terms of the future as well as the present (There was a time when the steam engine was the future. However, not now).
7. **Generate several alternatives that are superior**: Don't default to a Tradition just because you're having a hard time selecting the best alternative. Make a decision. The best way to find out if you're moving in the wrong direction is to start moving in a direction. Usually, people will let you know in the wrong direction.

TRAP #7: aRousal

A significant life event can rouse our thinking and emotions. These arousals can cause us to view the world and our future through the lens of that circumstance (Box 13.5).

> *As a child, I fell off of my bicycle.*
> *It was at that moment that I knew I was not an athlete.*

TRAP #8: Abstract Comparisons

Comparative words include yardstick words like—more, beyond, less, trivial, better, preferred, superior, worse, and inferior, below par, fewer, good, satisfactory, badly, poorly—anything that suggests an evaluation against some standard. The difficulty in understanding what these abstract comparisons mean occurs when the yardstick is omitted. Typically, in the communication process, the yardstick is not stated. It is left to others' interpretation. The use

Box 13.5 Counters to the Overconfidence and aRousal Traps

1. **Develop a disciplined approach**: Discipline your mind to test your own thinking when making forecasts and judging probabilities. Ask yourself, "Why that outcome, and why no others?"
2. **To reduce the effects of overconfidence, consider the extremes**: Consider the low and high end of the possible range of values. This will help you avoid being anchored by an initial estimate.
3. **Use your imagination**: Try to imagine circumstances where a decision would fall below your low or above your high, and adjust your range accordingly.
4. **Challenge estimates**: Ask for the precise source of all estimates.
5. **Always state your estimates honestly**: Explain to anyone who will be using them that they have not been altered. Emphasize the need for honest (documented) input to anyone who will be supplying you with estimates.
6. **Test estimates over a reasonable range to assess their impact**: Take a second look at the more sensitive estimates. Are you testing the impact against both the negatives and the positives?
7. **Carefully examine your assumptions**: To minimize the distortion caused by Trigger Mechanisms, ask what assumptions you are making to ensure that they're not unduly influencing you through the impact of your reminiscence effect. Children see the world differently than adults. When did you form this memory?
8. **Get actual statistics whenever possible**: Averages, means, and mediums are not concrete statistics. For example, a 100% increase could be increasing the quantity of "one" to the quantity of "two." This is convincing in distinction to the percentage, but may be insignificant in terms of the actual number.
9. **Do not be trapped by impressions**: Demand of yourself clear articulated thoughts. Yet, demanding mental precision can trigger feelings of frustration, anger, and hypersensitivity. Ultimately an accurately thought out position.

of adjectives is a part of the English language that describes objects. Comparisons almost always take the form of adjectives. For example, measures of job performance commonly use adjective-based comparisons. The question is, compared to what standard or person? For example, "We want to have 'fewer customer complaints.'" The counter is, "Fewer complaints than what?" or, "We want 'more sales leads.'" The counter is, "More sales than what or than whom?"

> *You will need to do much better than this, said the manager.*
> *How much better than this must I do? said the employee?*

TRAP #9: Psychological Cul-de-sac of the Past

Another trap is to make choices in a way that justifies past choices, even when the past choices no longer seem relevant. Former solutions were made to answer past problems. When those problems have been solved and new scenarios challenge the organization, the past decisions become unwanted decisions. If past decisions are no longer deemed relevant to the present context, then we should cut our losses by letting go of past "cul-de-sacs" and move toward the future (Box 13.6).

> *We have already started climbing the mountain on this side. There is no logical reason to think about climbing it from any other point of view.*

TRAP #10: Playing it safe

This trap takes the form of being overcautious or overly prudent. When faced with high-risk decisions, people may tend to "just be on the safe side," One way that people have overcompensated for the tendency to be overcautious is to develop an approach often termed "worst-case scenario." Using this scenario, decision-makers construct the worst possible conditions under which a product or a decision could be enacted, even though the odds of those circumstances actually occurring are negligible. This approach can add enormous cost with low to no practical benefit. The point is that too much caution can sometimes be as unproductive as too little.

Box 13.6 Counters to the Psychological Cul-de-Sac Trap

1. **Seek out heterogeneous advice**: Listen to the views of people who are objectively uninvolved with earlier decisions and are unlikely to be committed to the past.
2. **Ask yourself, "Does admitting to an earlier mistake disturb you?"** Remind yourself that all decisions have unintended consequences. Even the best and most experienced people make errors in judgment. Perfectionism is an impossible taskmaster. Learn how to manage failure and cope with imperfection.
3. **Reassign responsibility**: If those in your charge are making ineffective decisions, perhaps reassigning that responsibility to someone outside the process may improve the outcome. It is possible, however, that ineffective decision-making may be related to the organization's structure and not a person's performance.
4. **Do not cultivate a culture that fears failure**: Fear can lead people to perpetuate their mistakes. In rewarding people, look at the quality of their decision-making (taking into account what was known at the time their decisions were made), not just the quality of the outcomes. It could be that the organization's culture punishes failure instead of learning from it so it does not happen again.

I recommend not to build an organization on the premise of achieving minimum standards in order to "play it safe." This is a formula for failure.

SUMMARY

Effective L-Ns must constantly think about their thinking. The more aware an L-N is of their reasoning, the more fluent their leadership effectiveness and competence, and the less likely they will be entrapped in their own thinking.

The 10 Hidden Leadership Traps are offered as a way to improve the way L-Ns reason about problem-solving, decision-making, building competent teams, managing failure, and crafting strategy. Even though we cannot completely rid ourselves of entrapment reasoning, we can construct check-and-balance disciplines into our work habits that will enhance effective leadership (Figures 13.1 and 13.2).

In summary, the 10 Traps are:

1. Giving disproportionate weight to information first received
2. Mental frames that limit perspectives and alternatives
3. Self-entrapping rationalized positions
4. Overestimating the accuracy of our calculations and consequent plans

FIGURE 13.1 The keys.

FIGURE 13.2 The door.

5. Generalizations, distortions, and deletions
6. Biases that promote the status quo
7. Giving undue weight to significant past experiences
8. Abstract comparisons
9. Perpetuating psychological cul-de-sacs
10. "Playing it safe" when making decisions.

> *"This is a good place to close this book. However, by no means is it the end; rather it is a beginning. You have been handed the keys. The door is waiting."*
>
> Ken Sylvester

Section VI

Appendices

Appendix A: Glossary of Key Terms

Accumulated mind: How a person's thinking is conditioned over time.

Alternatives: A choice between possibilities.

Ambiguity: When words or ideas are vague or uncertain.

Answers, Formulas, and Techniques (AFTs): Predetermined ways to solve problems and make decisions without consideration of context or assumptions that are unique to a particular negotiation.

Assumption: An assumption is something that is taken for granted or unquestionably accepted as true.

Attributes: Qualities or characteristics inherent in or ascribed to someone or something.

Audience: This refers to the different kinds of people that a business is marketing in order to remain in business.

Balanced Power: Power to achieve rather than power to control.

Behavior Theory: What leaders do; researchers in the 1950s thought that if they could discover what leaders and managers did on the job, the secrets of effective leadership might be revealed.

Blind spots: Inability to see all the probable options and alternatives of a negotiation.

Boundary crossing: Assigned job responsibilities that cross over into other employees' job functions.

Bureaucracy: The administrative structure of a large, complex organization; usually includes a policy driven structure that controls employee productivity through following written processes, rules, or procedures.

Catastrophize: To create a dramatized event or conjecture a traumatic calamity from a less than dramatic event.

Change: To become different or undergo alternation; To undergo transformation or transition.

Classification of Information: This refers to how the human mind interprets or categorizes information and subsequently records or files it—much like the Dewey Decimal System in libraries. This is also related to how computer systems are programmed to store and retrieve information.

Cognitive Filter: How information and experience are interpreted in human beings.

Collaboration: To work together, to cooperate; in a global context, this requires a synergistic mind-set that engenders shared vision, alliance formation, and the tolerance of ambiguity.

Common ground: A foundation of mutual understanding.

Competition: Rivalry between two or more entities striving for the same market.

Concessions: Acts of conceding or compromising in some way; persuading the other party to accept alternatives and/or solutions as a trade-off to achieving some but not all of their priorities.

Conflict: A state of disharmony or open hostility between incompatible or antithetical people, ideas, or interests; a "clash."

Context: Context explains a circumstance or event that imparts meaning and frames action; Refers to the circumstances or background of a situation that helps provide insight that helps explain what and why something happened.

Contextual intelligence: The ability to identify circumstances of a situation that provides insight into strategic planning and/or conflict management.

Convergent thinking: Involves searching for known and correct rules to find a proper solution.

Critical thinking: Thinking that is characterized by careful evaluation and judgment; this involves thinking about one's thinking (metacognition). Critical thinking may involve examining contradictory lines of reasoning and/or using different lines of reasoning to cross-examine alternatives.

Culture: The beliefs, customs, practices, and social behavior of a particular nation or people; a group of people whose shared beliefs and practices identify a particular place, class, or time to which they belong; a particular set of attitudes that characterizes a group of people.

Data collection: This refers to the various approaches used to collect information.

Decision-making: the process of making choices or reaching conclusions, especially on important political or business matters.

Deductive: To reach a conclusion by inference from a general principle or claim.

Depersonalization: Not interpreting others' words or actions as having to do with you personally.

Diplomacy: The skill and tact of managing communication and relationships between different parties.

Dissatisfactory closure: Effort is made to resolve conflict but something has been left unresolved.

Divergent thinking: Involves brainstorming in order to creatively expand alternatives in an effort to make decisions despite ambiguity.

Effective questioning: A task-oriented method of asking questions intended to uncover assumptions, thereby clarifying data, classifications of information, and arguments developed during negotiations and/or conflicts.

Emotional maturity: The ability to resist getting caught up "dancing" to other peoples' (psychological) music or drama.

Failure: The condition of not achieving the desired end results.

Fragmentation: When the sole function of a person is to do one thing only (such as the highly specialized concept from Henry Ford's original assembly line). Originally termed the "fractionalization" of jobs, this has been the core premise of the "Scientific Management" School of thought. It emphasizes "efficiency" of either low costs or time-and-motion criteria. This has been shown to increase boredom, resulting in high turnover, absenteeism, union strikes, and decreased productivity.

Frames: A frame is a mental map; a particular way of thinking within a particular context.

Framing: How communication tools such as words, metaphors, examples, diagrams, and numbers are used to design an agreement.

Gordian knot: A symbol of solving complicated problems

Group think: Tendency for all members of the group to think alike and suppress dissent.

Imperfection: Something that makes a person or thing less than perfect.

Inductive: Logic that involves reaching a conclusion based on one's observation and then generalizing that logic to produce a universal claim or principle.

Influence strategies: Intended actions that produce an effect on or modify the nature, development, or condition of a point of view, a process, or an outcome.

Integration: The act of "making into a whole" by bringing all parts together.

Interdependence: Mutually relying on or requiring the aid of another organization; The shifting of basic organizational structures and functions such that businesses must rely on or require the aid of another business for viability.

Interests: Often considered underlying interests, these are goals that underlie a disputant's aspirations and exclude consideration of values or basic human needs.

Interpretation: The unique ways that people translate others words and behavior; an explanation of the meaning or importance of something.

JABs: An acronym for judgment, attributes, and blame, that may influence one's self-image, self-worth, and efficacy of mind.

Joint goals: The combination of goals; often combining goals against a common enemy.

Leader: Any person holding a managerial or executive position of influence.

Leadership Zone (LZ): One of three Organizational Zones, characterized by thinking out of the box, complexity, ambiguity, responsibility, and bottom-line orientation.

Leadership: The ability to "pilot" an organization or division; to stimulate others to follow for the purpose of achieving a task. Also, the ability to adapt and abandon default modes of thinking when the situation demands the ability to motivate followers; and the ability to apply intellectually strategic principles to decision-making, hiring, and problem-solving.

Logic: A mode of reasoning whereby knowledge of earlier or otherwise known statements, events, or conditions is used to guide decision-making and problem-solving.

Management zone (MZ): The middle of the three Organizational Zones, where management acts as a communicator between those in the Leadership Zone and those in the Production Zone.

Management: The act, manner, or practice of supervising or controlling a business enterprise.

Manager: One who handles, controls, or directs business affairs such as resources and expenditures.

Manipulation: To indirectly, deviously, or exploitatively influence, manage, use, or control others or a situation.

Motivation: There are eight major theories that explain approaches to motivate people. The eight theories are: (1) Maslow's Hierarchy of Needs, (2) McClelland's Need for Achievement, (3) Alderfer's ERG theory, (4) Herzberg's Two-Factor Theory, (5) Equity Theory, (6) Reinforcement Theory, (7) Expectancy Theory, (8) Goal Setting Theory, (8) and the Reward System Theory.

Multitasking: The ability to manage a lot of things simultaneously.

Negotiation: A problem-solving process in which interested parties identify their differences and attempt to reach an agreement.

Negotiation: The changing of any relationship on a continuum spanning contractual and routine resource allocation to negotiating major organizational change.

Negotiator: A leader who interacts with anything that has to do with connecting internal and/or external organizational systems.

Nonclosure: Conflict that is not resolved and may never be resolved.

Organizational intelligence: The ability to figure out how the specialized functions of an organization can be holistically understood.

Organizational puzzle: When various units or divisions within an organization present perplexing or confounding dilemmas and/or engender confusion or bewilderment as to roles and responsibilities. In addition, not all of the "puzzle" pieces are seamlessly connected or integrated, which in turn is one cause of organizational conflict.

Perception: Perception is the understanding or view people have of things in the world around them. It involves why people viewing the same situation "see" it differently; it is why people viewing the same situation give different reasons for its occurrence; it is why the receiver of a message hears it quite differently from the way the sender intended it; it is why different perceptions of behavior and its causes likely affect a managers' evaluation of their employees' behavior. Often, this results in **perceptual disagreements**.

Perfectionism: A propensity to be displeased with anything that is not "right."

Perfectionism: The doctrine that perfection is possible in human beings and a rigorous rejection of anything less than perfect.

Personal power: Knowledge of one's self, an awareness of one's strengths and vulnerabilities, and the willpower to persist under stress.
Perspective: Point of view.
Persuasion: The ways that leaders influence others to achieve a task.
Policy: Written guidelines and/or rules that controls or influences what a company does.
Politeness barrier: Violation of or disregard for showing consideration, tact, and/or the observance of acceptable social protocols.
Power and influence theory: Leaders exert power and followers react; researchers in the 1980s assumed that leadership flows from the top down.
Power: Deliberate influence and control over a person or surroundings.
Problem-solving: Finding a solution to a situation via a method or process.
Production zone (PZ): The bottom of the three Organizational Zones; this is the level of the organization where goods and services are "packed and shipped."
Professional power: An LN's knowledge base and expertise.
Psychological Cul-de-Sac: Boxed-in thinking that limits an LN's ability to generate alternatives.
Psychological fear: The L-N's negotiation skills to use E-Questions to bring into focus the consequences and implications of not negotiating. The potential intent of using psychological fear is twofold: (1) to restore the negotiation toward a diplomatic environment, or (2) to engage in a period of hostile relations using dominating, Win–Lose tactics.
Questions: Expressions of inquiry.
Reason: To draw conclusions or inferences from observations, experiences of facts.
Reframe: Redirects the focal point of a negotiation; that is, it directs the viewer to consider certain features while ignoring or not being able to perceive a particular characteristic.
Relational thinking: The discipline through which we view ourselves and organizations as part of the whole.
Relevance: Having a bearing on or connection with something; pertinent to the matter at hand.
Resources: The human, physical, and financial assets that are the energy of an organization. These resources are both tangible and intangible.
Risk: The possibility of suffering harm or loss; Usually, risk involves the statistical chance that an action would pose a threat, resulting in a failure of some kind.
Satisfactory closure: Conflict is resolved.
Self-control: A person's ability to maintain disciplined composure while under stress; being in command of one's internal triggers or "hot buttons."
Self-entrapment: When one's thoughts and/or behaviors act as a trap of themselves, controlling that person to only doing what their thoughts and behavior dictate; confinement without alternatives.

Shared goals: Each party receives different rewards but each party gains advantages by working together.

Silo conflict: Refer to conflict as described under the term "Tribalism."

Situation leadership theory: A theory that assumes that a particular situation determines the leader's behavior; researchers in the 1970s thought that leaders are at their best in a particular context. This theory is also referred to as "Contingency" or "Path-Goal Theory."

Situation power: The combined wisdom and judgment needed to select appropriate negotiation strategies and tactics within a given situation or context.

Sorting: To arrange or classify.

Specialization: To concentrate on a particular activity or specific function.

Stratagems: A scheme or maneuver designed to provide an advantage in order to achieve an objective.

Strategic advantage: Selecting directions that are most favorable to a given situation.

Strategic planning: A process of selecting from alternative courses of action, matching that with the available resources, and combining these in a way that will most effectively achieve the objective; Intended action toward an organizational goal or objective.

Strategy: Strategy is characterized by a combination of inputs, processes, and outcomes. Strategy provides a framework within which to make decisions and to measure progress. Strategic thinking: the art of outdoing an adversary (and knowing that the adversary is trying to do the same).

Synergistic opportunity: Increasing the size and ideas of the "pie"; putting joint goals ahead of self-interest.

Tactics: Tools for how to achieve one's objective.

Team competence: Integration of an organization to work as a whole; a combination of people and/or job functions that work together.

Territorialism: In an organizational context, it refers to a protectionistic approach designed to keep others outside one's divisional or managerial territory.

The Leader-as-Negotiator Theory: The disciplines of leadership and negotiation are inseparable; the behavioral attributes necessary for effective leadership are complementary to behavioral attributes for negotiators. This theory contains three precepts, signified by the three parts of the LN Symbol: (1) Accumulated conditioning has the power to control or box-in an LN (middle square); (2) Unexamined assumptions, biases, prejudices, and premises may confine, encircle, and subjugate an LN's thinking process into a "psychological cul-de-sac" (inner arrow); and, (3) Willingness to be open to new ideas and perspectives beyond one's own (through the use of Effective Questioning) can sharpen an LN's awareness of others' and one's own thinking in order to optimize outcomes for all parties in a negotiation.

Theory: A theory is a set of ideas stated as principles (or precepts); derived to explain a phenomenon or phenomena; used to assist in comprehension or judgment and/or to guide action.

Thinking errors: This refers to the imperfect functions of the human brain, such as the "false memory" syndrome.

Trait theory: Personal attributes are what determine leaders' effectiveness; researchers in the 1930s thought that if they could discover leadership traits, that they could discover the secrets of leadership.

Tribalism: Refers to organizational members assuming that their roles and responsibilities are the only ones of importance and others are of lesser importance.

Trust: Involves how much can be believed; a necessary condition in securing cooperation and effective communication.

Values: Deeply held beliefs about the importance or moral integrity of a goal, a position, aspiration, and or underlying interests.

War: The act of using whatever tactics are considered realistic with the purpose to dominate another party. In reality, there is no universally agreed upon concept of war.

Win–Lose: A negotiation philosophy that seeks an outcome that benefits only the self-interests of one party.

Win–Win: A negotiation philosophy that seeks an outcome that benefits all parties.

Zone blindness: The condition whereby each of the three organizational "zones" concentrates on their own needs, interests, problems—so much, so that they are unaware that other zones exist or are interdependent with them.

Appendix B

EQ ASSESSMENT: THE NIAGARA–MEDINA EXERCISE

The purpose of Effective Questioning (EQ) involves examining undetected assumptions that influence how information is interpreted and as a result, used to develop strategic plans. The following analysis is based on the Niagara–Medina Exercise located at the end of Chapter 5. The Niagara–Medina Exercise was developed to advance effective reasoning by demonstrating how numerous assumptions go unquestioned in everyday conversation and problem-solving. This document reveals 40 unquestioned assumptions from that exercise; in addition, the nine assumptions that lead to thinking errors are noted.

The Assessment of 40 EQ Assumptions: Each line corresponds to the Niagara–Medina Case Study in Chapter 5.

"Niagara Manufacturing is a large corporation that uses..."

- How large is the Niagara organization? Large in comparison to what?
- Is the large size of this corporation significant or relevant to your assessment?
- Does the word large assume too many possible meanings to not be informative?

EQ assumptions: Previous knowledge, context, audience.

Case in point: If the word "large" indicates something of value or advantage, then specify what that value or advantage would be in economic terms.

That uses "thousands of hinges of various sizes..."

- How *many* hinges and how many various sizes does Medina use?
- Is the term *thousands* too vague to be of *measurable* significance?

EQ assumption: Assessment-measures.

Case in point: How would this be interpreted if the quantity of *thousands* meant 2001 hinges? Or, 1000 hinges? What does the ambiguous quantity of *thousands* imply? Does the quantity of hinges purchased influence your price? Are the sizes referred to the sizes you can use? The numerical price breaks could be a negotiated item. **For example**: Specifically, what are the numerical price breaks? Do the price breaks refer to each order? or to the annual quantity purchased?

Various sizes "for over a decade..."

- Precisely, how much time is over a decade *implying*? 10 years? 20 years?
- Is the sweeping statement of over a decade precise enough for a contractual agreement?

EQ assumption: Assessment-measures and time.

Case in point: The imprecision of this statement is so vague that it provides no informative value. So ask, would you clarify what you mean by over a decade? From what years to what years?

"the *current*..."

- What does the term *current* specifically refer to? Could it mean, "recent" in measurable terms such as—Hours? Minutes? Days? Weeks? Months? Years? Present? Today? Yesterday? The other day? In progress? Other?

EQ assumption: Time—the concept of time is too vague to be informative.

Case in point: Somebody might say to you—"I will get back to you in just a few moments." However, their idea of "a few moments" might be tomorrow. So, you might say, "Let's set a time and day when you will be getting back to me."

The "Niagara buyer has purchased all of Niagara's hinges from the Medina Hinge Company and the current Medina sales representative..."

- Can this statement be interpreted in any other way? If so, then will the interpretation of this statement be accurately understood? or does it open the interpretive door for additional interpretations? Is this important?
- Is this statement *inferring* that there is a motive for their business practices? Could an inference be interpreted in different ways?

EQ assumptions: Assessment-measures and context may assume a personal relationship rather than just a business association.

"40% of the Medina seller's total dollar sales..."

- What is 40% of the sellers *total dollars*? This is a *percentage* and not a number.
- *Over what period of time does the percentage* 40% *become informative? Has it been* 40% *for a day? A month? Over* 10 *years?*
- Is 40% an average? A mode? A median? These are translations and each mathematical approach changes the meaning of the actual numbers.

EQ assumption: Assessment-measures—percentages are an interpretation of numbers—but are not the actual numbers. Always get the actual numbers.

For example, a 100% increase could be an increase of one item to two items.

The Niagara buyer "purchases other items", from Medina...

- What are the other purchased items? Could the *other items* be of negotiation interest or advantage to you?
- How many other items? Five? One-thousand? A million? How many? Could other items influence the context of how this situation is interpreted?
- Could *other items* represent a bargaining position when combined with future purchases of the hinges? If the numerical quantity of the *other items* is sizable, that number could represent a *price break* when combined with hinge orders.
- If the other items exceeded current hinge sales, would this be an important piece of negotiation information?

EQ assumption: Assessment-measurement is ambiguous and needs to be clarified.

"The Medina hinge account is '30%' of the buyer's total dollar purchases..."

- 30% of what? How much is the buyers total dollars?
- Is 30% an average? A mean? A median?
- Are the buyers 30% similar to the sellers 40%? These are not similar percentages. The only similarity is that they are both percentages.

EQ assumption: As described above, 30% is an assessment-measurement.

Case in point: You cannot know what you are negotiating without the actual numbers.

For example: Would you provide me/us with the numbers from which you attained these percentages?

Total dollar purchases "over a period of time..."

- The phrase *over a period of time* could denote any period of time.
- Does the amount of time influence how this situation could be interpreted?
- Would the amount of time make a difference if the period of time were, for instance, two hours? Or, two weeks? Or, two months? Or, over a decade?
- Does this time period reflect only Medina's sales context or the all-inclusive global context of hinges?

EQ assumptions: Assessment-measures and time.

Case in point: Two hours is not a very long period of time from which to observe a financial pattern. However, 2 years might be. Is the period of time referred to characteristic of a normal period of time or is it unusual?

over a period of time "the price..."

- Is price in this context referring to the price or the cost? Is it important to define the difference between these two terms, or are they interchangeable?
- Is the price based upon a price index that is used as a basis for price comparison?

EQ assumptions: Assessment-measures and classification.

Case in point: The term "price" usually refers to what you pay to purchase something; the term "cost" refers to after you purchase something, what are the costs to service and/or maintain something.

The price "has more than kept pace with inflation..."

- What is the specific rate and pace of inflation?
- Has inflation kept pace over a specified period of time?
- How has inflation been calculated over time? A week? A Month? A Quarter? A Year?
- Did the rate of inflation occur during a normal or irregular period of time? If so, by how much?
- By how much *more* has it kept pace? What is the inflation number that supports "more"? Is this number significant? It may have kept pace but does that numerically translate into being significant?
- What inflation index, if any, is used now or has been used in the past to report that it has kept pace?

EQ assumptions: Assessment-measures and time.

Case in point: Get the numbers and not a percentage. When it is reported *that it more than kept pace with inflation*—over what period of time has it kept that pace up?

I am assuming you are getting the gist of this. From now on, take a look at the 9 EQ assumptions that result in thinking errors in Chapter 5 (Using Effective Questioning Strategically) and analyze the following statements:

"and complaints..."
"from the factory supervisors..."
"about degrading hinge quality..."
"are increasing..."
"Niagara's hinge buyer places the orders..."
the orders are placed "with the Medina chief hinge sales representative, who happens to be..."
happens to be a "fellow college alumni" of the buyer...
"the buyer and the rep share a condo in Hawaii..."
in Hawaii "during winter months..."
winter months "on a time-share lease plan arranged by the Medina rep's sister-in-law who figures prominently in the real estate business..."
the real estate business "in the town where both the buyer and the rep live..."
"things are going O.K...."
things are going okay "at Niagara in spite of the rising costs and slipping quality..."
slipping quality "mainly because manufacturing is at plant capacity, orders keep pouring in and no one questions any of it..."
no one questions any of it "particularly no one in the accounting or quality departments..."

"In the same city as Niagara and Medina is the Foremost Hinge Company, whose hinges are unsurpassed..."
hinges are unsurpassed "in both quality and price competitiveness. Foremost started producing and selling hinges four years ago, and thanks to the efforts of a well-trained sales staff, has consistently..."
has consistently "gained market share of hinges..."
"but not being able to crack Niagara is a sore point. The standing pun at Foremost is nobody from here sells to Niagara .... Nobody!..."
"Foremost has its top producer working on the problem, though, and that rep found out about the alumni/Hawaii connection..."
"the foremost rep accepted the Niagara case and is determined to crack it. This rep is consistently the winner of hinge sales contests and is a member of the million dollar hinge roundtable, an organization of top hinge salespersons that are envied by every hinge sales rep in the country..."
"the Foremost 'hot dog' sales rep wants your help..."
Frames that are not explicit or written in this Case Study. Consider the following questions.

1. What is the context of this document?
   a. What is the source of this scenario's information? Do you know the source to be reliable? Is the source first hand? Second hand? Rumor? Other?
2. Was this information designed to be deceptive or misleading?
3. Are the three people in this Case Study men or women?
   a. Would the gender of these three people influence how situations were interpreted?
   b. Where is this case study geographically taking place? The USA? Other?
4. Does Maslow's seven stage diagram influence one's thinking?
   a. Are human beings able to be categorized into seven simple classifications?
   b. In your opinion, do people have more than seven needs?
5. The directions for this Case Study stated: "*Determine the needs of the Niagara buyer, the Medina seller, and the Foremost seller. Use Maslow's Hierarchical matrix below to check the appropriate needs. Remember, you need convincing evidence to support your assessment.*"
   Did you provide convincing evidence?

Maslow Needs Theory	Niagara Buyer	Medina Seller	Foremost Seller
7. Aesthetics			
6. Know and Understand			
5. Self-actualization			
4. Self-Esteem			
3. Love and Belonging			
2. Safety and Security			
1. Survival			

The following E-Questions involve questioning the context or frame of the exercise, which was Maslow's Hierarchy of Needs Theory.

a. Did you recognize that Maslow's Hierarchy of Needs Theory was a frame and needed to be questioned?

b. Are Maslow's Seven Hierarchy of Needs adequate to assess the complexity of human needs? Are human beings only seven levels of needs?

c. Could the oversimplification of this model influence one's thinking?

d. Is Maslow's Hierarchy of Needs model a universal, global model for the world?

e. What happens to our reasoning when we categorize people into marginalized stereotypes and simplistic biases?

f. Do people behave predictably within the idea of a "hierarchy"? That is, do people move lock-step in seven step-by-step linear progressions as inferred by Maslow's Model?

6. Was there a "sense-making" frame assumed in this exercise? In other words, was it assumed that because this document was provided as an exercise, that it was okay to set aside critical thinking? Was this a choice or a routine habit?

CONCLUSION: CONTEXT AND ASSUMPTIONS OF MASLOW'S MODEL

Did you realize that one of the assumptions was buy-in to Maslow's Hierarchy of Needs being the only and best way to assess and classify human behavior? In my experience, no one doing this exercise evaluated the assumptions of Maslow's Model. Without questioning assumptions, we may make conclusions or statements of fact. If Maslow's *sense-making rationales* are accepted without question, they could become absolute "fact" rather than an alternative point of view.

Appendix C

MOSSEY ROCK SIMULATION

In this simulation, participants are asked to read the background information below. This simulation is explained in Chapter 8 Strategy.

Mossey Rock is a quaint little town located in the heartland of our great country. Although it is only a 30-min drive to a major metropolitan center, most of the townsfolk prefer to do their shopping at one of the two general stores located in Mossey Rock. At these stores, one can buy a variety of goods, ranging from groceries to hardware equipment. Both establishments boast a soda fountain, which is quite popular among the younger generation as well. Like most small towns, Mossey Rock is proud of the fact that it has been able to preserve its many traditions, some of which date back to the 1890s. One of these grand traditions, which became official in 1923 when the town hall passed a resolution to this effect, is the cessation of all commercial activity on Sunday. Times have changed, however, and "Sunday shoppers" are becoming more and more prevalent. In fact, every Sunday there is a mass exodus to the nearby metropolitan center, where Sunday shopping has been permitted for years.

You are a member of the management team from one of the two general stores in Mossey Rock. Both the Country Market and the Corner Store have been consistently losing profit as Sunday shopping becomes more popular. Your management team, as well as the team from the competing general store, has recently contemplated opening the store on Sunday, in spite of the municipal resolution that prohibits this. The ramifications of such decisions are important since the profitability of such an action will depend upon the decision made by the competing store. For instance, if neither store opens on Sunday, it will be business as usual, and both stores will profit $100,000.

- **If only one store opens Sunday**, the open store **profits $150,000** for that week.
- If only one **store is closed Sunday and one store is Open, the closed store would incur a loss of $100,000**.
- **If both stores are closed on Sunday, they will gain $150,000**.
- **If both stores are open on Sunday, each store loses $125,000**.

The most notable preference of customers is to continue their shopping throughout the week at whichever the store that remained open on Sunday.

If both stores open Sunday, both businesses would encounter financial consequences. Although town hall may be able to turn a *blind eye* to one store violating the municipal resolution, two stores would be looked upon as a conspiracy against the political leadership of Mossey Rock. Eukariah Hampton, Mossey Rock's Mayor and direct descendant of one of the town's founders, would no doubt insist that town hall levy the highest possible fine allowable by law. The penalty for both stores opening would be $100,000 each week. While your lawyers have suggested that the municipal resolutions prohibiting Sunday shopping in Mossey Rock might be overturned in court, this legal pursuit would be financially expensive and involve a lot of time. In either case, **if both stores open on Sunday**, they will each incur losses of **$125,000**. Your management team must decide each week whether to **Open**, **Close**, or select the **Arson** Card. The decisions made for the first 3 weeks must be made without prior communication with the other management team. Both teams shall reveal their decisions simultaneously. **Your goal is to maximize profit**!

Business Overview

- If both stores are closed on Sunday, each store gains $100,000.
- If only one store is open Sunday and one store is closed Sunday, the open store gains $150,000 and the closed store loses $100,000.
- If both stores are open Sunday, each store loses $125,000.
- If an Arson Card is played, the team that played Arson will gain $125,000 for all remaining weeks in that round. The Arsoned business will lose $150,000 for each week it is out of business. However, if both businesses play the Arson Card on each other at the same time, both teams lose $150,000 for each week remaining in that round.

Preparation

Discuss the negotiation situation with your team; plan your strategy.

Objective

Your objective is to maximize profit.

Schedule

There are two sequences or 6-week rounds in this negotiation. Each sequence consists of six decisions (each decision represents one week).

1. Each business will receive instructions regarding how their choices will be communicated between each business team.
2. There are three decisions: (1) Open; (2) Closed; (3) Arson.
   a. The **Open** choice specifies that your store has decided to open on Sunday
   b. The **Closed** choice specifies that your store has chosen to close on Sunday

c. The **Arson** choice specifies the incineration of the competitor's store
d. Both stores will be asked to specify one of the three decisions each week

Gains and/or Losses

Profit and/or loss should be calculated each week. Profits and/or losses are *cumulative* throughout the 12 weeks.

Timetable: The 5-second rule

Each team has 1 *min* between each week's decisions. Your team's spokesperson has the responsibility to communicate your team's weekly decisions within 5 s of a request, and it will be assumed as an Open decision the first occurrence; and, assumed as an Arson decision the second incidence.

Communication of Each week's Decisions

Both teams will be informed of each team's decision at exactly the same time. In this way, neither team has an advantage during decision-making. Dr Sylvester will *shuttle* these decisions among each team.

Arson Protocol

Arson involves the burning of a building or other property for financial advantage. When the Arson Card is played, it burns down the other management team's store, forcing them out of business for the remainder of weeks in *that round*. Once an Arson Card has been played, that 6-week round concludes. Each team may use the Arson Card *only once* during the 12-week negotiation.

- Arson may be communicated ONLY during one of the 12 decision-making periods. Arson may not be rendered in-between decision-making periods.
- If a store has been Arsoned, it is out-of-business and therefore, is incapable of earning revenue for the number of weeks remaining *in that round*.
- *An Arsoned store loses* $150,000 *each week that it is burned down during each round*.
- *The Arsoner gains* $125,000 *each week*.
- If the Arson Card is used during the second round, this terminates the negotiation.
- In this business context, there is no legal penalty for using Arson.

Negotiation Protocols: 20 min to Prepare

- Neither business is allowed to communicate with the other business until the scheduled negotiation, which is planned to occur between weeks 3 and 4. Communication with the other team will be penalized $10,000 per team member for each violation.

- Each management team is granted a 5-min negotiation between the third and fourth weeks of round one; in addition, a 2-min negotiation between the ninth and tenth *weeks of round two*.
- When each team's negotiator returns to their respective teams, they have 3 min to debrief their teams previous to the next decision-making period.
- Each business team may request *one "additional*" 1-min negotiation at any time following week 4. **Note**: The party *requesting* an "additional" 1-min negotiation will be *assessed* $5000 per team member; the other party will gain $10,000 per team member irrespective of the other party chooses to accept or refuse the additional 1-min negotiation.
- Negotiators may negotiate whatever terms they choose and make agreements that are beneficial to themselves and/or their teams. They may employ whatever ethical or moral approach they consider appropriate. Management teams are not obligated to adhere to agreements made by the negotiator.

Three Decisions to Make Prior to the Start of the Negotiation

Select three people to perform the following roles: Do this as soon as possible.

1. A **Negotiator's** activities are described under "The Negotiator"
2. A **Spokesperson**'s responsibility is to communicate team decisions.
3. A **Financial Accountant's** responsibility is to record financial activity.

How the Negotiation Begins

- The seminar leader will indicate that the first round of negotiation is about to begin.
- Each team will have 60 s between each decision period to decide its' next move.
- The Spokesperson conveys all decisions to Ken Sylvester—generally, this is conveyed by displaying one of the three decision-making cards or via telephone/computer.
- The negotiation will proceed week-by-week except in the case of Arson. If an Arson decision is made, it terminates that particular 6-week round. For example, if an Arson Card is played in week 2 of round 1, two outcomes will result:
  - The team that Arsoned will gain $125 K; the Arsoned business will lose $150 K for all remaining weeks in round one.
  - However, if the Arson card is played in week 7 of round 2, this *terminates* the negotiation. The team using the Arson Card will gain $150 K for the remaining 6 weeks of round 2, or $750,000. The Arsoned store is out of business, and therefore, loses $150,000 for 6 weeks, or $900,000.
- There will be no further negotiation beyond the conclusion of round 2, week 12.
- Each team will calculate its financial status. Profit and/or loss are cumulative for 12 weeks.

PROFIT AND LOSS REPORT

Round 1	**Country Market Profit**	**Country Market Loss**	**Corner Store Profit**	**Corner Store Loss**
Week 1				
Week 2				
Week 3				
Week 4				
Week 5				
Week 6				
R1—SubTotal				
Round 2				
Week 7				
Week 8				
Week 8				
Week 9				
Week 10				
Week 11				
Week 12				
R2—SubTotal				
Total P/L				

Appendix D: Thirty Tactics

Thirty tactics are listed and defined below. Knowing what these tactics are, identifying and naming them even if you do not intend to use them yourself, will help you read negotiations you are in.

ACTING DUMB: THE "COLOMBO" EFFECT

The "Colombo" television show character (played by Peter Falk) solved cases by acting as dumb and as "sly" as a fox. His dumbness caused those around him to underestimate him. His behavior helped diffuse a competitive atmosphere.

BANDWAGON—JUMP ON

This tactic involves creating the perception of momentum. This assumes you possess skills in the power of suggestion. The suggestion leads others to believe that some plan is highly popular and that they had better join in support of it lest they be left out. This tactic is most effective against those who do not hold attitudes firmly or who feel insecure, strongly desire to please others, or desire to be part of the majority. The illusion of a bandwagon can be created by the sequence of contacts with significant people in the organization.

DO NOTHING OR INACTION

This passive tactic, sometimes called "pocket veto," involves letting something die on the vine. This tactic is effective when there is no advantage to action. The power of this tactic is in the difficulty of detecting its usage. This stall tactic is designed to wear the other party's interest down until they get the message and decide the matter is not worth pursuing.

DON'T BURN YOUR BRIDGES BEHIND YOU

The wisdom of this tactic is in not saying or doing things that permanently alienate others. Actions and words are often enacted with the assumption that certain people will never be able to influence your future. Remember: We never know what the future holds, or with whom you will later come in contact. A reasonable person goes out of his or her way to keep his or her relational-bridges in good repair. Nevertheless, in the momentum of passion, when intense emotion decreases perception, logic and judgment, people are capable of saying and doing things that create increased obstacles to reaching an agreement.

FAIT ACCOMPLI

Do whatever it is you want to do, thereby presenting the adversary with the accomplished fact, instead of risking the chance of having the plan disapproved. If your actions are successful, there is usually no argument with success. This tactic is recommended for minor matters. Disadvantages: some higher-ups dislike subordinates who seize power and proceed with some unapproved plan, particularly if it is a significant success. This could result in disciplinary action. It can also be interpreted as you trying to upstage your superior. Advantage: it is effective in dealing with people who are indecisive, inactive, and too conservative. Strong indifference may allow this tactic to go unchallenged, if not unnoticed.

FLAT TIRE

This tactic is like trying to drive a car with a flat tire. You cannot get far. Flat tires come in many forms, but the result is the same; the vehicle goes nowhere. A group may be controlled by the people who are selected to do it. In other words, they go through the motions for appearance's sake, and then place the responsibility for heading the project on someone who is incapable of causing anything to happen. Sometimes this is referred to as the hollowness of committees. Not infrequently, this is the very reason a committee is launched in the first place. Futility and ineffectiveness are the goals. Therefore, by bogging down the various power seekers in a morass of organizational committee structures, the top power structure can go about its business relatively unencumbered. It has been said that committees are where people waste hours and keep minutes.

FLINCH

Facial and body language communicating shock and unpleasant reaction to the offer you just heard.

GOOD GUY–BAD GUY

This gambit attempts to get your trust. It works only if there are two or more people involved in the tactic. Typically, one person acts as the "bad guy" through the use of aggressive and threatening words and behavior. The second person steps in as if to "save" the target from the "bad guy" hoping that you will let down your guard. When the "bad guy" is under control, the hope is that they target will tell the "good guy" whatever needs to be know.

GUERRILLA WARFARE

This tactic avoids direct confrontation when it is not advantageous to engage the enemy. Direct battles often result in causalities. This is a type of hit and run approach. Emphasize your strengths (hit) and minimize your weaknesses (run).

HOT POTATO

This tactic relates to issues that become so potentially sensitive that it is wise to avoid being connected with them. Therefore, passing on the "hot potato" helps one avoid the heat. No matter how adept one is at handling difficult situations, a hot potato could damage your career and reputation. This is a "time sensitive" tactic. Certain explosive situations will pass with time, but this does not mean to look the other way! Organizations can punish members who do not take care of business. The key is to pass it on!

INCOMMUNICADO

This tactic involves limiting or preventing certain people from being able to contact you. In certain circumstances, it is advantageous to see no one, or not be available to talk with anyone, if you are to keep from getting into difficulty. Sometimes, no matter what you say, it will be wrong; to remain silent will anger some; to speak will anger some. Hence, incommunicado! This tactic is best used in highly explosive situations in which all parties need to preserve the longevity of the relationship. Incommunicado can be an effective way of saying "no" without actually being forced to say it. This lets the situation pass by with no comment or confrontation.

KNOW WHEN TO FOLD'EM

In certain circumstances, the best tactic is to know when to quit. When there is no prospect of victory, and to stay and fight would only result in further loss, it is important to know when to fold em. There are two primary advantages to this tactic: (1) It conserves resources that may be needed in other situations and (2) If observed, others may be impressed by the wisdom of someone who knows when to quit. However, cutting your losses could mean resigning a position, dropping a product, selling off a division, selling a losing company, selling a bad investment, or canceling a plan of action. Admittedly, this is difficult to do because conceding failure is not pleasant. The trick to this tactic is to behave in such a way you do not give your opponent the satisfaction of realizing what is happening.

LET ME HOLD YOUR COAT

At times, it is strategic to not involve oneself in conflict. There are situations in which one can be burned, and so it is better to stand on the sidelines and watch. However, you may have an interest in the outcome, so then you may choose to "hold their coat" by providing support, but not be involved. This tactic is used best when you believe that the person whom you support may go down in defeat and you do not want to go down with them. This is most often used when your allies are going up against very strong adversaries and will most likely win.

LET THE SITUATION WORSEN

Sometimes, the best you can do is to let a bad situation get worse. If you act too soon, you will be criticized as taking unwarranted action. There are risks to this tactic: sometimes the situation worsens to the point that it cannot be corrected, and sometimes letting the situation worsen can be viewed by others as a lack of leadership.

MUDDLING

This tactic involves not having a strong agenda in mind to start with. Muddling is entering a situation with a mind to do whatever is expedient to solve a problem. It is best used when the tactic or policy cannot be determined beforehand due to the ambiguity of the situation. The concern of this tactic is that one can appear inconsistent and uncertain. The advantage is to get into a situation and then deciding what the best thing to do is as it unfolds. This tactic requires good judgment, the ability to think well on one's feet, and several alternative courses of action from which to choose.

NIBBLING

Wait until end of the transaction, and then ask for a little bit more. The rationale for this tactic to work effectively involves timing. It assumes that you are the buyer and that the seller has successfully sold you a product. Just before the "closing" of the deal has been completed, you ask for a concession or an additional product. The idea here is that the seller may not want to say "no" for fear that they buyer will walk away from the deal. In addition, the seller may not want to take the time and risk to go all the way through the sales process again in fear that you will change your mind. However, if the person does not need your sale, then this gambit may not work.

PICK YOUR BATTLEFIELD

This tactic concerns where a meeting should take place: Their office, your office, someone else's office, a neutral place, a social or political place where it is difficult for someone to oppose your plan because of the witnesses who are present? The place is determined by what influence a person wants the atmosphere to have on others. Intimidation? Relaxed in order to lower the others' guard?

Meeting on someone else's territory can have advantages, particularly if you succeed. This communicates your strength and emphasizes their vulnerability.

RATTLE THEIR CAGE

This tactic is suitable when a clear-cut victory is not likely. Harassing your opponent is conducted in such a manner that they eventually give-in. This is best demonstrated in a subtle and clever design. This is generally effective at forcing someone to resign when outright firing is not possible. Budgets can be reduced to an awkward point. Authority can be reduced. Social snubbing could occur on a frequent basis, overtly bypassing the person for consideration of promotion or reward. Usually, people have enough pride that unfair treatment and continual lowering of status will cause them to go elsewhere. Harassment tactics can backfire. If the person becomes angry and has sufficient power to counterattack or withstand the harassment, it can cause you more energy and headache than it is worth. The psychological disposition of the person is significant in determining the successful application of harassment. Some people have no tolerance for harassment. Others thrive on it. It is usually ineffective to harass someone who has nowhere else to go, or has no alternatives.

RED HERRING

This tactic involves giving false justifications for certain actions when you do not want to reveal your true reason. This tactic developed first in England. English Lords would hold a "foxhunt." English dogs were trained to detect by nose, the fox's path. Consequently, the dogs would lead the hunters to the fox's location. If a competitor in the foxhunt who desired to win at any cost were to drag a red herring between the path of the fox and the dogs, an inexperienced dog would take the stronger, more alluring smell of the red herring. This distraction for the untrained dogs, and their English Lords, would lead them astray—toward a false goal. Eventually, success in the foxhunt meant training the dogs to ignore anything but the scent of the fox. The key to overcoming this tactic is refusing to be distracted from one's true objective. This requires emotional and intellectual discipline and self-control to resist distractions.

RELUCTANT BUYER/SELLER

This tactic includes: (1) projecting an unwillingness to negotiate, (2) a casual "take it or leave it attitude," (3) mild disinterest (4) not sure, (5) just shopping.

RETREAT WITHOUT SURRENDER

This tactic comes into use when the opponent is so strong and the situation so explosive that to start a battle would be extremely unfavorable, no matter how right you may be and how wrong the opposition is. At times, this tactic could be described as a timing tactic: retreat for cover until you are better prepared to fight—then fight! There are sayings about "discretion being the better part of valor" and "that one should run away to live and fight another day." Remarks intended to minimize the seriousness of a situation is frequently a grave tactical error that only serves to infuriate one's adversary. This only makes reaching agreement more difficult. This tactic is most advantageous when a highly emotional adversary comes onto the scene that, because of their state of mind, cannot be reasoned with. If you cannot cope with the immediate situation because of such circumstances, it is reasonable to retreat to cover until the situation calms down. Retreat is a space and time to marshal your forces and/or obtain additional support for your position. A closely related tactic to retreating without surrender is to "clear out." In retreating, other people do not know where you are.

SET ASIDE

A technique used to build momentum by moving around or away from resistance zones or emotionally sensitive issues by moving on to other less tense issues. *Let's just set that aside for a while and look at other areas in which we share agreement.*

SPLIT THE DIFFERENCE

Always get the other person to split the difference. Never offer to split the difference yourself. The primary approach to this tactic is asking questions concerning how close your tow positions are apart, noting that it would be a shame to get so close and not close the deal. Typically, this must be repeated several times. Patience is important for this tactic to work. You must have the time.

THE STING

This tactic—ADD a bit like you did when you named the "Columbo Effect."

1. Upping the Mark—finding right person to fleece.
2. Playing the Mark—befriending and gaining confidence.
3. Roping the Mark—steering mark to inside con.
4. Telling the Tale—opportunity to show the mark a large sum of money can be made dishonestly.
5. The Sell—allowing the mark to make a substantial profit in a test run of swindle.
6. The Breakdown—mark invests large sum of money for big financial gain.
7. Sending—sending mark to get money to invest in big gain.
8. The Sting—fleecing the mark in the "big score."
9. Blowing off the Mark—getting mark out of the way quickly and quietly.

STRAW MAN

This tactic involves setting up straw men for the opponent to knock down, thereby leading them to believe that they have won a victory. The straw man is some demand or condition that you put forth solely for the opposition to knock down. You are not at all serious (internally) about the straw man. There may be several straw men in order to build a type of momentum from your opponent. Straw man must be logical and have some support; otherwise, the opponent may not view their attainment as a gain.

STRIKE WHILE THE IRON IS HOT

See opportunities and take advantage of them. You may fail, but most people admire those who try. The problem with this tactic is that too many people take on more than they are capable of handling. If this is the situation, others usually feel dispassionate about helping others get out of trouble more than a great once in a while. Taking advantage of an opportunity assumes you have the necessary resources, support, and expertise to capitalize on the opportunity.

TRADING OFF

If I do that for you, what will you do for me? The primary principle of this gambit is, any time you are asked for something you always ask for something in return.

TRIAL BALLOONS

This tactic involves testing the temperature of the organizational water before introducing a plan. If the reaction is adverse, then reevaluate and revise your plan. This will help you to save face. If it is positive, then continue to implement the plan. The strategic part of this tactic is that little, if anything is lost by testing the waters.

VISE

The vise involves pressuring someone into revealing their position or attempting to force the other party into stating their position by saying something like, "you'll have to do better than that." Trained negotiators will counter such a device by saying something like, "How much better than that must I do?"

WALK AWAY

One of the most important gambits in the negotiation process involves letting the other person know that you don't need what they are selling or can get along just fine without what they want you to accept.

Appendix E

1. **6 Ways Companies Mismanage Risk.** René M. Stulz, Harvard Business Review, March 2009.
2. **A Manager's Guide for Evaluating Competitive Analysis Techniques.** Grant, John J., and Prescott, John E. Interfaces, May/June 1988, pp. 10–22.
3. **Ackoff's Fables: Irreverent Reflections on/Business and Bureaucracy.** Russell L. Ackoff, John Wiley & Sons, Inc., 1991.
4. **American Communication In A Global Society.** Glen Fisher, 1979.
5. **Applied Economics: Thinking Beyond Stage One.** Thomas Sowell, Basic Books, 2009.
6. **Art and Science of Negotiation.** Raiffa, H.
7. **Art of Negotiating.** Advanced Management Research International Inc. Contains guide to reinforce the concepts presented in the audio program, the art of negotiating, and facilitates the applications of these concepts to real life situations.
8. **Art of Negotiating.** Nierenberg, G.T. Covers 3 areas of negotiation, personal, large organization, and international. Describes step-by-step methods.
9. **Art of Negotiation.** Rule, G.W.L. Purpose is to better equip those who negotiate on behalf of others, particularly those who represent nations and governments.
10. **Artful Negotiating.** Cohen, Herb. (Video recording) – Deals with time, style, strategies, tactics, and high expectations.
11. **Blind Spots: Why Smart People Do Dumb Things.** Madeleine L. Van Hecke, Ph.D., Prometheus Books, 2007.
12. **Business Leadership.** Tichy, Kotter, Goleman, Hesselbein, Kouzes & Posner, Bolman & Deal, Blanchard, Bennis, Quinn, Drucker, Collins, Schein, Bridges, McCall, Hamel, Wheatley, Heifetz, and Bossidy, Jossey-Bass, 2003.
13. **Business Negotiations with the Japanese.** Tung, R.I. Based on a survey of over 100 US. firms that have been involved with the Japanese.
14. **Collaborating: Finding Common Ground for Multiparty Problems.** Gray, B. Describes a process-oriented approach to problem solving among organizations. Emphasizes conflict resolution and the advancement of shared visions.

15. **Collaboration in Organizations.** Kraus, William. Discusses the need for collaboration within organizations, with suggestions on how to develop collaborative environment.
16. **Competitive Strategy: Techniques for Analyzing Business, Industry and Competitors.** Porter, Michael E., New York: Free Press, 1980, pp. 396.
17. **Competitor Intelligence: How to Get It, How to Use It.** Fuld, Leonard M., New York, John Wiley & Sons, c. 1985, pp. 479.
18. **Conquering a Culture of Indecision.** Ram Charan, Harvard Business Review, 2001.
19. **Contract Management and Negotiations for the Project Manager.** Cavendish, P. Includes section on organizational issues, contracting systems, and contracting process.
20. **Contract Negotiation Handbook.** Marsh, P.D. Covers planning and decision techniques, establishment of the target objective, and strategy selection; the organization and administrative environment of negotiation; structure and sequence of the negotiation, and tactics.
21. **Cultures and Organizations: Software of the Mind – Intercultural Cooperation and Its Importance for Survival.** Geert Hofstede and Gert Jan Hofstede, McGraw-Hill, 2005.
22. **Diplomacy.** Henry Kissinger, Simon and Schuster Publishers, 1994.
23. **Disputes and Negotiations: a cross-cultural perspective.** Gulliver, P. Studies the way in which two parties negotiate with each other to resolve a dispute between them and to discover a mutually acceptable, tolerable outcome. Discusses the process of negotiation, the study of joint decision-making; basic concepts for the study of negotiation; process models for negotiation; mediators; and dynamics of negotiation.
24. **Don't Say Yes When You Want To Say No.** Fensterheim and Baer, 1978. Explains the psychology of compromising good agreements by yielding to others.
25. **Don't Take It Personally: The Art of Dealing with Rejection.** Elayne Savage, Ph. D., New Harbinger Publications, 2002.
26. **Dynamite Salary Negotiations: Know What You're Worth and Get It!** Ronald L. Krannich and Caryl Rae Krannich, PH. Ds, Impact Publications, 1998.
27. **Ethics in America.** Newton, Lisa H. Study Guide, Prentice Hall, 1989 (paperback).
28. **Excellence: Can We Be Equal And Excellent Too?** John W. Gardner, Harper Colophon Books, 1961.
29. **Framing Public Life: Perspectives on Media and Our Understanding of the Social World.** Stephen D. Reese, Oscar H. Gandy, Jr., and August E. Grant, Lawrence Erlbaum Associates, Publisher, 2003.
30. **Friendly Persuasion.** Woolf, Bob, G.P. Putnam's Sons, 1990.
31. **From No to Yes.** (Video recording). Gould, P. Uses a meeting about reaching an agreement in acquiring a new computer system to illustrate

techniques in reaching consensus. Covers such topics as listening, communicating your ideas, handling territorial issues.

32. **Frontal Attack, Divide & Conquer, The Fait Accompli and 118 Other Tactics Managers Should Know.** Richard H. Buskirk, John Wiley and Sons, Inc., 1989.
33. **Fundamental Issues In Strategy.** Richard P. Rumelt, Dan E. Schendel, and David J. Teece, Harvard Business School Press, 1994.
34. **Getting To Yes: Negotiating Agreement Without Giving IN.** Roger Fisher, William Ury, with Bruce Patton, Penguin Books, 1991.
35. **Getting Together: Building a Relationship That Gets to Yes.** Fisher, Roger, and Brown, S., Penguin Books, 1988 (paperback).
36. **Give and Take: The Complete Guide to Negotiation Strategies and Tactics.** Karrass, Chester L., Thomas Y. Crowell, 1970.
37. **Good Communication that Blocks Learning.** Chris Argyris, Fellows of Harvard College, 1994.
38. **Heuristics and Biases: The Psychology of Intuitive Judgment.** Edited by Thomas Gilovich, Dale Griffin, and Daniel Kahneman, Cambridge University Press, 2002.
39. **How Bell Labs Creates Star Performers: Any training program for improving the productivity of professionals must first target taking initiative.** Robert Kelley and Janet Caplan, Harvard Business Review, July–August 1993.
40. **How to Fight a Price Increase.** Karrass, C. Applies negotiating strategies, tactics, and psychological insights to gaining price reduction.
41. **How to Win Government Contracts.** Greenly, R.B., Clarifies ingredients that make up a successful proposal, and then tells how to prepare a strategic business plan, gather competitor information, and take effective pre-proposal steps.
42. **Human Development Theories: Windows on Culture.** R. Murray Thomas, Sage Publications, Inc., 1999.
43. **Influence: Science and Practice.** Robert B. Cialdini, Allyn and Bacon, Fourth Edition, 2001.
44. **International Negotiation: A Cross-Cultural Perspective.** Glen Fisher, Intercultural Press, Inc., 1980.
45. **Is There A Best Way To Build A Car? A collection of best practices does not make a successful production system.** Michael Maccoby, Harvard Business Review, November–December, 1997.
46. **Judgment: How Winning Leaders Make Great Calls.** Noel M. Tichy and Warren G. Bennis, The Penguin Group, 2007.
47. **Leadership Secrets of Attila the Hun.** Roberts, W.
48. **Makers of Modern Strategy: From Machiavelli to the Nuclear Age.** Edited by Peter Paret, Princeton University Press, 1986.
49. **Management of the Absurd: Paradoxes In Leadership.** Richard Farson, Simon & Schuster, 1996.

50. **Manager's Negotiating Answer Book.** George T. Fuller, Prentice Hall, 1995.
51. **Managing by Negotiations.** Brooks, F.
52. **Mindsets: The Role of Culture and Perception in International Relations.** Glen Fisher, Intercultural Press, 1997.
53. **Negotiate to Win: Gaining the Psychological Edge.** Schoonmaker, A.N. Demonstrates the key to successful negotiating. Discusses methods for analyzing one's own negotiation style, its impact on others and the type of situations it suits or conflicts with. Provides effective techniques for coping with the ramifications of team negotiations.
54. **Negotiate.** Mastenbroek, W. Presents a range of typical negotiating strategies, followed by simulations designed to exercise negotiating skills.
55. **Negotiating Game.** Karrass, C. Tells how to analyze power and improve strengths, how to make concessions without weakening position, how to set goals which reflect high aspirations. Deals with status and the influence it exerts on people, traits of the effective negotiator, and the strategy and tactics to prepare for negotiation.
56. **Negotiating in Organizations.** Razerman, M.H. Introduces and reviews organizational negotiations. Covers negotiated decision making, third party use in organizational disputes, negotiating within the organizational environment, and suggests organizational applications.
57. **Negotiating Tactics.** Levin, Edward, Fawcett Columbine, 1980 (paperback).
58. **Negotiation Procedures and Strategies: Training manual.** National Contract Management Association, Teaches negotiations strategies and techniques.
59. **Negotiation Techniques: How to Work Toward A Constructive Agreement.** Guder, R.F. Explains principles and practices of negotiating. Discusses negotiating process, strategy and tactics as well as team negotiations.
60. **Negotiator: A Manual for Winners.** Coffin, R.A. Behavior guide for successful business transactions.
61. **News and Numbers: A Guide to Reporting Statistic Claims and Controversies In Health and Other Fields.** Victor Cohn, Iowa State University Press, 1989.
62. **No Contest: The Case Against Competition.** Kohn, Alfie. Philosophical discussion on the negative impact and consequences of competition in society.
63. **No Easy Victories.** John W. Gardner, Harper Colophon Books, 1968.
64. **On Leadership.** John W. Gardner, The Free Press, 1990.
65. **Philosophy: History, Ideas, Theories, Who's Who, and How To Think.** Stephan Law, Metro Books, 2007.
66. **Power and Interdependence: Power and Interdependence in the Twenty-First Century.** Robert O. Keohane and Joseph S. Nye, J.R., Pearson, 2012.
67. **Purchasing Negotiations.** Barlow, C. Wayne, and Eisen, Glenn P. CBI Publishing Company, Inc., 1983

68. **Reframing Organizations: Artistry, Choice and Leadership.** Lee. G. Bolman and Terrence I. Deal, Josey-Bass, Fourth Edition, 2009.
69. **Resilience: Why Things Bounce Back.** Andrew Zolli and Ann Marie Healy, Free Press, 2012.
70. **Robert's Rules of Order.** Robert, H.M. Presents parliamentary law and the basic guide to fair and orderly procedure in meetings.
71. **Secrets of Question Based Selling: How the Most Powerful Tool in Business Can Double Your Sales Results.** Thomas A. Freese, Sourcebooks, Inc., 2000.
72. **Self-Defeating Behaviors: Free Yourself from the Habits, Compulsions, Feelings, and Attitudes That Hold You Back.** Milton R. Cudney Ph.D. and Robert E. Hardy, ED.D, HarperSanFrancisco, 1991.
73. **Semantic Aspects of Collective Bargaining.** University of California. Emphasizes the use of specific language in agreements.
74. **Smart Questions.** Leeds, D. Presents with anecdotes, case histories, lists of queries and quizzes such topics as training, problem solving, negotiating, getting a raise, delegating, and corporate culture.
75. **Spin Selling.** Neil Rackham, McGraw-Hill Book Company, 1988.
76. **Strategy Safari: A Guided Tour through the Wilds of Strategic Management.** Henry Mintzberg, Bruce Ahlstrand, and Joseph Lampel, The Free Press, 1998.
77. **Sun Tzu: War and Management.** Chow-Hou Wee, Khai-Sheang Lee and Bambang Walujo Hidajat, Addison–Wesley Publishing Company, 1991.
78. **Talking to Terrorists.** Rand Corporation. Suggests ways of dealing with political kidnappers.
79. **The Art of Conflict Management: Achieving Solutions for Life, Work, and Beyond.** Professor Michael Dues, The Teaching Company, 2010.
80. **The Art of War by Sun Tzu.** Edited and with Foreword by James Clavell, Delta, 1983.
81. **The Art of War.** Tzu, S. Presents an English translation of the book written in China 2500years ago. Describes the philosophy of successful leadership that is as applicable to contemporary business as it is to war.
82. **The Change Masters: Innovation & Entrepreneurship In The American Corporation.** Rosabeth Moss Kanter, Simon & Schuster, Inc. 1983.
83. **The Chinese Mind Game:** The Best Kept Secret Of The East. Chu, C.N. Discusses negotiating strategies used by Chinese business persons and the cultural origins of many of them. Identifies some effective counter-strategies.
84. **The Conflict Resolution Toolbox: Models and Maps for Analyzing, Diagnosing and Resolving Conflict.** Gary T. Furlong, Wiley, 2005.
85. **The Future of Power.** Joseph S. Nye, Jr., Public Affairs, 2011.
86. **The Global Negotiator.** Griffin, Trenholm J., and Daggatt, W. Russell, Harper Business, 1990 (has a comprehensive bibliography).

87. **The Global Negotiator: Building Strong Business Relationships Anywhere In The World.** Griffin. T.J. Focuses on global negotiation skills exploring the nature of a relationship as the link allowing both parties to create and claim value. Identifies strategies and tactics that can be used in international negotiation. A four-stage model is set to increase the understanding of the negotiation process describing preparation, bargaining, ceremony, and implementation and dynamic negotiations.
88. **The Hidden Traps In Decision Making: In making decisions, your mind may be your worst enemy.** John S. Hammond, Ralph L. Keeney, and Howard Raiffa, Harvard Business Review, September–October1998.
89. **The Mind and Heart of the Negotiator.** Leigh L. Thompson, Pearson, 2015.
90. **The National System of Political Economy: Translated From The Original German by Sampson S. Lloyd.** Friedrich List, Augustus M. Kelley Publishers, 1991.
91. **The Psychology of Judgment and Decision Making.** Scott Plous, McGraw-Hill, 1993.
92. **The Psychology of Negotiation.** Rackham, N. Focuses on the positive approaches used by skilled negotiators such as the use of questions in persuasion, and creating trust on the part of those holding other positions.
93. **The Real Reason People Won't Change: It's a psychological dynamic called a "competing commitment," and until managers understand how it works and the ways to overcome it, they can't do a thing about change-resistant employees.** Robert Kegan and Lisa Laskow Lahey, Harvard Business Review, November 2001.
94. **The Set-Up-To-Fail Syndrome: How bosses create their own poor performers.** Jean-Francois Manzoni and Jean-Louis Barsoux, Harvard Business Review, March–April 1998.
95. **The Seven Military Classics of Ancient China.** Translation and commentary by Ralph D. Sawyer with Mei-chün Sawyer, Westview Press, 1993.
96. **The Zen of Listening: Mindful Communication In The Age Of Distraction.** Rebecca Z. Shafir, M.A. CCC, Quest Books, 2000.
97. **Thinking.** Gary R. Kirby and Jeffery R. Goodpaster, Prentice Hall, 1999.
98. **Thinking Qualitatively: Methods of Mind.** Johnny Saldaña, Sage, 2015.
99. **Tribal Warfare In organizations: Identifying The Tribes In Your Organization.** Peg Neuhauser, Ballinger Publishing Company, 1988.
100. **Turf Wars.** Robbins, H. Examines the causes and effects of territorial frictions in the office and explains how to encourage employees to compete with the outside, not with each other. Provides strategies, techniques for fostering cross-functional alliances.
101. **What You Don't Know About Making Decisions: Decision making is arguably the most important job of the senior executive and one of the easiest to get wrong.** It doesn't have to be that way – if you look at the process in a whole new light. David A. Garvin and Michael A. Roberto, Harvard Business Review, September 2001.

102. When Women Work Together. Duff, Carolyn S., Conari Press, 1993. Discusses the invisible competition among women in the workplace.

103. Why Do Employees Resist Change? Organizations have personal compacts with their employees. Change efforts will fail unless those compacts are revised. Paul Strebel, Harvard Business Review, May–June 1996.

104. Why Good Leaders Make Bad Decisions: Neuroscience reveals what distorts a leader's judgment. Here's how you can keep your own judgment clear. Andrew Campbell, Jo Whitehead, and Sydney Finkelstein, Harvard Business Review, February 2009.

105. Why Incentive Plans Cannot Work: When reward systems fail, don't blame the program – look at the premise behind it. Alphie Kohn, Harvard Business Review, September–October1998.

106. Winning Through Cooperation. Orlick, Terry. Discusses competition.

107. Win–Win Negotiating: Turning Conflict Into Agreement. Jandt, F.F. Explains specific defusing techniques, including unpacking; the mini-mix solution, bone throwing, issue substitution, and getting past "yes". Describes different types of adversaries.

108. Working With Difficult People. Muriel Solomon, 1990. Hundreds of office proven strategies and techniques to get cooperation from tyrants, connivers, badmouthers, and others.

109. World-class Negotiating: Deal Making In the Global Marketplace. Herndon, D.W. Outlines why international negotiating skills are so important today from the dramatic changes taking place in the new European Economic community and growing global economy power of Japan, to the emergence of developing countries in the Third World and the race for the lead in high-tech industries. Includes over 70 negotiating tactics of international executives, "critical incident" exercises and cultural self-awareness inventory listings to help to communicate with intercultural values, assumptions, and body language.

110. Writers On Strategy and Strategic Management: The Theory of Strategy and the Practice of Strategic Management at Enterprise, Corporate, Business and Functional Levels. J.I. Moore, Penguin Books, 1992.

111. You Can Get Anything You Want. Dawson, Roger, Fireside Book, 1985 (paperback).

112. You Can Negotiate Anything. Cohen, Herb, Bantam Books, 1980 (paperback).

Appendix F: About the Author

Dr Ken Sylvester has more than 45 years of experience as a leadership and management consultant and professional negotiator in the areas of business, law, education, government, and the nonprofit sector. He consulted and/or negotiated for organizations *such as* Boeing, Microsoft, Google, Nike, Apple, Coca-Cola, Edison Electric, Chrysler, the National Basketball Association (NBA), the National Football League (NFL), the National Collegiate Athletic Association (NCAA), the Oregon U.S. Attorney's Office, TransAlta Canadian Power Company, the National Highway Traffic Safety Administration, lead negotiator for the United Salmon Association (USA) of Alaska, Associated Grocers of America, United Grocers, and others.

As President of Organization Strategy Institute, Inc. (OSI) since 1989, OSI's business concentration included the United States of America, Canada, France, Germany, Britain, Wales, Belgium, Ireland, Scotland, Austria, Italy, Greece, Poland, China (Beijing, Shanghai, and Hong Kong), Japan, South Korea, Taiwan, Argentina, Brazil, Columbia, Peru, Venezuela, Ecuador, Philippines, Australia, New Zealand, and Mexico.

His educational background includes a Doctorate in Leadership and Management from Seattle University, a Master of Science in Organizational Leadership and Management from Pacific Lutheran University, a Bachelor of Science in Health and Education from Pacific University, an Executive Certificate in Production Operations and Management from Stanford University, and Legal Certification in Conflict Resolution from the State of Colorado.

After retiring as President of OSI in 2014, he served as adjunct instructor at the University of Colorado in the College of Business and Administration, where he was awarded Instructor of the Year on four occasions. He continues to be a keynote speaker at numerous organizations.

Index

Note: Page numbers followed by b, f, and t indicate boxes, figures, and tables, respectively.

D

E

M

N

O

P

Q

R

S

T

Printed in the United States
By Bookmasters